LONG ROAD TO LIBYA

AUTHOR'S NOTE

Where necessary a number of names, dates and places have been redacted to protect the identity of the individuals and companies involved, due to the sensitive nature of some of the contracts and locations in which we operated. Everything else has been described as I remember it.

LONG ROAD
TO LIBYA

DANGER, EXCITEMENT, TENACITY,
RESILIENCE, OPPORTUNITY AND SUCCESS

JASON WOODS

Matador
9 Priory Business Park,
Wistow Road, Kibworth Beauchamp,
Leicestershire. LE8 0RX
Tel: 0116 279 2299
Email: books@troubador.co.uk
Web: www.troubador.co.uk/matador
Twitter: @matadorbooks

ISBN 978 1800461 161

British Library Cataloguing in Publication Data.
A catalogue record for this book is available from the British Library.

Printed and bound by CPI Group (UK) Ltd, Croydon, CR0 4YY
Typeset in 11pt Adobe Garamond Pro by Troubador Publishing Ltd, Leicester, UK

Matador is an imprint of Troubador Publishing Ltd

DEDICATIONS

My Dad, who sadly passed away during the writing of this book, after a long, hard-fought battle with illness. I miss him and thank him for his unwavering support, sensible advice and for always keeping me on the right track.

My wingman, Des. From young Paratroopers in Aldershot and N. Ireland to working together on The Circuit in Iraq and Libya; one of my oldest, closest friends and confidants. We all miss your uncompromising nature. See you again soon my friend when my time comes to join you in the Final RV.

My family, 'past and present', who all provided so much support and love during this journey and who had to put up with me being away for so long and bear the brunt of my stress when home.

CONTENTS

FOREWORD

BY PHIL CAMPION

Former D Squadron, 22nd Special Air Service,
Security Operator, TV Personality & Author of *Born Fearless*,
Desert Fire, *Killing Range*, and *Who Dares Wins*

I first met Jas in Kabul, at a time when the city was still in turmoil, just after the Afghan war. He joined me on a small close protection team looking after a European Ambassador. It was a great job and Jas brought a great deal to the security team.

A typical former paratrooper, he was a proper operator and also a great geezer to have around off duty too. We had so many good times, it's impossible for me to catalogue them all and I am sure he will have discussed more within the chapters of this book. Jas was game for anything at any time, if there was something going down he was getting his kit together without having to be asked. There is nowhere on this planet I would not go with him and no better trooper to have by your side when the red mist is coming down.

There are two times in particular where I remember him best. The first was when a crowd surrounded our vehicle near Chicken Street in Kabul. Whilst I was trying my best to drive out without squashing anyone too badly, Jas had already brought his Glock into a position where from the outside you couldn't see it but should anyone make the wrong move he would have flat packed them in a heartbeat. A totally unrehearsed move and instinctive, showing his true colours in the face of drama. He never flinched and I have no doubt he would have been taking names if the need arose.

The second was in Dubai when we had been for a night out. I was flying home the next morning and he was flying into Kabul. We always did our handover in Dubai and had a few beers together. I woke in the morning a little worse for wear and, struggling to get dressed in time to catch my flight, I was searching for one sock. I was going mad looking for the bloody thing, which Jas had stolen. To take both would have been no fun. Letting me believe I had a chance of finding my sock, now that would have made him laugh all the way to Kabul.

We did safely operate in Afghanistan, Iraq and Sudan over the years and my only regret with Jas is that we never did enough together.

INTRODUCTION

Do I believe I am something special? No, I don't. Have I done anything that no one else has ever done before? Probably not. Do I think I have a story? Yes, I do. I think everyone has a story, some more interesting than others for sure, but there is a story in us all, and this is mine.

I have named my book, 'Long Road to Libya' because it refers to the personal journey I took and challenges I encountered along the way, through my time in the army, then on the security circuit and finally as I built my own business to get to my final destination where it all culminated, Libya.

Over the years, I had some unbelievably great times and the absolute pleasure to serve in the Parachute Regiment, and work on the Private Security Industry 'Circuit' with some of the finest men you could ever wish to have around you. I also encountered those who attempted, for whatever reason, to derail my journey, knock me down and stifle my road to success.

After selling my business, the time had come for a change of direction in my life. When I was originally approached to write this book, even though I was sceptical at first about the idea and how it may be received by my peers, I soon realised it was the perfect ending to my own very personal journey. The process allowed me to enjoy reminiscing and to put down on paper the exciting and sometimes difficult times I endured reaching this point in my life.

Within this book I talk about The Circuit, a term we who work in the private security sector use when referring to our sometimes murky and secretive industry. Many people simply view us as mercenaries, only interested in money and power. Yes, we get paid for our services, but it is nowhere near as much as people might believe and in return for this, we risk our lives in the course of our duty.

For the vast majority of us who work in this industry, it is purely an extension of our military careers, but mostly without the logistical and political support you receive in the armed forces. The tasks we are contracted to perform always have one purpose in common, to protect and save the lives of those clients who are entrusted into our care. This role tends, in many cases, to bring us up against old foes and the common enemy: radical terrorist groups wanting to disrupt and destroy our very way of life.

As in every industry, there are various types of people who work on The Circuit. In my time, I was lucky enough to operate for the smaller, more selective companies and was mostly surrounded by guys who were ultra-professional and many of whom I am fortunate to call my good friends to this day. Of course, there will always be an element that will spoil the reputation that our industry has built over the years. During my time in Iraq, in particular, this element grew out of control and tainted what the security industry had always stood for and will always truly be about in the future. There were those who were only motivated by greed, power and notoriety, if only in their own little towns or social media circles. These people had no regard for the safety of the local population in whose country we were living and operating. Trigger happy, poorly trained, and inexperienced Walter Mitty types, they were pretending to be something they most certainly are not, living out their own bizarre fantasies.

These types came from all walks of society during the boom time on The Circuit in Iraq. Fortunately, most of these people and their companies have now gone back to wherever they crawled out of and the industry has become far better regulated, self-policed and high quality once again.

Along with many of the great guys I worked with over the years, I was proud to serve in Her Majesty's Service and I was also proud of the work I did on the security circuit after leaving the forces.

PROLOGUE

The sprawling city of Kabul had been quiet since the official end of the war against the Taliban, but insurgent activity was bubbling away under the surface. On high alert inside our armoured Mercedes G-wagon, with my MP5 close to hand, we made our way along the roads between the embassy villa and the UN compound where my client wanted to play his weekly game of squash. In the side streets, old, clapped-out cars, trucks and mopeds made their way along the same streets as donkeys and carts. Women fully covered in burkas, men in loose, baggy trousers and shirts with jerkins over the top made their way along the dusty, dirty sidewalks. People carrying their belongings on their heads weaved in and out of street stalls and avoided men and boys on bicycles as they passed shabby buildings riddled with bullet holes, a stark reminder of the recent hostilities.

In the dying day, the mountains surrounding the capital city loomed in the background, their giant forms silhouetting on the horizon as we reached our destination without incident. I went into the squash courts with the ambassador and watched for a while as he and his playing partner smashed balls and themselves into the echoing walls. After a while, I wandered outside to the empty square in front of the main building and sat down on the low wall surrounding a flowing fountain. The air was warm and pleasant as I looked up at the starry night sky. I was vaguely aware of the hum of traffic and the tooting of horns beyond the compound walls; the noise muffled by the constant, soothing flow of water from the fountain. Looking up at the clear, star-filled sky, I lit a cigarette and drew in deeply.

The explosion split the air and rocked the walls. A violent blast of hot air lifted my whole body and threw me like a rag doll across the fountain, smashing me against the small stone wall to the rear, cracking the top of my head open. Blood ran out of the wound and streamed down the side of my face.

CHAPTER 1

JUST AN ORDINARY BOY

I was just an ordinary boy. There was nothing special or extraordinary about my childhood. Born in Basingstoke on the 20th February 1972 as the only child of hard-working and loving parents, Bob and Elaine Woods, my father was a carpenter who could easily turn his hand to most parts of the building trade and my mother worked in retail, mostly in Marks & Spencer and Owen & Owen. My father was a private man, but behind his introverted persona, he was very kind, fiercely loyal to his friends and family, a humble man with a wickedly quirky and outspoken sense of humour. My mum was a stunning young woman, brought up by her mother and aunty in Farnham after the Second World War. My mother was dating one of my dad's friends when they first met. My dad instantly fancied her and when she became single again a few weeks later, he began calling on her at her home, only to be met by my nan, who would give him what's for and send him on his way. My mum was not that keen on him in the beginning, mostly due to his NHS glasses, which was a bit harsh for sure, but my dad was persistent and gradually wore her down until she succumbed. Even though he was clearly punching above his weight, my dad won her heart and they began what turned out to be a lifelong romance. I obviously get my good looks from my mother.

We didn't have loads of money, but we weren't poor, we were just a normal working-class family. I was totally unaware of the struggles some people in the country went through with the oil shortages, strikes and short working weeks of the seventies; I was too busy riding my BMX, playing football and organizing war games with my mates. My parents weren't particularly demonstrative in their love and affection; typical of that generation, I suppose, so I never felt that I was missing out. I think all of my friends had a pretty similar upbringing. I didn't see much of my dad in the early days because he was working away a lot, but he was at home most weekends and then weekday nights when I was a bit older. He was a really lovely guy and would do anything he could to help anyone. He was a super hard grafter and he took great pride in his work. He made lots of things for me such as wooden machine guns with which I ran around the local estate, or roman swords that I took to school and used to beat my mates' swords until they broke in half. One Christmas he made me a two-metre square scaled model of a town in Europe during World War II. It had its own airport, bridge and beach and I used to play there with my toy soldiers re-enacting the D-Day landings and Arnhem parachute regiment raids.

All I wanted to do as a young boy was play war and be a soldier. My mum says that I had so much energy and she could not calm me down or control me; I was always running around outside organising all the other boys into teams and planning attacks. We built camps in the local woods and stole the farmer's bales of hay to pad them out and enlarge the defenses against the other groups of kids in the local area. At every opportunity, we would raid their camps, destroy their infrastructure, nick their gear and then run back to our own base. I dug holes in the back garden of our house in Basingstoke, cooked up and ate my meals from mess tins and slept outside overnight trying to simulate what I thought the army would be like. It was mad stuff, but great fun and I always felt totally at home in this military type environment. When I was in the house, I would constantly watch war films, *The Longest Day, The Eagle Has Landed* or my favourite, *A Bridge Too Far*. I was totally focused on one thing and one thing only, the army. I had no idea where it came from. All I ever wanted to be was a soldier. There is a photograph of me when I was five wearing camouflage gear at a street party to commemorate the Queen's Jubilee and another photo of me wearing the famous airborne maroon beret at an army show when I was six or seven. I dreamt that one day I would go on to earn a Para beret of my very own.

Dad was never in the army, but his father had been. I never met my grandfather, whose name was Clarence; he died before I was born, but I knew that he had been in the military serving in what became known as the Royal Corp of Transport. He had also been attached to the Long-Range Desert

Group which was a reconnaissance and raiding unit of the British Army during the Second World War, founded in Egypt in June 1940. I heard some great stories from my dad about my grandfather's experiences during the Second World War. One tale was from his time in North Africa. His unit, a group of drivers, stopped for the night to rest up and parked their vehicles on the rough track in the middle of the vast desert. Most of the men slept in and around the vehicles but my grandfather decided to make himself a bed in the sand dunes a short distance away. When he awoke in the morning, he discovered all of his comrades dead with their throats cut. An enemy patrol had come past in the night and silently killed them all. He was the only survivor because they had not seen him asleep behind the dunes.

It may have influenced me, who knows, but what was really interesting was that it was not until much later that I found out even more about my grandfather. When King Hussein of Jordan died in 1999, my dad received a letter thanking my grandfather for his service. It turned out that he had been a bodyguard to King Hussein when he was at Sandhurst Royal Military Academy training centre for officers in the early 1950's. When my military career ended, it would lead me to work in the private security sector, which was a relatively unknown business even then, and yet there was the evidence that my grandfather had moved into the same line of work many years earlier. My dad always said it had skipped a generation and that I was just like my grandfather who was a hardnosed disciplinarian man and very short tempered, even around his own family! Not sure I liked the whole comparison, but to be fair it was reasonably accurate.

Another revelation came when I found out about my maternal grandfather. My mother never knew who her father was, and my grandmother never talked about him. However, just a short time ago, my dad decided to trace our family trees and became interested in DNA testing. My mum's DNA tests revealed that her father was called Earl and had been a French-Canadian soldier based in England during the Second World War. My grandmother had had a relationship with him and discovered that she was pregnant after he had left for the D-Day landings in mid-1944. In those days, it was all kept very quiet and nobody ever spoke about the pregnancy or the father. My grandmother was shunned by most of the family for many years to come, which I always felt was very sad and totally unfair. They always presumed that my maternal grandfather had died during the landings, as did thousands of others and, as she never heard from him again, she left it at that. The DNA findings traced him to the island of Nova Scotia in Canada where he had died in 1999, aged seventy-two. Sadly, my mum never got the chance to meet her father, and we very much doubt that he ever knew she even existed, but perhaps all the military connections have been passed on down to me from both my grandfathers and run through my blood today.

When I was nine, I joined a junior section of the local army cadets in Basingstoke called the Wessex Rangers, which was run by a guy called Colonel Smith, not the A team leader, just to be clear. They installed a bit of personal discipline into me, which was much needed at that time. There were weekly drill nights and they took us out camping at the weekends to teach us how to live in the field and cook up military rations. They also introduced us to replica weapons and patrol techniques. I absolutely loved it and spent several nights a week and weekends involved with their activities. However, Dad had a dream of building his own house and wanted a change in the pace of his life, so when I was twelve years old, we moved to Cornwall. I was not happy about this at all, I had a great life in Basingstoke with my friends and the cadet group and did not want to move to Cornwall and live amongst the backward, tractor driving, Cornish bumpkins, as I saw it at the time.

I tried to make the best of things and joined the official Army Cadet Force (ACF) in Cornwall, but I didn't stay for long. It wasn't as well run as the set-up in Basingstoke and I didn't like it at all, or the people who were involved. I've always been the same that way. If I don't like someone or something, I generally say so and don't hang around any longer than necessary. As a young teenager in Cornwall, I began arguing with my mum over just about everything. It was the beginning of a theme that took a long time for me to understand and attempt to change; an inability to cope with women I love challenging me. I include the three lovely women I have had the pleasure to marry in my life and my beautiful daughter in this bracket, and to be brutally honest, I still haven't totally mastered that one today.

I hated school, always did. I had no problem with the discipline installed by the army cadets but just had no interest in learning the way they wanted to teach me in school and I always felt out of my depth. I reacted to that by rebelling and constantly messing around. That is when I actually went to school at all. Funnily enough, my teachers all thought I was quite bright and capable of a lot more than I was showing. They placed me in the higher sets and said that I just wasn't concentrating or applying myself in the correct manner to reach my potential, but I felt like I wasn't any good and so to cover that I just didn't bother. I remember dreading the English teacher asking me to read aloud because I didn't feel as though I could read properly and had no confidence in that skill set. I just hated the whole environment. I was constantly sent out of class and instead of waiting to be let back in or for the start of the next class, I just went into town or hung around the local park until home time. I was getting into more and more trouble, fighting with other lads and in scraps with the local older bullies who used to try and throw their weight around on the school bus, from which I tended to come out the worst.

I did love sport; the only days I looked forward to in school were when I had Games – two double sessions per week. I was in all the school teams for football, rugby, cricket, basketball and athletics. The only teacher who ever seemed to like me or pay any attention to me was my P.E teacher. I was not a good student and I'm sure looking back now that they just got frustrated with my lack of commitment and the disturbance I would cause in class when I was there.

I really thrived on individual sports where I could properly channel my competitive streak and had no one else to blame if I did not win. I was very good at tennis at an early age, but, unfortunately, I never received the encouragement or opportunity to pursue it to the next level. My P.E teacher at school spotted my talent and coached me for a while. He encouraged me to go to a private tennis club, but there was not the money or time in my parents' lives to support that dream.

In my mid-teens I found snooker, I had always had an interest in snooker and closely followed it on TV, supporting Jimmy 'Whirlwind' White each time he got to the world championship final and sadly lost on each occasion. I started to become a very good snooker player. I spent hours and hours in the local snooker hall in little, old St Teath, the sleepy Cornish village we were living in at the time, either just practising or playing against my mates Gary, Mark, and Digby. The hall only had one table and was hardly ever used. We had the keys and the technique for getting the ten pence to stick in the electricity meter so we could play for hours without paying. We raised money via a sponsored twenty-four-hour snooker marathon to pay for a new cloth. Together with an older guy called Bob, we formed and entered a very young team into the local Cornish league when I was fifteen. We won the second division that first year going unbeaten all season, reached the later stages of the cup where we were only just beaten by the league one champions and current cup holders and I reached the final of the doubles knockout tournament with my mate Gary.

We should have easily won that trophy, and our parents were there to watch us in our moment of glory. Unfortunately, we both froze on the big stage and literally could not pot a ball between us. We ended up losing to two old boys, two frames to nil, well they seemed like old boys to us. I thoroughly enjoyed snooker and again, in my dreams, I thought I could have taken it to the next level. However, I stopped playing the following year as the army came calling and nothing, not even snooker, could get in the way of that ambition.

I never lost the desire to join the forces. With my poor old dad trying his best to act as referee, my mum and I argued constantly. I was causing nothing but trouble in school and out and so it was probably best for all concerned when I went down to sign on a few months before my sixteenth birthday. I have to say that my relationship with my mum improved after that; I get on great with Mum now and love her very much.

At the time, I was obsessed with the Parachute Regiment having seen the television series, *The Paras* in the early eighties about 480 Platoon recruits going through the Para training. I was transfixed; that was what I wanted to be, and this was compounded by the amazing feats accomplished by the Parachute Regiment in The Falklands War in 1982, which were widely reported on TV at the time. Little did I know then, that I would one day be a member of 557 Platoon. My dad and I went to the Army Careers office in Redruth, Cornwall and the career officer we spoke to was in the Light Infantry. I did not realise it at the time, but he was clearly recruiting for his own regiment and did a very good job of persuading me and my dad that I couldn't join Junior Para at this time and that by joining the Light Infantry I would be eligible to become a Junior Leader, which he made sound very exciting. I was desperate to start, the thought of waiting another year or more and joining as an adult recruit did not appeal, so I signed on the dotted line and applied to join the Junior Leaders Light Division.

Not long afterwards, I travelled up to the army selection centre at Sutton Coldfield for initial tests. It was the first time I had been on a train on my own for any significant distance and sitting on that train I was nervous but exhilarated at the same time. This was a challenge and I have always loved and thrived on challenges, any form of competition, and I wanted to win. I could not bear the thought of going home on the train and telling my dad that I had failed, it just could not happen, and I would not allow it.

The initial tests that took place over a couple of days were fairly straight forward compared to the actual training. I had to sit a written test to be eligible for the Junior Leader section and if I didn't pass that, I would go in as a normal junior soldier. There was a medical test, a couple of reasonably simple physical challenges including a one and a half mile run and some gym tests such as pull ups and sit ups. I had been training hard at home and was a naturally fit kid, so had no issues with the fitness tests. Finally, there was an interview, after which they told me there and then that I had passed. I was ecstatic on the train home and only had to wait for the official confirmation by letter with a start date. I could not wait to tell Mum and Dad.

I was accepted into the Light Division Junior Leaders' platoon to start a one-year training cycle at the newly built Sir John Moore Barracks in Winchester on the 12th September 1988, a date I will never forget. A letter came through confirming my start date and containing a travel warrant for my journey to Winchester train station. The time came and I said goodbye to Mum and Dad at Bodmin train station in Cornwall. There were no tears on either side, I now had to man up fast. I now know that Mum cried once I was on the train, but even though they were both sad to see me go, they were also pleased for me. They both knew it was what I had always wanted to do. I was just so happy to finally be on my way. It may not have been my preferred choice of the Paras, but for now that did not matter and the opportunity to join the Parachute Regiment would come again in the near future. I set off on the train to Winchester where new recruits from all over the country were heading to a new life in the army. I was full of the excitement and anticipation of making my dream a reality.

CHAPTER 2

JOINING UP

Arriving at Winchester train station, I was greeted by a big, burly, giant of a man, a Corporal, shouting at the top of his voice. He called out our names and I was ordered to grab my kit and get onto the back of a large four-ton truck. I joined a load of other new boys who had arrived on another train a few minutes earlier. All in civilian dress, many with long straggly hair, apprehension was etched into their faces for what lay ahead. We were taken to the camp up on the hill above Winchester to be processed on arrival and then divided up into our platoons and different sections. It was a newish training establishment, purpose-built for the Light Division. I was designated as a Junior Leader and my first section commander was a guy called Corporal Lewis. He was a small, wiry character from 2nd Battalion the Light Infantry (2LI) with a funny, squeaky voice and a dodgy tash who definitely seemed to have some sort of chip on his shoulder. We were shown to a big room that had a small divide down the middle with five small beds on either side. That was my section and would be my home for the next year.

We had our kit issued and our hair shaved off. Corporal Lewis sat down with us the first night and laid down the ground rules: unpacking our kit, our locker lay out, standing up whenever he or any of the other platoon instructors came into the room. He immediately began installing discipline, shouting at us and making it very clear that he wouldn't accept any nonsense; we were not kids anymore and it was time to grow up. Anyone out of order got a clip round the ear and if you were not up to the mark, then you would be binned, in other words sent home. That scared me; failure was not an option, and to be honest, I had no other paths open to me in life, so I had to pass.

As sixteen-year olds, we were the babies of the camp. The other recruits in the adult platoons, who were at least eighteen and many of whom were in their twenties, looked on us as kids, which is exactly what we were. I think the instructors secretly liked the juniors the best because we had all chosen to join up at a young age and most of us were clearly obsessed with the army. We were also young enough for them to properly train and mould into exactly what they were looking for over the year ahead. Some of the older recruits in the adult platoons may have just drifted into the army because they didn't know what else to do or were just simply unemployed. Despite that, the general feeling was that I was in an elimination competition; only the strongest would survive and this was the attitude I carried through the entire training process.

There were forty young starters in the 1988 Corunna platoon, split into four sections of ten. All the instructors wanted to do at this early stage of the process was to get rid of those of us who were not fully committed to the job ahead and should not have been there in the first place. They wanted to root out those they initially believed did not have what it took to serve in the various battalions and to find out who had the mental and physical qualities for a career in professional soldiering. I love and have always thrived on competition and so for me it was just sheer determination to win through and not throw in my hand, get back squaded or even kicked out. As sixteen-year olds, we were not on full time contracts due to our age and could actually leave at any time. All you had to do was let them know and you would be straight in front of the Platoon Commander. The Officer Commanding (OC) would chat to you, check why you did not want to stay, ship you straight out, and put you on the train home. The thought of not making it through and letting Dad down was a great motivator for me.

Each day started very early in the morning around five-thirty with Corporal Lewis kicking the door open, turning the lights on and shouting at us to get up and ready; a week down the line we became responsible for getting ourselves up and ready for his inspection. We all jumped out of bed to get to the shower and to shave, regardless of whether we had any facial hair growth at that age or not. I didn't have any and could just as easily have stuck my head out of the window and allowed the morning wind to blow my bum fluff straight off, but shaving made us feel like real men. We got all our kit ready the night before, ironed our uniforms to perfection and the rest of our kit was in the lockers looking like a picture from a perfect home magazine. We then spent an hour cleaning our rooms, communal washrooms and block area before Corporal Lewis carried out his daily morning inspection.

We were all given certain block jobs to do each morning; if everyone did their bit then it worked well. The block needed to be cleaner than a hospital operating theatre to pass. This involved sweeping and washing the floor each morning, carefully laying down floor polish and allowing it to dry before using hand bumpers, which weighed a ton, to polish it up so that you could see your face in it. The sinks were cleaned with toothbrushes to make them look like they had just been installed and every ledge and under your bed was carefully dusted to make sure every single speck of dust or fluff was gone. Every morning, Corporal Lewis, followed afterwards by either the platoon sergeant or commander, inspected the entire room, our uniforms, lockers and bed blocks. Bed blocks were a challenge, similar to a Rubik's cube, but with blankets and sheets. It was a skill we all had to learn fast, or else it simply got thrown across the room or out of the window. In essence, you folded your spare blankets and sheets to a certain specific size, then laid them on top of each other like making a sandwich, fifty centimeters by twenty centimeters with sharp ninety degree corners, then wrapped the remaining blanket around so it fitted perfectly and clearly showed the front of each of the other sheets and blankets. This was placed on top of your mattress cover which was pulled tight under the bed with sharp hospital corners and pillows sat on top in perfect order. Difficult to explain let alone make! Needless to say, some fun was had with our efforts. It reminded me at times of an episode of Bruce Forsyth's Generation Game where an expert came on and made something which looked reasonably simple and then asked the contestants to copy, which would, of course, go badly wrong and be nothing like the expert's example!

Even if there was nothing wrong, Corporal Lewis would find something to pick on and went berserk, yelling, overturning beds, throwing kit and bed blocks around the room. To be honest it made me laugh a lot and we would all stand there trying not to giggle as someone's entire belongings were thrown out of the window, unless they were yours, of course. This was all designed to see if you had the mental aptitude to handle the stress and work under time pressure. One morning, it was my turn to be picked on and my bed and all my kit were literally thrown out of the window onto the ground below. The corporal then picked me up and hung me out of the window by my belt, all the time yelling at me and telling me I was useless and asking did I really think I deserved to be there after whatever it was that I had done wrong. Our room was two floors up and I really wasn't sure that he wouldn't let go; at least my mattress was on the ground below, which I hoped I would land on, if he did.

As juniors, we had a year of training before we could pass out and go to our respective regimental battalions. The older adult recruits only had six months to make the grade. Over the next few months, I really bonded with the guys in my section and made some good friends throughout the platoon as we were put through our paces. The guy in the bed space next to me was called Young and he was from Mansfield. He was a very calm guy and brilliant at organizing his locker and ironing his kit; he had this great, all singing, all dancing steam iron that made light work of the ironing. All I had was a little travel iron, which was not up to the job at all. Young used to lend me his iron once he had finished and sometimes ironed my shirts whilst I bulled his boots, a skill I had mastered in the cadets and could do quite quickly and well. It was teamwork at its very best and was actually what the army was all about.

In order to punish us as a collective, one of the instructors' favourite techniques was what they called 'change parades'. This was utilized when they felt that as a group we were not performing or working hard enough, or, if truth be told, no matter how we were performing, it was still going to happen. It usually took place in the evening after we had prepared all the kit in our lockers and they were immaculate, ready for the next morning inspection. They got us all formed up outside the block, delivered a bollocking and then gave us two minutes at a time to change into a new set of clothing and the time only stopped once the last man from the entire platoon was back outside dressed correctly, and we were all formed up in three ranks. They would then find someone who was not in the right clothes, not smart enough or too slow and pin the blame on them for another change and the whole process would start again. The change of clothing could range from working dress to barrack dress, or PT kit to shirt sleeve order. However, there were a lot of other weird orders such as full NBC (Nuclear, Biological, Chemical) suit with respirator; this meant all of us trying to run down the stairs with gas masks on that we could hardly see out of and wearing cumbersome suits. Then there was mess tin order which consisted of the two mess tins, which you eat out of when in the field, attached to a plastic belt around your waist just covering the front of your tackle and the back of your arse. Apart from the tins, we had nothing else on except our boots. This was a favourite choice of the instructors and clearly made them chuckle, as it did us. It was total mayhem during each clothing change. All the recruits ran as fast as they could to the stairs. Not wanting to be the last man back, we all tried to clamber up at once. We would arrive back at our own bed space to find the lockers had been thrown all around the room by the other instructors who were roaming around the block, so you could not find what you needed to wear anyway. As you can imagine, the odds were not stacked in the recruits' favour, and by the end of the evening, we were knackered and cold, with kit everywhere. Every item of clothing needed to be ironed again and rearranged perfectly back in the locker ready for the following morning inspection. It didn't leave much time for sleep, if any at all.

Every so often, I heard that someone else had gone to the Officer Commanding (OC) to sign off and I saw them back in their civvy clothes with their bag on their back being marched out of the block by their section commander. They just could not handle it for whatever reason and didn't want to stay any longer. I remember one lad called Powell in the bed space opposite me who just looked shit scared like a rabbit caught in the headlights from day one. It came as no surprise at all that he didn't last long and left before the first milestone of six weeks. However, it wasn't always the obvious ones. There were other kids who were real hard nuts; they were fit and not afraid to stand up for themselves but even some of them left. It just showed that it was about mentality and not so much physical strength. For me, it was all good. Every time someone left, I was one step closer and I thought, 'Hey, I must be doing okay, because I'm still here.' At the end of the six weeks was the first time we had any contact with the outside world and our families were invited up to see us.

The whole one-year training programme was a well-oiled and tested machine. It was split into four quarters and each individual day consisted of intense training. We had physical and mental challenges to push us further and further, all the time they got harder, and new skills were introduced. It was designed to weed out the weaker ones amongst us, who left.

We did runs and gym sessions that got progressively longer, and the physical training became gradually more intense. We first ran in trainers, then in boots and progressed to adding our webbing and Bergans (rucksacks) and carrying weapons over various distances and terrains. I have always been naturally fit and to be honest never really found this part too hard; I always seemed to do well. This of course went down well with the platoon staff; there was nothing they disliked more than unfit recruits who did not show the will power or heart to keep up with the pace.

Weapon skills was of course a large part of the training, and very early on I was introduced to my personal weapon the SA80 and over the following few weeks I learned how to strip it down and put it back together again, how to clean it and handle it with absolute precision. This was an ongoing process and every week there were tests and if you got something wrong you were 'beasted', which mostly involved some stress positions or running around outside with your weapon above your head, before having another go to get it right. Once you got close to mastering one weapon system, you were introduced to another such as the Light Support Weapon (LSW), General Purpose Machine Gun (GPMG), Browning 9mm pistol, Cargustof anti-tank weapon, and the 51mm mortar. All of these had to be mastered during the training process and fired live on the ranges at various stages throughout the year. Once you arrived in your battalions, you would be expected to be able to use all of these weapons as and when required with precision and confidence.

A huge amount of time was spent on field craft that involved learning the key skills of an infantry soldier in what was our true working environment outside the barracks; this was our bread and butter and what we would be judged on by our instructors and going forward, our peers. We learned everything from the basics about how to live and survive in the field: establishing harbour areas (a place where we slept overnight), putting up our bashers that we slept under, cooking our rations, patrolling as a section using various formations, reacting to contact, carrying out close target recces and ambushes, as well as blank and live fire attacks, to mention but a few. We were also taught about health and hygiene, which was key; if we did not look after our bodies in these challenging conditions, then we would be in no state to do our job and fight effectively beside our team mates when the time came.

As we were juniors and had an entire year of training, a fair bit of adventure training was mixed in with the intense military syllabus. This involved going away for a few days at a time and doing such things as rock climbing, canoeing, and hill walking where our navigation skills were honed. We also had some relaxed down time away from the intense grind of the camp training programme. There was a skiing trip to Italy, where most of us learned how to ski for the first time and, more importantly, we had a great week away from our usual instructors with plenty of time for beer, girls and more beer.

We could not legally drink in the Winchester pubs. On the odd night or weekend we were given off and allowed out of the camp, we had to seek out those pubs which turned a blind eye to your age or try to bluff our way in using our military ID cards and hope that the landlord didn't look too closely at the date of birth. My mate Vas and I went down to Bournemouth one weekend and arrived back at the camp totally pissed. I could hear Vas singing in his bed when the duty instructor walked in that night and hauled him out. We were charged and ended up in front of the OC to explain what we had been up to and received one week's show clean, which meant that on top of everything else we had to parade down the guard room four times per day and had restricted privileges.

Joining up as a non-swimmer was a major disadvantage for me, and something that I soon had to learn the hard way. Whilst the rest of the platoon was up one end of the pool having advanced swimming training, I was down in the shallow end with armbands on learning how to doggy paddle. As you can imagine, this was not something I enjoyed and I got a lot of stick for it, so I quickly learned enough to join the others in the big boys' pool. Everything was aimed at encouraging you to grow and mature as a man.

It was all fantastic and a lot of fun at times. I had come through the difficult early stage and I was thoroughly enjoying every part of the process, but then after six months, everything changed. A lot of the lads had signed off and gone home and those of us left in Corunna platoon, around twenty of us, were then amalgamated with another group of Junior Leaders being trained across the way in Anzio platoon. I had finally become comfortable with Corporal Lewis, and suddenly I found myself in a completely new group of guys under Corporal Spoon, who had his favourites amongst the Anzio lads and had a completely different way of doing things. Rather than building individual and team spirit, they seemed to actually get involved in and encouraged bullying amongst the recruits. I went from really enjoying it in a strange way to not liking it at all. Corporal Spoon had the few that he liked, and he did not seem to like me or care much at all for those of us who came over from Corporal Lewis' old section and he criticised what he had been teaching us. For a while, Corporal Spoon actually seemed to have very little concern for any of us from Corunna platoon. I lost a little interest during this time and started to struggle with the whole thing. I went from being right up at the top of my old section and platoon to somewhere in the middle. The rest of the training became a real effort for me, but I kept going, just kept my head down and motivated myself with the thought of how disappointed Dad would be if I quit.

Over the last few months of training, everything got progressively harder. Those of us left at this stage were unlikely to leave now unless injured and the finer skills of our training were being honed and tested ready for our final exercise and live firing package which was held up at the famous Garelochhead training camp in Scotland. Set up in 1940, it was the training ground for over twenty thousand American servicemen preparing for Operation Overlord, the Allied operation that launched the successful invasion of German-occupied Western Europe during World War II, also known as the Normandy landings.

The final exercise consisted of various scenarios that our training platoon had to deal with, including a vehicle borne insertion into the training area in Scotland followed by a long, day-night march to our chosen patrol base, which had some relatively basic facilities and cold running water. We then patrolled out of this base over the next couple of weeks. It all culminated in a march and shoot competition. On a cold and wet Thursday afternoon, we ended up on a live firing range far worse for wear than when we had arrived two weeks earlier. We had to fire an assortment of weapons and we were marked on our performance. We needed a certain team score and an individual point tally to be able to pass out back in Winchester the following week.

I got through this final exercise and all the tests by sheer determination not to fail and managed to pass out on the square the following week. This was a great day and a proud moment for my parents who also had the opportunity to meet my first proper girlfriend, Faith, who I had met in Southampton on one of our drunken weekends off during the training.

After a short leave at home in Cornwall celebrating and attempting to drown myself in alcohol, I was ready to move to my new battalion. At that time, in the late eighties, most newly qualified recruits tried to get a posting to a battalion either in, or about to deploy to Northern Ireland because it was really the only active theatre around at that time. Everyone wanted to be where the action was in order to put their training into practice. However, you had to be eighteen to go to Northern Ireland and I was still only seventeen and a half, so in August 1989 I was posted to Berlin and the battalion I was assigned to (1st Battalion the Light Infantry) had come back from a six-month tour of Northern Ireland a few months earlier.

I was on the train to Luton airport from where we were flying to Berlin later that day. I looked across and caught the eye of some guy staring back at me. He was one of the adult recruits who had passed out the same day as me. I remember thinking, who the hell does this idiot think he is? Neither of us looked away or broke the menacing stare. Damien or Stu, as I came to know him, was joining the same company as me in Berlin and we ended up becoming lifelong, best friends. Stu also followed my path to the Paras, was the best man at my first wedding and worked alongside me in Iraq and Libya once we got out of the army. All of this was in the distant future, right then he was a stranger, staring across at me on the train.

Berlin was considered a good posting at the time and the battalion had taken on a role as a quick response unit as part of the NATO forces based in Germany in the eventuality that the Russians should invade the West. Due to this, all the training was geared around lots of exercises and manoeuvres with the other countries' troops based in Berlin and Germany as a whole, including the Americans and the French which was very interesting and a lot fun, especially when working with our American cousins. Throughout the British sector of Berlin, there was also a huge amount of guard duty that the battalion was responsible for, and this kept us pretty busy and in a good work routine.

The Berlin Wall was still up when I arrived, and the city was divided into four clear sectors, the British sector, American sector, French Sector and a large Russian sector in the East. Within the first few weeks of being in Berlin, our company commander arranged for us to go over to the east of the city. This could only be done with permission from the East German police and we had to wear number two dress, so that we could be clearly identified. Times were clearly changing as a visit to the East would never have happened a few years earlier. The guys enjoyed it because we got around seven East German Deutschmarks to one West German Deutschmark and this meant that everything was cheap to us. It was also way behind the times and there was not much worth buying and bringing back, so we just settled for a few cheap glasses of Steiner beer.

Little did I know when I went, but after a couple of months of being in Berlin, on the 9th November 1989, the Berlin Wall came down. The checkpoints opened up with East Germany allowing those trapped in the East since 1961 to travel freely to the West. This was a momentous time in history and looking back on it now, it was great to be part of and to witness it transpire, even though I don't think I actually appreciated that at the time and probably did not soak it up as much as I should have. That evening my platoon was posted to one of the checkpoints, which had been designated to open up and allow the East Germans across. We were briefed to look smart and to be welcoming and I was tasked, along with a few of the other blokes, to hand out hot tea as the people came through. Hundreds streamed through that evening, with huge smiles on their faces, most of them were driving the classic East German Trabant, a small box-like car which had become synonymous with the Eastern Bloc regime. Crowds of people massed around the wall, climbing on top of it and over it. Many were smashing at the concrete with pickaxes and mallets. It was a huge party as people celebrated the momentous announcement that travel restrictions had been lifted marking the symbolic end of the Cold War. At the first opportunity, I borrowed a local guy's hammer and chisel and chipped off a bit of the Berlin Wall with some graffiti on as my own souvenir from this historic time.

Looking back at my short time in 1LI, the first thing I remembered was the culture of bullying, especially of the new recruits. This is something I have never liked to see or ever wanted to be a part of, and I remember thinking at the time that this was not what I was expecting at all. When you first join a battalion you know that you have to prove your capabilities and your worth to your peers and I had high hopes of becoming part of a close-knit team, making some great friends, and getting involved in some exciting soldiering. However, whilst there were some very talented and committed soldiers in 1LI, many of whom I greatly admired, unfortunately, the majority of my memories were of guys who were more worried about doing as little as possible, were not that good at their jobs and had no great pride in who they were. Considering the time that a lot of them had been serving, their previous N. Ireland experience and the role we were supposed to be fulfilling, it was disappointing. I did have some good times whilst there and I made some friends, one of them being Stu, and we totally embraced the German drinking culture and got to know the women in town. After a few months of being in 1LI, I was quite disillusioned and began to think again about my dream of being in the Parachute Regiment. I believed that was my destiny and where I should have been in the first place if I had not been sneakily steered in the wrong direction all that time ago in Redruth army careers office.

My plan was to apply for P Company, which many considered the hardest physical training course in the army apart from Special Forces selection. This I believed would allow me to then transfer to the Paras. However, the LI did their best to block this and I consequently found out that the only way to actually achieve my dream was to apply for a full transfer and go back to basic training with the Paras. This sounded like a nightmare at first, considering that I had only just completed a year's training as a recruit to get to 1LI, but if that was the only way, then I was prepared to put myself through it again.

Once I started thinking about the Parachute regiment again, I couldn't let go of the idea and being as headstrong as I am, even though I was still considered a new bloke in my current unit, I was determined to follow up on my dream and make it happen. I asked around, mentioned it to my platoon commander and kept on pestering him. They eventually said that I could apply for it if that was what I really wanted to do. I had to wait a few months for my transfer, and of course, the other guys in my platoon were understandably not particularly impressed or happy about someone like me, so new to the battalion, choosing to leave them so soon and wanting to move to the Paras, who they clearly disliked. Some of them naturally gave me a hard time about it. Every now and again after a night out, some of the senior private soldiers, usually those who were the worst soldiers, kicked in the door to my room and attempted to rough me up a bit. They then sent me on some stupid errand to go out of the camp to buy them some takeaway food. To be honest all the new guys went through similar things and I just got on with it.

I learned in the future that the Paras were a very different breed of guys, far more professional, much fitter and tougher, but not bullies. They believed in developing team strength and individual spirit and you got a hard time in the Paras if you were seen not to be up to the mark with regards to your soldiering skills, not just because you were new to the battalion. In the Light Infantry, bullying went on for months and months and I just wasn't impressed by that behaviour, especially when it was being done by guys whose own soldiering skills were nothing to boast about at all. It was probably worse because they knew that I was transferring. I also got into a few silly scrapes in Berlin, got into some fights and even ended up getting arrested and spending a night in a German jail. I was brought back to the army jail at first and I was waiting for the German police investigation to send their findings to the regiment. Fortunately for me, they took a long time to send them and by then my transfer had come through. This was a stroke of luck and I packed up all my kit in a military flight box and collected what little money I was due from the pay office. I was then taken to the airport with my bags and left to get on a plane back to the UK. I never heard from the LI again and that investigation must have ended up in a bin somewhere along the line. I had been lucky and it was even more incentive, not that I needed any, to pass Para training and never have to return to the Light Infantry.

I arrived back in the UK and made my way to Aldershot, 'The Home of the British Army' as it was known, dressed in civilian clothes. I ended up getting a train to Aldershot and a taxi to the barracks with all my kit bags, which cost me a lot of money and I didn't have much at the time. I remember arriving at the gates to Browning Barracks without a clue about what I had to do or to whom I should be reporting. The barracks have all gone now and just a museum and the famous Dakota plane remain, but it was the most amazing place. Across the road from the training depot (which was known as 'The Factory') was Montgomery Lines where Five Airborne Brigade, with its two permanent Parachute Battalions and attached support arms, was based. I could see the guys over there in their famous maroon berets at the gate of the Lines and all I wanted to do was to join them. First, I had to get through the factory. The next phase of my journey began, and this time it was exactly what I wanted to do.

CHAPTER 3

THE PARAS

I arrived at the gate of Browning Barracks, also known to the Paras as 'The Factory' in May 1990, with all my personal kit, alone and a little worried about what I had let myself in for and what lay ahead. I had no idea where to go and was faced by two 'Joes' (trainee Paras) in their crap hats on guard duty, who asked me who I was and what was I doing there. I tried to explain that I was from the Light Infantry and was there to transfer to the Paras. They weren't expecting me, my name was not on any list, so they got on the radio asking the guard commander what to do with me. I ended up going from one person to another, all of them asking who the hell I was and telling me, 'Get out of here!'

Eventually, I ended up at the Falkland's platoon accommodation where I was met by a sergeant who had the classic Para beret hanging over the front of his eyebrows with the cap badge on the left side of his head, a thick, long, wiry moustache and monster sideburns. After finding out who I was, he threw me in with a bunch of recruits who had either been injured during their training or had been back squaded from one of the platoons for failing P Company. Anyway, I was what was known to them as 'a hat' (a derogatory term for all other regiments in the British army); I was already a trained soldier who had been in another regiment. I was an easy target for their jokes. They ideally wanted lads who had come straight to training as a Para, to mould them in their own unique ways. They told me to go away and return with my P.T kit on in five minutes. I did as I was told and then this PTI, who was a tall, muscular, black guy, gave me some long-winded instructions to run out of the barracks, down past the canal and onto the main straight road heading towards North Camp to a specific lamppost a couple of miles away and to get back within a certain time. He told me that they would be watching me and if I wasn't back within the allotted time, I would be straight back on the train to my hat regiment, before I knew it.

I don't know whether they were watching or not, and I was not even sure which lamppost he actually meant. Either way, this was what I had wanted to do for so long, so I decided it was time to get to it and absorb whatever mental games they threw at me and pass any physical tests I was given. I was so determined not to fail. I got back just within the allotted time, absolutely exhausted, but that was just the start of a few days of physical 'beastings' at the hands of the Falklands platoon training staff. They threw whatever they could think of at me, but I was very fit; I'd been training super hard on my fitness in Berlin in preparation for this. It felt like mayhem at times and seemed like none of the Para staff seemed to actually know why I was there or what to do with me.

Finally, after a few days of constant runs, gym sessions and making endless cups of tea for the instructors, they told me to grab my kit and to go over to the other side of the barracks to join 557 platoon who had just reached week six of their training program and had just returned from their first few days of leave. This meant I was going back to basics. I started off thinking that I already knew everything. After all, I was a trained soldier with eighteen months experience in the army already under my belt. However, the Paras have their own way of doing things and I was soon learning new and different skills, even down to how I held my personal weapon.

I went into three section and met my new section commander Corporal Sid Marrant. He was a scary character from 3 Para, built like a brick shit house and exactly what I envisioned a paratrooper to be. He very quickly made it clear what he thought of me and my and previous military experience and that I was now a recruit again and in the factory. If I had any expectations whatsoever of becoming a paratrooper in his beloved regiment then I had to prove myself to him over the next few months. Corporal Marrant was a veteran of the 1982 Falkland Islands' conflict as were two of the other instructors; the rest of the staff including the platoon commander and sergeant were all from 1 Para. It became clear very quickly that the instructors from different regiments had their own ideas on how things should be done and there was a lot of banter between them. The 1 Para instructors had not gone to the Falklands because they were stationed in Northern Ireland at the time the conflict started.

The other recruits, split between the five sections, were a mixed bunch from all over the country. There were some real characters, and I started to get to know my new platoon mates. One of them, who joined around the same time as I did, was a guy who had been a corporal in the Ulster Defense Regiment (UDR), and we had another from the Guards Division. This just showed what pull being in the Paras had throughout the army: if they could relinquish their ranks to become recruits again, then I could certainly start again with the prize of the coveted maroon beret at the end.

Four and a half months of intense training followed, with the intention of making us twice as fit and twice as good as normal infantry soldiers by the time we passed out and joined our Para battalions. It was extreme, emotional hard work, but fun and rewarding at the same time. Long Tabs (a Para term for tactical advance to battle) ranging from six-mile speed marches to longer eighteen-mile slogs, were mixed in with field craft and weapon handling lessons. We learned new skills and every few weeks we went on exercises honing and testing our patrolling and live firing drills. It was all aimed at putting our new skills into practice. The standard of training and pure pride in the regiment we were all hoping to join was clear to see in everything we did, and totally outshone anything I had ever experienced in the past.

We were able to get out into town some evenings and weekends and we tended to head for the Alexander pub, up on the hill in Aldershot, and get as many pints and vodka oranges down us as we could, before we headed back for the eleven pm curfew. This was the only pub where the Para recruits were allowed to drink. Further down the road in town were other pubs such as The George, 5's The Airborne Inn, The Exchange and The Rat Pit, where all the Paras from the battalions and our instructors drank. This was where we all wanted to go, but certainly did not dare at this time.

Just like in other regiments, the training was designed to weed out those who were not up to the grade, but in the Paras the standards and targets were so much higher. Many of the recruits who failed P Company transferred to other regiments as trained soldiers but just did not make the grade for the Paras. We still had the daily cleaning routines and inspections from the instructors. I personally experienced and witnessed on many occasions when recruits flew into the back of their locker after a chest punch from one of the staff. It was all good character building stuff to be honest; in today's world, they would never get away with that sort of thing. One of their favourite punishments if things were not up to standard in the block was 'show clean'. They made you, or, as I experienced on a couple of occasions, your whole section show clean your entire room outside the guardroom at seven o'clock at night. This involved carrying every bit of kit that was not attached to the walls to the guardroom. We had to take beds and all down the three flights of stairs and across the square to be inspected in exactly the same layout as it was in your room that morning. Every item had to be laid out in order and to look immaculate. This was a military manoeuvre in itself and a test of all our will power, organization and teamwork to pull it off successfully. Again, it was all designed to test our mental strength and how much we really wanted that beret.

Time was also spent learning the somewhat short, when compared to other regiments, but undeniably action packed and glorious history of the Parachute Regiment, which was formed on the 22nd June 1940 during the Second World War, on the direct request of then Prime Minister, Winston Churchill. During WWII, the Paras quickly built a reputation as an elite, flexible and fearsome fighting force with operations in North Africa, Sicily, Italy, Normandy, South of France, Ardennes, Rhine Crossing and of course the famous operation, 'Market Garden' in Arnhem, Holland, which was famously dramatized in my favourite film, *A Bridge Too Far*. The modern-day Parachute Regiment is an elite airborne infantry regiment. The first battalion is now part of the Special Forces Support Group (SFSG) under the operational command of the Director of Special Forces. The other battalions are the parachute component of the British Army's rapid response formation. The Paras are the only infantry regiment of the British Army that has not been amalgamated with another unit and since WWII has served in the Far East, Palestine, Cyprus, Suez, Kuwait, Aden, Malaysia, Northern Ireland, the Falklands, the Balkans, Sierra Leone, Iraq and Afghanistan. This is what I wanted to be part of, it is special, as simple as that, and once you have served in the Paras, you will always be part of the airborne brotherhood. There is no such thing as an ex Para.

The staff of 557 platoon still gave me a hard time, saying that any time I wanted, I could go to the office and throw my hand in and they would happily send me back to the Light Infantry. Comments like, 'I'll drive you to the station myself,' were the norm. They did everything they could to test my will to stay and become a paratrooper. However, I thrived on all of that. The thought of being sent back to Berlin was motivation enough. I could imagine very clearly what reception I would receive on returning there as a failure. My life would just not have been worth living if I threw my hand in and returned to unit (RTU). It just wasn't going to happen.

All the way through the training, I kept that in my head. Whenever I was feeling exhausted, flagging or any negative thoughts found their way into my mind, I would just think about arriving back in Berlin and that would be enough to keep me going. There was no way they were going to get rid of me; there was no way I was going to fail, and gradually I got to know the other recruits, made some great lifelong friends, adapted to the Para way and started to do well. Corporal Marrant could see how fit I was and how strong I had become and was now using me as a motivational tool on tabs to push others in the section who were struggling by saying, 'Don't let a hat like Woods beat you.' However, I wasn't there yet and to get into the Paras I still had to pass P Company, which was generally acknowledged throughout the regular army as the most gruelling physical and mental test imaginable; a test of strength, speed, and endurance that pushes you to your mental and physical limits.

CHAPTER 4

P COMPANY

The time finally arrived for P Company. In order to qualify for my place in a Para battalion, this five-day, gruelling selection course had to be overcome. It would take everything I had and a maybe a bit more to pass; I was so close, but at the same time so far. This beast of a test seemed like a mountain standing between me and the maroon beret, that I had dreamed about for so many years.

P Company, an abbreviation for Pegasus Company, was the rigorous training and selection organisation based in Aldershot, at least it was when I completed it. Now it's based at the Infantry Training Centre, Catterick, North Yorkshire. P Company run the pre-parachute selection courses for trainee Parachute Regiment soldiers (known as Baby Paras) and officers as well as an all-arms course for Regular and Territorial troops. Unless candidates for trainee parachute training have already undergone a rigorous training course such as one run by the Special Forces, they must pass the pre-selection course, P Company. Only then can candidates go to Brize Norton RAF base for their Basic Parachute training course. The age-old debate on whether the course has got easier since moving to Catterick still rages on today. I have my own opinion, but will leave that subject to be discussed by others, as I'm sure it has been many times in the past and will continue to be in the future over a few beers by those who have successfully completed one version or the other.

The P Company that I was on took place over five days. The first two were in Aldershot and the last three days were over the hills in the Brecon Beacons in Wales. There was a short weekend break in the middle when we sorted out our admin, and were transported between the two locations. There are ten gruelling events in P Company. Each event carries a maximum of ten points, with three events, the log race, the trainasium and the stretcher race also being a pass or fail i.e. if you come off the log or stretcher, or do not complete the trainasium, then you get an automatic fail – you are off P Company and that is that.

The first half of P Company, held in Aldershot, started on day one with the steeplechase, followed by the log race and then the assault course. On day two we had the legendary Aldershot ten-miler, followed by a test of heights and nerve with an aerial assault course called the trainasium and then lastly the milling. Then it was up to Brecon for the second phase that started with a gruelling seventeen-miler endurance march on day three. Day four commenced with a twelve-miler over Pen Y Fan and Fan Fawr, followed by a six-mile speed march. P Company then culminated on day five with the fearsome stretcher race. If you got through all of this without failing any of the key events, managed to amass enough points and were also deemed in the eyes of the P Company permanent staff as worthy, you then hoped to hear that awesome word 'Pass' as your name was read out on the cattle grid and to receive the coveted maroon beret.

I was ultra-fit by this time, had been lucky enough to get this far through the training with no injuries of note and was probably classed as one of the fittest of all the guys left in the platoon. If I could remain injury free, I was reasonably confident that I was capable of passing. I was mentally ready and I just wanted to get on with it. Although I was nervous, the inability to accept failure and its consequences was all the motivation I required.

Early on a hot Thursday morning, dressed in lightweights, boots and red PT vest, with my heart beating through my chest, we all gathered in the woodland ready for the first P Company event, the Steeplechase. It's not like you see on TV or in the Olympics, a gentle run around a track in trainers with a few minor hurdles to jump over at regular intervals on each lap. This is an extreme cross-country course over two miles of uneven ground with numerous obstacles, mud and water to overcome and a mass of other men heading in the same direction, clambering over one another and pushing each other out of the way as if their lives depended on it. You have nineteen minutes to complete the course for your ten points, and you are docked one point for every thirty seconds you finish over this time. Everyone aims to beat everyone else and complete the course within the allotted time, desperate to collect their points and get their own P Company off to a good positive start.

The gun fired in the background and we all set off. By the time we got through the first obstacle, my boots were full of water and mud. It was absolute madness with guys all around me pushing, shoving yelling, jumping over obstacles and landing on top of each other. There were bodies everywhere and I pushed myself forward as fast as I could to get away from the crowd and find some space where I could get into some sort of rhythm. I started to control my breathing, which was getting out of hand, as my adrenaline took over. This was an individual event, different to many others where you were encouraged to work as a team, and to be honest, I was out for myself on this one. I pushed past one of the other guys as I scrambled through the thick mud and squeezed past the edge of the trees; the branches cut and slashed at my face. I splashed through the water jump and fought my way through the woodland. Leaping over one of the wet and muddy obstacles, I slipped as I touched the ground, and while I was finding my feet, another recruit coming up fast behind landed on top of me. A little dazed and now completely covered in shit, I stumbled up and regained my composure. I was even more determined now to push on hard. I had to make up for that fall. I was in the zone and making good progress around the course, gradually overtaking a few of the lads as I moved on, trying my best to get to the end within the allotted time. Getting those ten points was my only focus as I forced my way forward to a space near the front-runners, away from the melee behind me and headed for the finish line. I called upon a last spurt of energy and sprinted across the line as P Company staff clocked my number and time. First event under my belt, it was time now to settle the nerves, a little like a challenger feeling out his championship opponent's power in the first round of a world title fight. Nine more events to go. After I had finished, I discovered that one of my mates had pulled out after sustaining an injury and his P Company was sadly over. For me, it was back to the block for a quick shower, change of clothing and ready for the next challenge, the log race.

We formed up later that morning on the sandy area in the middle of the Aldershot training site. This time dressed in boots, light weights, white PT top, helmet and webbing, we were ready for the second event, the log race. Fifty metres or so ahead of us lay four shortened telegraph poles, weighing sixty kilograms each with toggle ropes for your hands to slide through on each side, which would enable us to lift the log and carry it. One guy was at the front pulling the log with his rope wrapped around his shoulder and setting the pace. As a team, we had to carry the log, which was meant to represent a battalion anti-tank weapon, across two miles of undulating, sandy, wet and muddy terrain. I was in a team with other guys from my section taking turns to hold the ropes and we were racing against three other groups. We were all pumped up, ready to go; I could feel the adrenalin running through my body from nervous anticipation of what lay ahead.

A thunder flash went off to our front that was the signal for the start, and we were off. The burst of adrenalin in that short sprint to pick up the log was incredible. It felt like I was running the one hundred metres in the Olympics and it used up so much nervous energy. I grabbed my rope and wrapped it around my right-hand wrist. Feeling the weight of the log for the first time, we all lifted together and headed down the two-mile course, across the sand towards the first steep hill. It was heavy and the rope cut into my skin, but I blanked it from my mind. The P company staff, dressed in their distinctive blue tracksuit tops and berets, kept their beady eyes on us all as our own section commanders ran alongside, shouting at us to move faster, to work as a team, getting a grip of those who were not pulling their weight and encouraging their own particular sections to win the event, which of course reflected well on them.

We made our way up steep sandy hills, down the other side, slipping and sliding all over the place as we came down with guys going headfirst but desperately making sure they held onto the ropes at all times. After the steeplechase in the morning, I was pushing my body to keep up as I felt like I was running on an empty tank. Around corners, through the mud, and then up the sand dunes we went. Regularly changing over positions on the log, encouraging each other to keep going, this time we were very much working as a close-knit team over two miles of pure hell. All I thought about was staying on my feet as guys around me slipped and scrambled to get up. If you let go of the rope and fell away from the log, you were out. The heat seared down on us all and the sweat was pouring down my face from under the helmet that served no purpose other than to make me feel hotter and more uncomfortable than I already was as it flopped around on my head. My hand was bleeding from the rope but there was no way I was going to give up. I was now back in the zone, totally focused on finishing the race, pushing my team on, doing whatever it took to win. It wasn't until the end, I realised that more guys were missing. They hadn't made it. I felt wrecked, totally exhausted, but exhilarated.

In a really weird and masochistic way, I had actually really enjoyed it. I was so relieved that I had got through the event and stayed on the log. I put everything I had into the race and was absolutely knackered, but that was only the second event of day one; I still had the assault course to go in the afternoon. It was time to get back to the block again for another quick shower and change of clothes and then off to scoff at the cookhouse to refuel the body ready for the next event.

The Assault Course, another test of individual fitness and stamina, was located at the back of the camp and consisted of a combination of around fifteen high and low obstacles on a circuit which had to be completed three times within seven and a half minutes. We formed up ready for the start of the event, this time wearing our red PT tops, which we had washed and dried since the morning's first event, with lightweights, webbing and helmet. I really hated running in the helmet, as it just would not stay still and kept falling over my eyes, but this was, of course, all part of the test and it was what you would be wearing if and when you went into battle with your battalions in the future. It would also be handy if you fell off one of the obstacles onto your head! The course was never dry, and the muddy conditions just added to the difficulty level of the energy-sapping test. I was pretty nimble and fast in those days and managed to keep up with the leaders as they sprinted off and got a good start making a bit of room away from the main pack as we clambered over the first obstacles. I stayed up near the front as we went round once, twice and by the third lap, my legs were working in automatic as I pushed on with sheer determination to the finish. By the end of this event, I was truly exhausted, but just so relieved to have got through the first day with a decent point tally in the bag and no injuries. The P Company staff don't tell you what points you have at any stage; this is so you don't get overconfident and think you have made it or relax too much in later events. However, you know yourself pretty much how well you have done and can reasonably approximate your points.

The day was not over yet. We had to go back to barracks and clean all our kit again ready for the following day's events. We only had two P.T shirts (red and white) so they had to be washed and ironed and my boots, crusted in thick mud, had to look as if they had just been taken out of the box brand new. Even though we were on P Company, our kit still had to be immaculate each day. This was all part of the test and reminded us of the self-discipline and dedication required to serve in a Para battalion.

Once everything was prepared, I got straight into my bed and slept like a log, no pun intended. I was so tired that almost as soon as my head hit the pillow that night, I was asleep; the only thoughts I briefly had whirling around in my head were for the upcoming events. In the morning was the legendary ten-miler with a 35lb Bergan on my back and a weapon. This is tough but I'd done it many times in training. My biggest fear was the event after this, the trainasium. This is the real test to make sure that you can hack it as a paratrooper, have a head for heights and nerves of steel. I wasn't absolutely sure that I did and I knew that if I made one slip, it would all be over.

The ten-miler is the flag ship event of P Company, and, as I found out later when I got to battalion, a test that the Paras like to do on a Friday morning usually after a heavy night out on the town to check their fitness levels. Hangovers or not, everyone in the company takes part and it's a great check on how fit you are at any time in your career. Today there are Paras 10 events, as they have come to be known, held in the UK each year that anyone can apply to do and match themselves against the Paras' fitness levels.

The ten-miler we had to do was the same route as the Paras had been doing for many years in Aldershot. Starting after we had gone under the bridge, by the Basingstoke canal next to Malta Barracks, we then headed down past the army golf course and over Engineers Bridge. The iron bridge was a well-known landmark. As recruits, we had to climb up onto it, walk over the top girders and then climb down the other side. It was another impromptu test of our nerve; there were no health and safety regulations in those days. The route then went out past Rushmore arena and onto the training area, up Hungry Hill, Flag Staff, through Long Valley, Miles Hill and then back around towards the Driver Training Circuit, again past Rushmore Arena, over Engineers Bridge for a second time and along Laffan's Road to the finish line. Sounds easy, but far from it; we had to complete the run in one hour forty-five minutes to get the ten points and pass.

I had a Bergan weighing thirty-five-pounds on my back, water and my weapon in my hands. A member of the P-Company staff weighed your kit at the start of the event, to make certain you weren't cheating and then led the way making sure that the pace he set would bring the main pack who stayed with him in on exactly the one hour forty five minute mark. This meant that those that kept up with him would get the full ten points for the event. We also had a support team with us, as in most of the events, consisting of a medic and a wagon to pick up stragglers who weren't going to make the cut off time, and these were always as close by as they could be.

Off we went. We headed off over Engineers Bridge and towards the training area, where Hungry Hill would be our first major climb. This is a very steep hill. I pushed myself up the slope, my calves burning, my legs feeling like jelly from the sheer exertion, my heart pumping and sweat pouring out of me. At times, some of us were literally on our hands and knees getting up this steep and narrow hill. At the top, there was a chance for a quick water break and then the P-Company staff checked which of us were on the pace with him and designated other members of the training team to stay behind and mop up the stragglers. Then he was off again, and I knew I had to keep up with his pace or I would not get to the next much-needed water break or have a chance of receiving ten points. Behind me, guys who were dropping off the pace were picked up by the medical staff, checked over and allowed to continue if they showed they were still with it, or otherwise put on the back of the wagon. They knew which guys were not going to make the cut off time and made them stop.

The route took us back down the other side of Hungry Hill, over the training area and towards Flag Staff. After this, we hit Long Valley, an area of undulating sand tracks used for training and testing army vehicles. It was bad enough trying to move quickly on normal dirt track terrain but getting through the deeply rutted sand and waterlogged tracks of long valley with all the weight we were carrying was another thing altogether. It was like running through thick treacle. I felt as though my legs were weighted down and I just had to keep picking them up and moving forward step by step. We eventually made it through the valley and headed to Miles Hill for the final water stop. By now, the main pack had shrunk and there were only around ten of us left who were on the pace. We started to head for home. Once back on the main road, we turned the corner and headed back over Engineers Bridge. We knew we were getting close and could see the finish line, but it was still a mile or so away. My tank was running on empty by this point, but somehow, I managed to drag up my final mental reserves to keep myself going and get in with the main pack. The end was in front of us; I crossed the line with the pack and thankfully got my ten points.

With the ten-miler completed successfully, there was no time to rest and I quickly started to prepare myself for the next test. This was the part I was dreading the most; I was more nervous about this than all the other events, the trainasium.

This was the Para Reg confidence test. Located in the depot grounds at the back of our block was a course purely designed to see how a would-be paratrooper will react when faced with a problem whilst fatigued and under stress. There is not a great deal of physical effort or fitness needed for this event. However, a huge amount of mental strength, fortitude and nerve is required. The P Company staff are not only looking for confidence in the air, but total obedience to orders in stressful and scary moments. The test is designed to mimic the fear that we would face when jumping from a plane in operational conditions with dozens of our fellow paratroopers at our side. This aerial course had been well thought out and designed specifically to test recruits in this particular area with the help of psychologists, psychiatrists and not least the Parachute Regiment themselves. Hesitation or refusal to jump is not an option and it is quite obvious that you can't expect to be a paratrooper if heights are an issue or you cannot quickly overcome any hang-ups you may have at this key time.

The trainasium itself was a bit of a big boy's playground and consisted of a series of scaffolding poles and wooden planks built some forty feet above the ground in many places. It may have looked harmless to some, but not to me. The planks were wonky and unbalanced, they were placed in awkward positions and were replaced in many areas with wet slippery poles, which you had to walk or shuffle over, and they were high enough to kill you if you fell. Many so-called celebrity tough guys have attempted the trainasium over the years. They have failed to get around and have ended up climbing down with their tails between their legs. Later in my career, I had the opportunity to take the United States 82nd Airborne troops, who were over on an exchange trip, to the trainasium and around fifty percent of them did not make it around and climbed down in fright. It was no easy test for baby Paras to do, but it was instrumental in setting us apart from the rest of the army.

I was one of the last to go, I watched as the other recruits from my platoon navigated their way across the fearsome obstacle with my heart in my mouth. When my time did eventually come, I quickly climbed up the cargo net onto the first scaffold platform, moved along the planks safely until I reached a metal ladder. I climbed up until I reached the first of the confidence tests, the shuffle bars. I was now forty feet above the ground and the metal was unsteady and slippery beneath my feet when the instructor below shouted at me to go. I took stock of the situation, still trying to maintain my balance, as he called for my name and number. All I could think about was not falling or looking down at those little figures below, and from somewhere I had to find my voice and call out the answers. Somehow, I managed to call out, 'Number 19, Woods,' and then continued shuffling along the poles until I came to the two uneven metal stoppers which I had to lift each of my legs over one by one, whilst still maintaining my balance. I continued to shuffle over to where I was told to stop and touch my toes, and finally got to the other side of the structure to climb back down to the platform below.

I continued to move along and over further parts of this difficult and testing obstacle until I reached the illusion jump. There was a large gap between the plank I was standing on and the next plank, which was a couple of feet below and all I could see was the daunting distance to the ground in that gap. The wooden plank I was standing on and the other I was supposed to then jump onto had been designed and positioned in such a way that it created an optical illusion and gave you the feeling of a long, impossible distance. In fact, it was not that far and was quite possible if you committed to the jump. You had to stand with your feet and knees together and jump exactly when you were told to by the P Company instructor, just as you would from an airplane with your parachute on, but you had no parachute. This was a crucial test to find out if you had the balls to do the job. I don't particularly like heights, and this was the hardest thing I had faced. However, I knew I would rather fall than fail, and so I forced myself through the fear barrier and jumped on his command. I landed safely and then continued around the obstacle, over the wooden seesaw and across more metal runners until I eventually got to the final cargo net leap, what is now known as the Superman Jump. The only way to ensure getting a safe grip on the net is to land sideways and to punch your fist straight through the ropes and grab on tight the other side. By aggressively punching through, you part the ropes and your arm goes through enabling you to get a firm hold. If you try to dive at it or grab the rungs with your open hands, it is more than likely that you will miss and fall or bounce back off it. The jump I made back in 1990 was then known as Leopard's Leap after a guy called Private Leopard, who missed by trying to grab with his hands open and had fallen ten years earlier. Since then, they had installed a safety net below, which made it only slightly less scary. I completed the course and got my points with a huge sigh of relief, but the day was not over yet.

We went back for lunch, stuffed it down our faces in a few minutes as usual and then headed back to the block for a five-minute power nap! During lunch the platoon staff put us all into pairs for the next event, the milling.

Milling takes place in 'The Factory' gymnasium. Benches are moved into the centre to form a small, tight square and all the recruits sit on these benches to watch the various pairs fight in the space between the benches. If someone falls backwards, then the other recruits seated around hold him up in the absence of ropes. The Commanding Officer of P-Company sits on a raised platform flanked by two other members of his team where they can see and judge the fights clearly.

The pairs are carefully chosen so that everyone is matched with someone of roughly the same height and weight and I was put up against a good friend of mine, Andy, who was in the bed space next to me. In cases where there had been a bit of a feud between two recruits during the training, the staff would take the opportunity to pit them against each other in a grudge match to get the situation resolved. We had this in our platoon with Connelly, a hardnosed, racist northerner, and Dell, a black, Mancunian guy. They just did not like each other, and it had been boiling away under the surface for weeks. Our red PT tops were dirty from the ten-miler and trainasium, so we only had white tops which would show all the blood. For this event, half of us were fighting bare-chested so there was no confusion during the fight. The instructors took us out into the block corridor in two lines before heading over to the gym. Everyone was standing opposite their chosen opponent, first eye balling each other and then shouting abuse and swapping a slap here and there. It was all designed to wind us up into a frenzy and prepare us for the fight.

The pairs got up to fight in the order they'd been placed. We were already physically and mentally exhausted from running the ten-miler and completing the trainasium, but this event was a test of pure manhood and mental courage. Milling is not boxing; boxing skills are actually discouraged, and you are not permitted to defend yourself. You just have to throw everything you have directly at your opponent's head, whilst keeping your own head up and fully focused on the target. All the P Company staff want to see is the will to fight, the guts to take a punch full in the face and keep moving forward. If you get knocked down, you get back up and go forward again. Even if the person you are matched against is clearly stronger and more skilled in the fight, you can still earn a good score by showing you have the heart to continue and the refusal to give in.

The gloves were eighteen ounces, there was no protective headgear and there were no gum shields in those days. The bell rang and the first pair launched into each other while the rest of us cheered and yelled as they fought, pushing them back into the middle when they fell on top of us. Blood was flying across the ring. It was only meant to last one minute, but sometimes they let it go on for much longer if one of the fighters was not showing them what they wanted to see. If someone was knocked down, the referee stopped the fight and then set them off again. The aim was not necessarily to just win; what they were looking for was those who could keep going in the face of adversity with the spirit of a warrior.

It was a ferocious and often gruesome battle. The P Company OC did not mince his words at the end of each fight. If he thought both fighters had given it one hundred percent, then he congratulated them. However, if he was not impressed, as with a couple of the fights on that day, then he told the offending recruit and left them in no doubt about what a weakling, pussy or big girl's blouse he thought they were. This, of course, could be a bit embarrassing for that person and left his chances of passing P Company and ever going to a Para battalion in great jeopardy.

I wasn't first up, and all I could do was wait and think about my fight. I just wanted to get in there, get on with it and get it over with. I can't stand waiting, it makes me nervous; I just want to get on and do things. Eventually, it was my turn. I can remember standing up and facing my opponent, my heart started to beat faster as the adrenaline ran through my veins and when they rang the bell to start us off, I just went for it and flung my right fist out with all my strength and caught Andy full in the face with a couple of clean shots. He went straight down which was a relief, but to be fair he also bounced straight back up again. I hit him with everything I had, but he jumped back up again to face me with blood pouring out of his nose. After this we exchanged numerous combinations of punches, it was a good fight and my own nose was bleeding as well now and my eyes were glazed over. He came at me hard with anger in his face and I punched again and again, nearly blowing myself out at one point. I kept catching him with good clean punches and he was taking each one of them and was still there standing in front of me wanting more. The last good right hook I caught him with knocked him down again and I kept thinking, 'Stay down, just stay down, for fuck's sake!' I got more and more tired and he kept coming back landing further punches of his own on me. In the end, the final bell rang and I was awarded the fight. I would imagine I got nine or ten points – there was not much more I could have done – but Andy was strong and would also have scored very well, which the OC acknowledged, due to his pure bravery and heart to keep getting up and continue fighting, which is exactly what they are looking for in this event. Andy was a top guy, very strong and resilient, a former body builder, and he went on to have a great career in 2 Para and the Red Devils free fall team.

The staff didn't want to see any defensive movements they just wanted you to go at each other and not give up. With the pressure off, I watched the following fights and joined in the yelling and cheering. There was blood everywhere as guys went at each other, neither wanting to give up. Finally, the fight that everyone had been waiting for arrived, Connelly vs Dell, and it lived up to the hype. Connelly was a beast and he went at Dell with everything he had but Dell, even though he was not as skilled, just kept getting up and dishing it back to Connelly. The OC declared it an awesome fighting draw and congratulated both fighters for the airborne spirit they had shown. Unfortunately for Connelly, he failed P Company in the end. Dell made it through and joined me in 1 Para, but this just showed how hard the ten-event test actually was.

Once the milling was over, we were told to stand down for the weekend with the wise words of advice not to drink too much because we still had a long way to go before passing P Company. Of course, nobody took that advice and in the proud traditions of the Parachute Regiment, it was with very heavy heads early on Monday morning that the diminished number of us got into the back of a four-ton truck and were driven to the Brecon Beacons in Wales for the second phase of P Company.

After a long, bumpy, four-hour drive, trying desperately to get some sleep the best we could, we arrived in Brecon, debussed at the side of the narrow mountain track, got our Bergans on and immediately prepared to set off on the seventeen-mile endurance march over the Brecon Beacons to where we would camp that night. This was the sixth of the ten events we had to complete. The seventeen-mile endurance march is a very long and arduous test. A lot of the guys were already carrying niggling injuries; the next seventeen miles was not going to be easy and would test all of our resolve.

The Brecon phase was, in the eyes of our instructors, the most important part of P Company, as it replicated the conditions in which we would, maybe one day, be expected to operate and fight. Our instructors constantly reminded us of the Falklands campaign, which they had fought in eight years previously, and how they were required to march, carrying heavy loads, across the Falklands' interior and stay switched on throughout to fight and win a battle at the end of it. The Falklands had a very similar terrain to Brecon and mirrored the hideous weather conditions.

As usual, the P company instructor set the pace – stay with him and get in within the allotted four hours and you passed and got your ten points, simple as that. The first leg was straight up the hill to the ridgeline and we then contoured the beacons up to the top of a large feature where we had a water stop and a head count. One of the guys, who was very fit, had dropped out before this point with a foot injury that he had picked up on the ten-miler.

We finally reached the end of the march in late afternoon with everyone managing to get in within the cut off time. I was feeling good and I finished with the main pack and got another ten points. However, my feet were starting to show real signs of wear and tear with some huge blisters appearing. The medical staff popped them with a needle and then put iodine on them to stop infection and assist in recovery. This was unbelievably painful, but it clearly amused the P Company staff as each of us in turn went through the same process.

That night we bedded down in some corrugated iron buildings where we ate our evening meal, an airborne stew knocked up by the chefs and delivered in a huge urn. We ate it with as much bread as we could get our hands on and washed it all down with a gallon of sweet tea.

The following morning, we were up bright and early, went through some kit checks with our platoon instructors, wrapped our blisters with zinc oxide tape and talcum powder and put on fresh socks in preparation for the day's two marches.

The first was the twelve-miler over Pen y Fan and Fan Fawr, which were mountain climbs totalling more than three thousand feet, and this was quickly followed by the six-mile speed march to that night's stopover point. The twelve-miler in itself sounded a lot easier than the seventeen miler the day before, but the miles were now taking their toll, especially with the six-mile speed march coming straight on the back of it in the afternoon. Another tough test with the field stretched out, I found the going hard on this one and had to dig deep into my reserves to keep up in the early stages. I just managed to hang onto the back of the lead pack as they got to the top of Pen y Fan. We had a quick water stop being careful not to get blown off the top as Pen y Fan is the highest peak in south Wales, 2,907 feet above sea level.

The second major climb of the twelve-miler was up Fan Fawr, which itself was 2,408 feet high with a cairn marking the summit. I felt far more energized on this leg of the tab and was determined to stay on our instructor's shoulder until we got to the top of the mountain. Again, there was another short water stop and head count before the steep descent down Fan Fawr to the finish point. The hardest part of this was staying on your feet as it was so steep and slippery, and in the back of everyone's mind at this point was the worry of turning an ankle as we slipped and slid our way down. This would have been disastrous with just two more events to go. I got through it okay with my second wind and finished on the shoulder of the P Company instructor to receive another ten points.

We stopped for a break, got a brew on and some food inside us and had time to change our socks and dress the blisters again. These were getting progressively worse and causing some of the guys major problems, but none of us was going to allow blisters or minor injuries to thwart our charge to the finishing post of P Company, which was now only two events away.

One hour later, we were off again on the six-mile speed march. Most of us who had been doing okay seemed to have found a new lease of energy and there was a spring in our step knowing at the end of this was dinner and another night's sleep followed only by the final event, the famous stretcher race. We could start to smell success. I was pushing my body to its absolute limits and although I was in pain, I found it exhilarating and, I have to say, I was loving the whole experience.

The six-mile speed march seemed to pass quite quickly, and the whole platoon got through it okay, generally keeping up with the P Company instructor. That night at our overnight camp, there was an eerie silence as guys got their heads around what we had already achieved and what still lay ahead of us in the morning. Morale was high, but no one wanted to get overconfident until the stretcher race was completed.

The morning came and it was finally time for the last event, the stretcher race. This was a team event and one which we would also be assessed on individually. It was made clear to us at the start that no matter how well any of us thought we had done so far, if we did not perform on this final event, then we would fail and it would have all been for nothing.

The stretcher race was six and half miles long and uphill for the vast majority of the distance. Weighing one hundred and forty pounds, the 'stretcher' is made of scaffolding poles and old tank tracks. Those of us who were left were split into three teams with team members taking turns to carry the stretcher or run alongside. We had our helmets on and our weapons slung over our backs as tight as possible to stop them from swinging around.

The instructors ran alongside us and if anyone looked as if they were not taking the weight or carrying it properly, they were out. If you tripped over a rock or fell away from the stretcher, you were out. They would back squad you, which meant that you had to do the whole thing again: all the training, P Company, everything.

By this point, most of us were verging on physical and mental exhaustion and we were all digging deep to squeeze that last bit of energy out of our bodies to get us through this final energy-draining test. The P Company staff were looking for those who in times of adversity could up their games one more level and they could then see who the strong characters were and on the other side of the coin, who was weak and could not handle it.

It was known that if an instructor didn't like someone, they might 'accidentally' knock them off the stretcher. When you weren't on it, you were expected to show encouragement to the ones who were and be ready and willing to take a turn at any time. The instructors were watching us like hawks all the time and marking us. The Log Race and The Stretcher Race looked like mayhem, but all of the P Company staff knew exactly what they were doing, and they were watching each individual to see how they reacted. My body ached, my hands and feet were covered in blisters and blood, but the determination and desire to complete the race and win were all consuming.

When the stretcher race was over, I knew deep down that I had passed, but the instructor still gave us a grilling, telling us all that we'd let him down, mainly because they all had bets on who would win and our team didn't come in first. In fact, our stretcher had come second out of three, just twenty seconds behind the winner. Not that it really mattered; we had all worked our socks off and given everything to get to the finish line.

We ended up back at the same cattle grid where the Brecon phase had started, and it was quite a momentous occasion. All the vehicles were there with the Officer Commanding P Company and you could see all the berets, which we had been measured for previously, lined up on a table. They already knew all the scores, they added on the final points from the stretcher race and all of us had to stand at ease and form up in two ranks with nothing on our heads and wait for our number to be called. They called out each number and just said one word, 'Pass' or 'Fail'.

I heard my number, 19. I came to attention and answered, 'Sir!' Then I heard that beautiful word, 'Pass' and accepted the much longed for maroon beret. Putting it on my head for the first time I grew a foot taller; it was the proudest moment of my life to that point; a day I will never forget.

About a third of the recruits who made it through to the end and formed up with me at the cattle grid failed. Their kit was thrown into the back of a truck, they got on and were taken back to Aldershot and were not really seen again. Those of us who passed got on a lovely, comfortable coach and were taken back in luxury so that we could prepare for the next phase of our journey, parachute training at Brize Norton RAF Base. We all went out drinking that night to celebrate our great achievement, but it was not over. We were still known as Baby Paras and I was nothing yet, as I still did not have my wings.

CHAPTER 5

PARACHUTE TRAINING

Nowadays, parachuting or skydiving is a very trendy, glamorous and thrilling hobby for some people. Military parachuting is nothing like that; it is purely a form of transportation, hardcore and not for the faint hearted. We usually jump at around eight hundred feet, three hundred in certain operational circumstances. This is so we are in the air for as little time as possible to avoid being seen or becoming targets whilst still coming down to the ground.

Most operational jumps are at night; we carry all our personal kit, weapons, ammunition and support equipment and the low-level parachutes we use are designed to get you to the ground as fast as possible. They are not really steerable, the landings are fast and hard in winds and on drop zones that are often not particularly receptive to parachutists, with hazards such as water, rocks, trees, buildings and uneven ground. The Paras principle role is to drop in behind enemy lines and to take and hold key strategic targets with little hope of support or reinforcement in the short term. Many injuries are sustained during the jumping phase including ankle, leg, wrist, shoulder and back injuries. Later in my career in 1994, I took part in the, now legendary, Sardinia NATO exercise training jump. Aptly code named 'Dynamic Impact', we sustained forty-four injuries due to landing on a rugged drop zone littered with rocks, potholes, and hard baked sand. All I could hear that day was the word, 'Medic!' being shouted out, as so many of my fellow paratroopers lay badly injured across the hazardous DZ. I actually had a very soft landing, must have been lucky again. I wasn't so lucky on the 50th Anniversary of the Arnhem jump, when I dislocated my left shoulder. However, I still managed to get down town that night and have a good evening with the lads.

On arrival at Brize Norton, which is a large RAF base in Oxfordshire, we bedded down in the accommodation block and then, with our new maroon berets proudly on our heads and stable belts around our waists, we headed to the RAF cafeteria for lunch. We were all absolutely gob smacked at, not only the amount, but also the standard of the food available. It was something that none of us had ever experienced before having only eaten in army cookhouses and the Aldershot depot was not exactly high up in the rankings of those. We were amazed by how the RAF was fed and generally looked after compared to the army. It was a real eye-opener and I'm not sure why that gulf in standards should exist. The RAF had become used to Paras on their base by now, so they were not surprised when we acted like a plague of locusts and went about trying to eat the entire contents of their dining hall in one sitting.

Our Para training started the following day and consisted of a week of ground training before we even got close to thinking about carrying out our first jump. We learned how to fit our parachutes and pack our containers, which carried all our personal equipment and weapon when jumping. This container is attached to a parachute harness by two bulldog clips. When jumping and once in the air, the clips are released, allowing the container to drop on ten-foot ropes and hang in the air below the parachutist. It then hits the ground just before he lands.

We also spent a lot of time in lift swings, which simulate being in the air. The swings helped us to learn how to exit the plane properly, and to check and deal with any issues the canopy might have once we were out of the plane. The trouble was they crunched your nuts up, at times raising the pitch of your voice, and definitely were not good if you had any expectations of fathering children in the future. It was humorous to watch guys in the swings who had their nuts caught up under a strap. They were trying to carry out the drills the instructor was giving them to do whilst clearly in pain throughout. We practiced how to steer the parachute into clear air space, which is not easy with hundreds in the air at any one time. We learned how to land and carry out our various Para roles safely and without injury depending on what angle and speed you came in. We ran up various sized ramps, jumped off and carried out what ever role the instructor called out.

The first jump we had to do was out of the famous balloon; a massive hot air balloon which looked like an old Zeppelin with a metal harnessed platform swinging below and metal bars around the edge to stop you falling out. The platform landed on the ground and loaded up with the PJI (parachute jump instructor) and five jumpers. The parachute instructor gave the signal and the balloon then rose to eight hundred feet. I still remember being able to see the faces of all the people below and make out who was who. It was pretty scary and quickly brought to reality just how low we actually jumped and how little time we would have in the air to get ourselves sorted and ready for landing. There was definitely no time for taking in the views or even slightly enjoying the whole process.

The PJI delivered a brief while we were up in the air explaining that he would call us forward one by one and when called forward we had to move in front of the gate, which was just a metal bar that lifted up and allowed us to jump off. He then instructed us to hook up, which meant we hooked the clip at the end of our static line parachute to the bar above our head. This automatically functioned our parachute when we left the platform and, from one hundred feet below, deployed the parachute above our heads. We also had a reserve parachute on the front of us in the event that the main parachute did not deploy by the time we had counted to three thousand i.e. one thousand, two thousand, three thousand, checked canopy and looked up to hopefully see a full, green parachute above our heads. This reserve parachute had to be deployed manually by pulling the red strap on top of it. As you can imagine, this was a lot to take in on your first jump and we all thought the chances of being able to deploy the reserve if the main one did not work were minimal, so we thought, 'Let's just hope the main parachute opens or else we can kiss our arses good bye.' We also hoped that whoever packed our parachutes had not been on the piss like us the night before and didn't have any grudges against Paras.

Once clipped on, the PJI raised the bar, told us to come forward, adopt the position, and standby. We had to cross our arms over the reserve parachute, get our feet into position and wait for him to say, 'Go!' As a paratrooper you are expected to jump immediately on go, or the green light when on the plane, with no hesitation at all. This is what a lot of our training had been about and why the trainasium had been so precisely designed. Everything was designed to prepare you for the moment when you had to jump. If you were on the plane with sixty-four other fully equipped paratroopers jumping out at half second intervals from a Hercules C130 using port and starboard para doors, they needed to make sure that no one slowed down or even halted the process. Any hesitation would endanger the lives of all involved. In the Paras, if someone refuses to jump when at the door of the plane, or in this case, the balloon, when told to go, they are pulled away, taken straight down and immediately kicked out of the regiment with no ifs, buts or second chances. This is what we do and there is no room for hesitation or weakness in this regiment.

I watched the first two guys go; the anticipation started to rise, my stomach began to knot and my heart was racing. As I said before, heights are not really my thing. However, I tried to keep my mind clear of all negative thoughts and concentrate on the job in hand; it felt like my whole life had been leading up to this particular moment. My turn was next; it was completely still, no wind, no sound at all. It is completely different to the noise and commotion of an airplane and many say the balloon jump is harder for these reasons. One way or another, it was certainly a test of nerve and one I could not afford to fail if I wanted to be a Paratrooper. I was called forward to the gate and told to standby. I crossed my hands over the reserve parachute, positioned my feet at the door and mentally prepared myself for the jump. The word 'go' rang in my ear, and I immediately threw myself out, falling in total silence, shouting as loud as I could, 'One thousand, two thousand, three thousand', as my lungs emptied of air. I threw my head back and looked up to check my canopy and saw this beautiful, green cover open above my head. I felt a huge jerk as it deployed from its case and ripped my nuts up into my stomach, but the sight of that canopy was a feeling like nothing else, pure relief, I guess. Not sure how many words actually left my mouth, but I remember saying, 'Thank fuck,' or words to that effect, as most of us did when we saw that green silk above our heads.

The next thing I heard was one of the instructors on the ground on a loud hailer shouting, 'Steer away, number 19', so I took a good look around and located the cable which secured the balloon to the ground; I did not want to smash into this on my maiden jump and look like a right idiot. I grabbed hold of my front right lift web and pulled down hard to try to steer the parachute away from the cable until I was in clear air space. The instructor was still talking to me from the ground, but I was now quickly preparing myself for the landing. This first jump was clean fatigue, so no container or kit to drop and take care of this time.

During the ground training stage, they taught us about ground rush, a phenomenon that when you get close to the landing zone in the last hundred feet or so, the ground suddenly rushes up at you and you must not reach for it. If you do reach then there is a good chance you could break a leg or ankle, as your legs are too taught and rigid, rather than relaxed and bent. To avoid any injury, you have to stay in a good Para landing position, accept whatever your landing is going to be, and perform which ever parachute roll is required depending on the angle of landing. I was preparing for the landing and the next thing I knew, the ground was upon me. I tried to perform a forward right landing, reached for the ground and got it completely wrong. I landed like a bag of shit and hit my helmet on the ground but I attempted to roll over once I actually hit the ground, trying to give the watching instructors the impression that I knew what I was doing. Of course, it did not work. However, I was alive, no injuries and had carried out my first parachute jump. I was on my way to earning my wings!

Now we were at Brize and had passed P Company, the platoon instructors were starting to treat us a little more like grown-ups and we were able to go to the bar at Brize Norton some evenings, have a few beers and relax a little. Of course, this had the potential to go wrong, and just like wild dogs once you let them off their leads, they don't tend to behave. The local crab bar (the term we used for the RAF) was called the Spotlight Club. A few of the lads and I went in there every night we could. We were seeing women for the first time since joining up – serving RAF girls, and the usual NAFFI ladies, who were all probably someone's wife. One way or another, we all managed to get ourselves into a lot of trouble and we were banned from going out for a few nights, due to our love of beer and certain other indiscretions.

There were a few fracas with some marines and TA SAS guys who were on our course. Our instructors had taken a major dislike to a couple of these guys, which I think went back to the Falklands' rivalry. For whatever reason, they ordered us to beat them up one afternoon outside our block, which of course as a group we duly did. It was no different from Darth Vader commanding his storm troopers to carry out an attack; the instructors' orders were carried out without question. These were trained soldiers who had served in their units for several years and wanted to join our Para course; they came through to get their wings and went back to their own units afterwards with these extra skills. In truth, neither the RAF, nor any other unit in the British army particularly liked us as a regiment, mainly, because we truly believed we were better than anyone else and God's gift to women. These characteristics were installed in us from day one of training and it is what makes the Paras what they are today. As any boxer will tell you, if you truly believe you are the best and can't be beaten, then you are already halfway to winning.

We had seven more jumps to complete out of a Hercules C130 plane, one of these jumps being a night jump. The ground training continued with the aim of improving our awareness and skills in the air, our ability to steer the parachute and deal with any potential emergencies that may occur. In addition, lots of work was done on a daily basis on our landing techniques and Para roles. My first two airplane jumps were again, clean fatigue i.e. no container or weapon. This was to get us used to the procedures and techniques of jumping from planes without the hindrance of the large cumbersome containers.

We then progressed to jumping with kit. I could barely move. I had to pack it all up ready, stand on the runway ready to load and then get onto the plane. I sat on a tiny, net seat fixed to the side of the fuselage with my parachute on and the heavy container with all my kit and weapon between my legs as we set off on the first low level test flight. The pilot was also on a training flight and as we set off following the contours of the land, some of the guys started being sick from the motion of the plane and the fumes we were breathing in. It was horrendous. I had the sick bag in my hands trying not to think about it. Twenty minutes out from the DZ I had to stand up with my partner, attach my container, hook up to the wire and stand there, waiting for action stations. The container itself weighed nearly as much as my own body weight and I stood there dying from the weight and the smell of the fumes mixing with the smell of vomit. Finally, we got called to the door, the red light came on followed by the green light which meant go, and we had to get out, jumping at half second intervals from both the port and starboard doors. I was desperate to get out, to feel weightless, and to escape the smells and weight of my kit. Jumping is scary; so many things can go wrong. Sometimes parachutes don't open: if you turn over, the parachute can get hooked up and drag you along the side of the plane or you can end up in twists where your rigging lines above you are so twisted that the parachute cannot fill with air properly. You can have air steals where another parachutist moves across you and takes your air and you then drop like a stone with no time to pull the reserve. People have died and been seriously injured in the past. Military parachuting is not for the faint hearted.

The rest of the jumps were like this, and went pretty well, with no injuries of note to me or my fellow recruits. This was good news as we had all worked too hard to get injured or even fail this part of our training, which was supposed to be and is regarded as the fun bit of Para training and what makes us unique in the British forces.

The night jump was an amazing experience; I could not imagine how the hell it could be organized and how you avoided everyone smashing into each other. Firstly, I noticed that when we were out of the plane how quiet it was in the air and you could actually see, depending on moonlight, the other parachutists across the sky and avoid them with no issues. Fluorescent sylooms were used on the ground to mark your RV (Rendezvous Point), so if you were lucky, you saw the colour you were supposed to head to on the way down and had a rough idea which way to head on landing after you had unpacked your equipment and packed up the parachute. The other interesting fact was that I, like many others, still found myself reaching for the ground in the day when we could see it. However, at night you had no idea when it was coming up so all you could do was brace for impact and accept your landing, which in itself forced you into a natural Para roll when you hit the ground. That aspect was surprisingly easier than I thought it would be.

Once the parachute training was complete, which was a great four weeks with a lot of fun, banter and drinking, we were awarded our wings and then headed back to Browning Barracks to proudly wear them and prepare for the final part of our training. This was a one-week live fire training exercise called Last Fence where we were able to put into action all the skills we had learned over the past six months including a parachute insertion. This is what it was all about, and I loved it.

After this was completed, we had our Pass Out parade. Family members, wives and girlfriends were invited up to watch us parade on the square and there was a small social event where they got the chance to meet the platoon training instructors. It was a very proud day for all involved and my mother, father, grandmother and aunties were all able to attend. This was followed by some well-earned leave before heading up the road to the Para battalions we had been designated to join. Ninety percent of us from 557 platoon were joining 1 Para, as they were about to start their preparation and training phase for a two and a half year tour of Northern Ireland. This was very exciting for me, and exactly what I wanted. It was the chance to join the battalion of my choice, who were about to go operational.

CHAPTER 6

NORTHERN IRELAND TOURS OF DUTY

After a great fun and alcohol packed leave following my Passing Out Parade, I was sent to join 1 Para, across the road in Montgomery Lines Aldershot, along with most of the others who had passed out from 557 platoon, to boost their ranks and prepare ready for a two and a half year operational tour of Northern Ireland (NI).

I was posted to 5 platoon B Company along with Rich, a good friend from the depot. It is always a daunting time joining your new battalion and of course, we were new guys and had to quickly earn the respect of our new peers. If we were deemed not to be up to the mark, then we would quickly pay the price. However, the guys, under the platoon leadership of Sergeant 'Taff' Edwards and Lieutenant Chris Titcombe, were great, very welcoming. They allowed us the opportunity to prove our worth over the first few weeks and quickly helped us to settle in and feel part of the team.

We were now able to go on the piss downtown in Aldershot, and drink in the Para pubs. Wow, what an experience; I doubt there has ever been anything like it anywhere before, or ever will be again. In the evening, the guys would head out on the lash. Depending on the time you went down, the first stop was usually the George pub for a couple of warmers and then everyone headed down through the alley and into the back door of the Airborne Inn, aka the 5's. There were no tables, no chairs, no windows and one large bar with a stage at the front, which was just used for the blokes to perform on – least said about that the better. There was a ledge around the side of the sawdust floor, and most of the women who were brave enough to go, stood on this and surveyed the carnage in front of them. It was just a mass of fit as you like, hairy-arsed paratroopers with crew cuts wearing a variety of Para Reg tops, and sporting tattoos that signified their particular battalion or company. Considering the amount of testosterone going around, fights were rare and usually only kicked off if two Para battalions were in town at the same time or some attached arms stepped over the line. I would walk in and see a mass of Paras drinking pints of milk. The only twist was that they had half a dozen or so shots of Malibu in them. It was an expensive round, but a couple of those and your night was near on over. Then there was Mad Dog 20/20, Snake Bite and Black and any other alcoholic concoction the blokes could get their hands on or was the in thing at the time. If this was not enough, then it was over the road via The Exchange pub, if you required a breather, before going into the Rat Pit to boogey the night away with the Para Reg shuffle and possibly find a woman drunk enough to take you home. On the way back to the camp, it was either via Johnny Gurkha's for a Ruby Murray (curry) or Tony's chip shop. Tony always pretended to remember everyone and asked if you wanted your usual, and then we had to remind him what it was. If you were out of cash by then, you could leave your ID with him or an IOU and pay the next day. Then it was the emotional trek back up the hill with your compass kebab and through the back gate of the camp. All to be repeated the following night if you were hardcore enough!

We had just over three months to prepare for a completely different style of soldiering: urban patrolling in West Belfast. We were taking over from 3 Para who were due to finish their two-year tour where they had been working hard to quell the hive of IRA terrorists who had been running riot in this area of Belfast before their arrival. One of the 3 Para teams had just been involved in an incident with joy riders that drove at speed through their checkpoint one night whilst they were out on patrol. The team had opened fire thinking they were under threat, and killed two of those involved. The incident was under investigation and tensions were running high.

The training was very intense, but great fun. We were split into four-man teams (bricks), and then split again into two groups of three bricks called a multiple. One was led by the platoon sergeant, and the other by the platoon commander (the Boss). My brick commander was Corporal 'Taff' Salmon (Sam), a highly professional and gritty Welshman with many years of experience. Sam had high standards and wanted his team to be the best in the platoon, simple as that, and aimed to prove this during the training phase. Jay and Tony made up the four-man brick. Tony was a Lance Corporal, unlucky not to have his own team, and Jay was a switched on, keen and super fit guy who had been in the battalion around six months before I joined. Jay and I became great friends and continually pushed each other to see who could be the best at each new discipline we learnt.

The training was full on. Firstly, our fitness levels had to be higher than normal because when your body is fit then your mind is sharper. Each morning, the platoon NCOs (non-commissioned officers) would take us out for early morning runs over the Aldershot training area, then it would be back to the accommodation block for a quick shower, breakfast and ready for whatever Northern Ireland orientated activity had been planned on that week's training program.

In the first few weeks, all the training took place in Aldershot and was run by our own platoon and 1 Para instructors. We worked on all our core skills to bring them back up to where they needed to be: weapon drills, patrolling in four man teams, medical training and navigation. We put a lot of work into the various contact drills we needed to master that required us to be fast and slick before we hit the streets of Belfast. We also worked on many other skills with lots of live firing taking place down at the local ranges. This was all preparation for when we moved to the next and main phase of training, which was held elsewhere in the country. The Northern Ireland Training Advisory Team (NITAT) ran this and we would be put through our paces properly as a battalion, making sure that we were one hundred percent ready to be deployed to the Province.

A month down the line, we moved into the cramped and cold thirty-man platoon sized temporary accommodation blocks of the NITAT training facility ready for phase two of the NI training package. This tried and tested training package has been refined and developed over the years, as the threats and technologies have evolved. In preparation for our urban Belfast tour, we were put through our paces by the NI training team and tested in Tin City, where low powered training rounds could be fired. Tin City was a mock town that had been built with streets, houses and even life-like dummies of people

I was always destined to join the army, never had any other ambition at all when I was a kid, apart from being a professional footballer maybe, but that was soon ruled out due to lack of skill.

Once I knew who the Paras were, there was never any other choice, the series *The Paras* in the 80's just confirmed that passion.

Due to a dodgy Army Careers Officer in Cornwall and my impatience to leave home and join the Junior Leaders, my path to the Paras would take a little longer than I had planned, however, I got there in the end.

Both my grandfathers had served in the army during World War Two.

Left: My mum's father who served in the Canadian Army.

Right: My dad's father who served in the British army and also worked as a bodyguard for the King of Jordan after the war.

Top Left: Earning my wings, Parachute training at Brize Norton in 1990.

Top Right: 557 Platoon on the P Company Steeplechase.

Right: Passing off the square, drill and number two uniforms were never really my thing, I was far more comfortable in the field or on operations.

Bottom: With Mum & Dad after my passing out parade.

Above: West Belfast tour in 1991 with Sam my first team leader and Jay my top cover partner.

Right: Chilling in the back of one of our armoured vehicles before being re-tasked back onto the Belfast streets.

Below: On patrol in the Twinbrook, a hardcore Republican area in West Belfast.

Above: Close Observation Platoon (COP) in an op keeping an eye on West Belfast.

Left: On a rural patrol in Northern Ireland.

Below: B Company, 1 Para in the UK after an Ireland tour, some top guys in this picture.

Above: Aldershot 10 Miler through Long Valley, led by Mad Mas, B Company, 1 Para.

Right: My best mate Stu and me on the back of a Chinook Helicopter.

Below: Passing on enemy troop movement from a cliff face observation post in Sardinia during a NATO exercise in 1995.

Above: On the way to a Liverpool match at Anfield with my parents and daughter.

Bottom Lef: Chelsea's Graduation day in N. Ireland, so proud of my little 'Pap'.

Middle Right: Baby Chelsea in our Army Pad in Aldershot.

Bottom Right: "Behind every successful man, there is a strong woman"; this was certainly the case with Dawn.

with microphones and cameras attached so that they talked to you – a strange experience for sure. As you patrolled these streets, you were faced with various possible scenarios that you were likely to come up against in real life Belfast. Obviously, because it was training, you knew that every time you patrolled in Tin city you would be faced with at least one possible incident as you made your way around on a pre-prepared patrol plan. You were under intense pressure at all times, carrying out thorough five and twenty metre checks each time you stopped. It could be a wheelie bin bomb, someone opening fire on you from a building or something as simple as one of the dummies wanting to chat and offer up vital intelligence on an upcoming event; around every corner lay a new challenge or threat. One of the dummies suddenly started talking to you, and then up the street, a window opened and you were under fire from a sniper. Everything was filmed on CCTV; there was no hiding from the many cameras and microphones strategically located around the area.

After each training exercise, you were taken back into the high-tech debriefing theatre to watch the whole thing being played back from various angles, catching every move you made, or didn't make in some cases. A member of the NITAT training team told you exactly where you had behaved well and where you had gone wrong and could improve for the future. They banged home the point that it was essential that we all engaged with and spoke in a polite manner to the general public in Belfast. Hearts and minds of the local population were very important and it was drilled into us that they were not the enemy, that the vast majority were law abiding citizens going about their daily business and could well become friendly towards the security forces if treated well, and a level of trust was built.

We also embarked on a new phase where we patrolled another training facility or small estate, this time with real buildings and real people acting as the Civilian Population, CIVPOP as they became known. It had shops and even a pub, where the soldiers playing the CIVPOP roles got pissed on cans of lager, which as you can imagine, did not help our cause. The CIVPOP, just like in Belfast, had 'known terrorists' amongst their ranks with certain roles within the organisation. Prior to each patrol, we were shown photos of these 'terrorists' and we had to memorise their faces, names, addresses, and positions within the organisation. When we spotted them out on patrol, we were to report their movements to our control room and, if required, stop, search and question them. It was intended to imitate life just as it would be when we hit the ground for real in the Province in a few weeks' time.

The NI training camp package culminated in a live riot scenario held in this village. For this purpose, the NITAT training staff acted as marshals and they brought in another army regiment to act as extra CIVPOP. That evening, we patrolled the village as normal and we were briefed to react accordingly to any incidents that occurred. Whilst dealing with a mundane stop and search, things started to escalate with a crowd building up around us, and our brief was to carry out normal drills and only escalate the situation as and when the need arose. As you can imagine, competition throughout the various British army regiments is high, so when a 'hat' regiment, as we affectionately refer to all other army regiments, gets the chance to act as 'CIVPOP' against the Paras then things can very quickly get out of hand. The NITAT marshals' role is very important and a degree of personal control from both sides is required. Suddenly, the situation turned into a full riot. We had handy stocks of old rubber bullets that are around three inches long and one inch in diameter and petrol bombs became available for the crowd to throw at us. We called out our Quick Reaction Force (QRF) who turned up in full riot gear, helmets, shields, and wooden batons, who then started to confront the raging crowd, and attempted to take control of the situation. The whole idea of the training was to prepare us for the real thing, which unbeknown to us was not that far away in the future. The petrol bombs were thrown in a reasonably controlled manner, aimed at the base of our shields to give us a realistic taste of what it was really like to be on the receiving end of these devices. As the flames roared up my shield and against my helmet visor, the heat was unbelievable. I could really get a feel for how extremely dangerous this situation was and would be for real and it was not a nice experience, I can tell you!

On the other side of the coin, we also practised with our baton gunners simulating firing plastic bullets at the pre-identified riot leaders and main troublemakers. This would, in reality, drop them to the floor and enable our snatch squads to run forward and drag these individuals back behind our lines where they were arrested and taken away back to the police stations. Again, as you can imagine, the other regiment were not too keen to have this happen to them, rightly fearing a kicking once they were captured. A fight started during one of these snatch and grab missions and Sam was hit in the face by a rubber bullet. Both sides at that point forgot why we were actually doing this and got stuck into each other until the NITAT training team was able to diffuse the situation and end the exercise. Our platoon staff spoke to me about keeping my cool afterwards, as I got so enraged during this process and lost control. One way or another, the training was so intense that I actually found the reality easier to cope with, which was of course the aim. As they say, train hard, fight easy.

Eventually, the time came and we were off to Northern Ireland. I was genuinely excited at the prospect of going operational. I had bonded well with the other guys in my platoon, an all-round great bunch of blokes and real paratroopers, and made some great friends for life; we were all ready for some real work, a chance to turn our training into reality. We were posted to Palace Barracks, a holding camp just outside Belfast, close to Hollywood and it was far more comfortable and a lot newer than our accommodation back in Aldershot. We were split into four-man rooms with plenty of space for all our kit. In Aldershot, we were in eight-man rooms and the blocks were literally falling down around us, so this instantly raised the morale of the guys. Before you knew it, most bed spaces were full of large, brand-new TVs and stereos that we all purchased from the camp NAFFI. You could put anything on a NAFFI debit card, which was easily obtained, and pay in monthly installments. We all felt a little better off due to the extra daily allowance of NI danger pay, however, many of these electronic niceties soon ended up being flogged off to each other for a fraction of their original cost so that cash could be raised for a few nights out on the beer in the local town of Bangor. Paratroopers are notoriously bad with money and tend to live for the day without too much concern for savings or thinking about the future.

During the two and half year posting, the battalion split its time between four specific roles, each one around a six-week cycle. Brigade Reserve included guards and duties at Palace Barracks. Province Reserve, we could be deployed to any area within the Province at short notice, Rest and Recuperation (R&R) home leave and training, and our primary role of supporting the Royal Ulster Constabulary (RUC) in the Woodbourne area of operations (AOO) in West Belfast.

Woodbourne was the name of the area where the RUC police station was based in West Belfast; an area, which up until 3 Para arrived two years earlier, had been out of control and was a stronghold for the IRA. Woodbourne RUC station was responsible for the Lenadoon, Poleglass and Twinbrook estates, which were all hardcore republican areas. Also, just outside the RUC station, was the small Suffolk's estate, known as the Oranges to us, which was made up of staunch protestant families who refused to move or be intimidated out of their homes. We would patrol through this estate on our way out or on our way back on a regular basis to give the locals some confidence that we were there and keeping an eye on them. 3 Para had gone in and had effectively restored a sense of normality in the area, but it was still rife with danger and the police required close support when patrolling to be able to enforce law and order. At times there could be up to twenty soldiers securing the area for one policeman to complete his duties.

Woodbourne Police station was heavily fortified and protected due to the number of attacks it had come under over the years and was still very vulnerable, particularly when patrols were going in and out of the station. I remember one night vividly; things got very heated and it wasn't from standing too close to a bonfire with my marshmallow. It was the anniversary of Internment, a British Army operation in Northern Ireland on 9-10 August 1971, which involved the mass arrest and imprisonment of three hundred and forty-two people suspected of being involved with the IRA. It had become almost traditional for Republicans to demonstrate on this date and that night was no exception. It was the perfect excuse in West Belfast to have a good old-fashioned riot and dust up with the security forces.

That night, our platoon was patrolling the Lenadoon area up near what was known as the Big Five, five tall blocks of flats at the top of the hill which dominated and overlooked the entire local area. Lenadoon was a staunch Republican and IRA supporting estate and had become famous way back in 1972 when 'The Battle of Lenadoon' took place. This was a series of gunfights over six days from the 9th to the 14th July between the Provisional IRA and the British Army in and around Lenadoon Avenue area. Twenty-eight people were reported to have been killed during this time, ending a two-week truce between the forces of the British Government and the IRA. Since then Lenadoon had not changed much and was home to many known, high-ranking IRA terrorists and was a tough and dangerous place to patrol.

You could cut the tension in the air with a knife that particular night. A huge bonfire had been built down the hill on the waste ground above the community centre and it was just a case of when, not if, it would all kick off. As the teams moved down the avenue towards the community centre, a mob started to descend upon them with stones, bricks and wooden pallets, which would end up being used as shields and a barricade. We were on vehicle patrol, and were the only teams on the ground at the time. We all moved quickly down the avenue to where we all managed to rendezvous (RV) around the community centre building. This was where we would hold our ground, it was important that whilst not inflaming the situation we were not driven out of the area by the mob and didn't show weakness in the eyes of the local people.

The light was fading and more and more local youths had joined the crowd who were becoming increasingly aggressive towards us. It was clear this had been organised and was not a spur of the moment incident. Petrol bombs began to appear from everywhere, and were now raining down on us, along with an assortment of missiles. The mob was using the wooden pallets as protection as they moved forward to get in range of where our defensive line was held up on each side of the community centre building. They were organized and reminded me of a Viking shield wall, which moved forward as one well drilled unit and then opened up to fire at us before retreating with the shields in place. The situation was becoming more tense and the decision was made to utilize the baton guns that we carried in each team; these used 25-grain plastic bullets designed for crowd disbursement and riot control situations just like this. A plastic bullet would not kill the person it hits, but would certainly knock them off their feet and leave them sore. We were always taught to aim for the body and not the head, and not to bounce the bullets off the ground as this could be very dangerous.

We fired our plastic bullets in volleys at the wooden pallets with an aim to stopping them from getting any closer and to disperse the crowd, but it wasn't working and we were getting low on ammunition. Suddenly, the Quick Reaction Force from Woodbourne turned up consisting of other members of our own unit as well as the RUC special response units known as The Blues. They were huge guys, highly experienced in dealing with situations like this, carried the power of the law with them and even more importantly, they arrived with a new supply of rubber bullets as our own were nearly depleted. The Blues opened their van to reveal boxes and boxes of rubber bullets. We were very relieved and rotated the use of the baton gun between us.

The Blues were keen to get hold of and arrest as many of the ringleaders and main troublemakers of the riot as possible. Following our training in the UK, we worked as a well drilled team to fire volleys of rounds at the mob and when the main perpetrators went down and the mob drew back, our snatch teams bravely rushed forward, grabbed hold of these individuals and dragged them back through our lines. We took them round the back of the community centre that had now become the centre of our operations. The RUC then arrested them and shipped them off in the wagons to the police station.

During the ferocious commotion, something quite surreal happened. We spotted a well-known local drunk walking down Horn Drive pissed out of his head as usual and blissfully ignorant of what was going on around him. He walked right through it all, not a missile or plastic bullet hit him; it was as if he had a protective shield around him. We watched him weave into the distance unaware and unscathed.

We battled against the mob and held our lines for around five hours with the constant threat that at any time the IRA could open up with live ammunition. This had happened many times in the past in the Province and was one of their favourite techniques of attacking the army and the police, using their own crowds and people as cover. Finally, the rubber bullets and mounting number of arrests deterred the attackers, and the crowd started to slowly disperse. More rubber bullets were fired that night at the Lenadoon community centre than in the previous five years of the Troubles, which just went to highlight the intense level of attack we were under and the resilience our guys showed throughout the situation. I have no doubt whatsoever that if any of us had been grabbed and fallen into the hands of the mob, that they would have been murdered without any hesitation at all. It had happened in the past when soldiers had been captured.

Part of our remit meant that sometimes we were seconded to go with the RUC Blues on patrol around other areas of Belfast and support in arrests and house raids. On one occasion, we arrived at the house in question and the police began battering at the front door with their ram. It took them a good few seconds before they broke down the door and rushed inside, only to reappear after a short search to announce that it was the wrong property. We all moved to the house next door and went through the same door-opening process to gain entry, which was quite comical. This time, Jay and I moved inside with the Blues and checked from room to room. I was moving towards the stairwell and heard a movement above. My finger was on the trigger ready to squeeze in an instant as I pointed my weapon up the staircase. A figure stepped out across the landing and I realised just in time that it was an old woman and lowered my weapon. The Blues went into houses that had been pinpointed as terrorist hideouts or stores and either arrested the occupants, if that was the aim, or searched the property for illegal material, such as weapons and munitions.

We spent four weeks at a time in Woodbourne. Our four-man team lived in a three metre square room with two bunk beds, eating and operating out of the RUC station. This was the part of the tour that I really enjoyed the most. This is what we were there for; guard and duties at Palace Barracks was boring and I wanted to be where the action was. It was hard and dangerous work, but really rewarding and exhilarating at times as we came up against the hardcore Republican terrorist cells.

Working day or night in twelve-hour shifts, we performed three or four patrols per shift, often carrying out vehicle check points (VCPs) and generally dominating the ground and supporting the RUC policemen performing their duties. Prior to each patrol, we were briefed on the names and faces we needed to know and recognise, and we were shown the route that we would be following. All the teams were in radio contact with one another and it was important that the radio net was kept as clear as possible for key information. If anyone came into any kind of conflict, there was just one word that indicated high alert. We were on patrol one evening when the word, 'Contact', come over the radio net. It was Jonah, known to us as Saddam, due to his uncanny resemblance to the then, Iraqi President. Jonah had Des and Davy the Jock Squad with him in an open-topped Land Rover, which held two men standing up facing outwards on what we called top cover with a driver and team commander. They had been attacked and within seconds, everyone was moving to the area to support. They were contacted whilst driving under a bridge; someone had hurled a 'coffee jar' bomb down on them. This is literally, an old coffee jar packed with nails, some explosives and a detonator. When the jar smashes, the detonator is released and it explodes firing the nails and shrapnel at the intended target; it is a nasty little device homemade by the terrorists. This bomb had hit the side of their vehicle whilst travelling under a bridge, but luckily, nobody was injured on this occasion with the armoured vehicle absorbing most of the blast.

At the end of each Woodbourne tour, we had some home leave or a getaway holiday together for a few days. We went to the likes of Ibiza and Tenerife to let our hair down and drink our own body weight in alcohol, de-stressing and properly relaxing. We felt as though we had properly earned these holidays, which of course brought other issues, but was a lot of fun. This bonded us even more closely as a strong-knit group and allowed us to relax away from the daily grind of the Province.

After our leave, it was back to Palace Barracks for more guard and duties as well as continuation training and while based there, we had time off in the evenings to go down to the local pubs in Bangor and Newtonards. It was in Bangor that I first met Caroline. We all loved the Irish girls; they were very different to the English we were used to in Aldershot. Many of the guys, like me, found girlfriends that we began to see whenever we could, and relationships grew. I was seeing Caroline's friend when we first met, however her friend wanted to go back out with another one of the guys who I served with and I fancied Caroline, so we swapped things around and we were all happy.

Caroline was a great girl, very loving and caring; she wasn't your typical fiery Irish lass, but she would still let me have it when required! She was very gentle and mothering and took good care of me when I was with her, which is exactly what I was looking for at that time, I guess. She took me home to meet her parents, who were both very welcoming, even though her Dad, who resembled a huge Viking, was wary of me. He always kept me at arm's length and gave me a look of 'don't mess with my daughter or I will rip your head off,' which, now I have a daughter myself, I fully understand. We got married a year after we first started dating and moved into our own house on the camp in Palace Barracks; it was fun setting up home together and we had a great time. It was the first proper home I had had since leaving my parents' place when I was sixteen. It enabled me to get away from the mayhem of the accommodation block and chill out for the little bit of time I had off, but I was still able to have my mates around and hold a few parties. Many of the guys married their Irish girlfriends and took them back to Aldershot at the end of the tour, but unfortunately, few of them ever went the distance.

We were not safe, even when off duty. The terrorists bombed a pub in Newtonards, which we used to drink in, and they planned an attack on a pub in Bangor that we all used to frequent along with Irish Protestant girls. This attack was only thwarted by the fact that an informant let the security forces know about it and the terrorist Active Service Unit (ASU) who was tasked to carry it out was apprehended on the way over to the bar.

I was twenty-one years old when I decided that I wanted to apply for the Special Air Service (SAS) selection. Looking back on it now, I was far too young and inexperienced, but my team commander Sam was training for selection and this had a huge influence on my decision. I was keen, ambitious and always in a rush to reach what I saw as my full potential and never stayed put anywhere for too long; it is a trait I have continued with all my life. I applied to see my Company Commander (OC) Major Mason, a fantastic man known to us as Mad Mas or just Airborne. He didn't have time for messing around, but he took the time to talk to me about my application and gently steered me in a sensible direction. He recommended that I first join the Close

Observation Platoon (COP) before trying for the SAS in a couple of years once the tour was over, I had gained some more experience, and I was back in the UK.

I took his sensible advice and applied to join 1 Para COP. This is generally made up of the more experienced, keener and all-round better soldiers in the battalion, but not strictly, as there were great soldiers right across Para Reg. There was a six-week selection course to get into the COP held back in England, which was run by Special Forces personnel, who specialised in covert operations in Northern Ireland. Like all courses in the army, fitness was the key to success. There were five of us on the course from 1 Para and as we were looking to join the COP mid-way through the NI tour, we had to do our selection attached to another regiment's course. Because of this, and being Paras, the pressure was on the five of us to excel in all areas; we were certainly expected to be at the front of all the fitness tests and we were looking to break any course records that we could, pushing our bodies to the limit to get into top physical condition.

As the COP worked in small teams, often isolated with little support close by, we were required to become experts in close quarter battle (CQB) and vehicle contact drills. Driving around Belfast, you could easily take a wrong turn or find yourselves in a critically dangerous situation with no support just like the two signalers back in 1988 that were murdered by a mob in Belfast. The two soldiers, wearing civilian clothes, both armed with browning pistols and in a civilian car, accidentally drove into the funeral procession of an IRA member. Dozens of people quickly surrounded and attacked their car. One of the soldiers drew his service pistol and fired a shot in the air but he and his partner were dragged from the car, bundled into a black taxi, then beaten, stripped, and searched. They were then driven to a nearby waste ground where they were shot and murdered.

We were taught about different scenarios and how to deal with them. I loved it. The primary role of the COP was to have eyes on key targets and `trigger' i.e. verbally transfer, any information, movements or updates to other specialist units on the ground. To do this we needed to become experts in firstly getting ourselves into positions to observe these targets without being detected and secondly, on how to use the high-tech surveillance equipment required to watch, photograph and record what we were observing.

The course was intense both physically and mentally. Most mornings, we went for an early run. However, before the run started we were taken into the lecture theatre and shown a number of words or pictures in a random order on a screen or on a table, which we were expected to remember. When we got in after the run and were physically exhausted, we had to write everything down in the exact order that they had been shown to us. This would test our mental strength as well as our physical ability, which was a key part of the COP's job. The course was great; I really enjoyed it and learnt some great skills. All five of us did well, passing the course with flying colours.

I flew back to Ireland in early 1992 and joined 1 Para COP. It was a completely different working environment to what I had become used to; we were treated like experienced soldiers and we were expected to keep ourselves fit and in good order at all times. We generally worked in small, four-man teams, we were able to grow our hair long, so we did not look like soldiers, and wore civilian clothing in camp and on many of the tasks that we were deployed. It was a complete change from the life I had in the rifle companies where everything was so regimented and disciplined.

The Boss was a captain known to the guys as 'Ed the Waff' due to the stories he came out with about his former career and life back in Africa; he was a strange character. In charge of operations was the Sergeant Major known as 'Dave and Dave' because he was a bit of a schizophrenic. He had been in the SAS and had been sent back to 1 Para to run the COP, again another eccentric character, but he certainly knew his stuff and had many years of high-end operational experience, which was exactly what was needed. I was the youngest and one of the least experienced soldiers in the COP at this time and I was surrounded by some of the most experienced and longest serving non-commissioned officers (NCOs) and private soldiers in the battalion. It was a bit of a shock to the system and none of the fun and close comradeship of the rifle company seemed to exist. It was all very intense, which of course it should be as it was serious business.

The jobs we were tasked with were very challenging and exciting, working alongside the other 'Special Forces' units in the Province as well as the covert RUC teams. One week we would be up on the mountain carrying out long distance observation tasks and the next we would be in the city driving around in unmarked vehicles using new weapon systems and working out of various inner-city locations.

I enjoyed the job, it was exactly what I wanted to do; I was learning fast and becoming a decent operator. However, my downfall was that I was still very immature when it came to my social life and spent a lot of my time back with my old mates at B Company drinking too much and going off the rails. The COP leadership team frowned upon this and I didn't do myself any favours.

Looking back on it now, I have no idea how I got away with it for so long. I was a good soldier with a growing reputation and on track to great things, but I was a wild child when I was on my time off. I have no problem sticking to the rules when I can see they are important and when soldiering I was completely disciplined. However, give me a few drinks and a bit of freedom and I kind of make up my own set of rules.

I had never taken my driving test, but in Northern Ireland, you needed a car to get around. When I was still with B Company, before I joined the COP, I decided that a license was not essential and bought a red XR3, which I taught myself to drive. My best mate Stu, who I had served with in the LI, had also transferred and arrived in Belfast to join our platoon. I had managed to claim him as my cousin, which was a complete load of bollocks, but it worked and it was great to have him with me. He soon settled in and won the respect of the guys. After a few months of being in the battalion, I sold the XR3 to Stu to clear some of my mounting debts. He gave me a cheque, which I put straight into my bank. That night was a Sunday, known as Pigs Ball at the camp when the local girls were allowed into our NAFFI for a disco. I got mega pissed and then had the bright idea of driving out of camp to buy some food. The trouble was that I had sold my car to Stu, so I popped upstairs and took the keys from his shelf. Jay and Geordie jumped in with me and off we went. We drove out of the back gate and along the road towards the junction. Before reaching the junction, I must have passed out and the car veered off the road and went straight between two trees. The gap was only just wide enough for the car to fit through, the two wing mirrors were sheered straight off and the car smashed into something before spinning round and ending up facing in the opposite direction. Jay and Geordie put me in the back and one of them drove the car back into the camp. We parked up outside the block and all made our way to bed, feeling the worse for wear. Next morning, I woke up to find Stu standing over my bed saying, 'What the fuck? You owe me a grand!'

I got away with driving without a licence back then, but it wasn't going to last. When I was home on leave from the COP, I took a few lessons and despite my instructor telling me that I wasn't ready, I applied for my test. I was absolutely sure that I would pass, but I didn't, I failed. The next time I was in Northern Ireland, I decided that it still wasn't essential to have a licence and this time I bought a black XR2. I was taking the odd lessons in my time off in Ireland, but nowhere near enough to enable me to pass my test.

The boss of the COP saw me driving around in my car without a licence and he warned me not to ever drive the car again. He didn't care what I did with it, but I was not to drive. It was sensible advice. I, very stupidly, ignored him and drove it again. Of course, he found out and called me to his office. He asked me straight out if I had driven the car again, which I had, down to Bangor to see Caroline the night before, but, even more stupidly and without thinking, I denied it. I don't know why, it was just my first reaction when confronted by him and of course lying to my Boss was the worst thing I could do. I was sent up in front of the RSM, a guy called Dave Collins who many years in the future would become a great friend and work colleague in the private sector. However, for now, he was the Regimental Sergeant Major (RSM) and I was a lowly private soldier. Firstly, he talked about how all my work reports were excellent and that I was an above average soldier with lots of potential, but then moved on to my social life. He said that off duty I was not behaving in the way that was expected of a member of the COP platoon and in particular, they viewed the driving of an uninsured car with no driving licence and then denying it to my boss, very badly. I was kicked out of the COP and sent back to B Company.

It was a big mistake, but it actually worked out well in the long run. I was back doing what I knew best, with guys that I genuinely enjoyed being around and had missed. I went back into Sam's team and they all laughed and took the piss out of me for why I had been sent back. I didn't learn any lessons though and continued to mess around when I was off duty. It was my way of de-stressing, I suppose. My next big cock-up was going to have more far reaching consequences.

I finished the two-and-a-half-year tour in B Company and moved back to Aldershot with Caroline into married quarters at Ramillies Park, which reminded me of an old Butlins holiday camp. Life back in Aldershot was good and I regularly went away for training in other countries including trips to Corsica, Sardinia, Germany, Holland, Kenya and the USA. Going to Fort Bragg in America was incredible. It is a fantastic site covering an area the size of a small town. It has two golf courses as well as all the training facilities, which gives you some idea of the enormity of this US base. We could actually take off and do our jump practice within the site. The Americans treated us really well and I loved socialising with them. The contrast in our cultural habits was huge. The Americans were astounded by the amount we drank. We would head down to Fayetteville with them; they would order a bucket of beers for a group of them, while we ordered a bucket each!

In Corsica, we trained with the Foreign Legion. One day we were doing an exercise with them that involved attacking a trench position at the bottom of a hill. There were umpires from both sides wearing white tape on their helmets to indicate who they were, and they would tell someone when they had been injured or were 'dead' i.e. out of the exercise. The Foreign Legion being the Foreign Legion paid no attention and when the first of our men reached their forward trench, they got back up again. One guy, who was officially 'dead', stood up, whacked one of our guys around the head with a shovel, and, as you can imagine, it all kicked off. The rest of us looking through our long-range sights from up above saw this happen. We all had the new combat 95 Bergens with a simple clip release mechanism, which we actually hated, but in one instant fifty Bergens fell to the ground and we rushed down the hill to join in the scrap. Even the OC was hit as mayhem ruled. The next day, the Foreign Legion OC and our OC apologised and they closed the bar for a week to prevent any continuance of the bad feeling. Things calmed down and the incident was kept very quiet.

Northern Ireland was never far away from our thoughts and it was only a matter of time before our battalion was redeployed back to the Province. Our next tour was to be a six-month tour in West Belfast again, this time based up in Whiterock RUC station which covered the Ballymurphy and Falls Road area, another well-known hive of hard-core IRA members and supporters.

We were also deployed at short notice in 1995 to support the RUC in West Belfast during the protestant marching season in flash point areas where the Protestants crossed over and moved into Catholic areas. This type of deployment lasted around two or three weeks, until the threats dissipated.

My final deployment to Northern Ireland was for another six months, this time a rural tour, based in Cookstown RUC station. By then, I had spent a year in the Mortar platoon, which had been great fun and I had then been promoted and sent back to C Company as an NCO and brick commander. Our boss for this tour was a young Lieutenant attached to us from another regiment, very inexperienced at the time, but a nice guy who generally listened to our advice. We had a good set of NCOs with a fair bit of experience between us of operating in the Province. My team was part of the boss' multiple as well as my mate, Rab's team. Rab was a good friend, who was very sadly killed in

Iraq in 2007 by a vehicle borne improvised explosive device (VBIED) driven by a suicide bomber whilst out on a vehicle movement task working in the private security sector. He was a man mountain of a guy with a huge personality; a gritty hard-nosed Jock and he will never be forgotten.

As always, we prepared ourselves rigorously back in Aldershot concentrating on rural patrolling skills, which in many ways was our bread and butter and came far more naturally than urban work. As before, we deployed to NITAT who ran the battalion through its paces before flying into the Province and deploying to our Cookstown base.

Cookstown is a small place, not far from Dungannon and just west of Lough Neagh, which were both in the battalion's area of responsibility. The IRA used Lough Neagh as a transit route across the Province sometimes ferrying men or munitions across the lough (lake). The Marines had a constant presence on the lough to help deter and apprehend those attempting these activities. We utilised this boat asset whilst on patrol to move us quickly and without trace from location to location, giving the IRA no idea where we may appear. Our Marine friends always gave us a hot cup of tea and biscuits when we were on their vessel, but a few of us would usually bring it back up before hitting land again.

It was hard work, but a rewarding tour and I was really enjoying it. I had been involved in an incident where my team was attacked by some local drunk hooligans late one night, which ended up with us having to use minimal force to defend ourselves and restrain one or two of those involved. This would end up in a court appearance further down the line where I would be required to explain and justify my actions. Halfway through the six months, our company commander arranged for each multiple to separately have one night off and the use of the bar in the RUC station for that evening. Normally, we could not go anywhere near a beer because these six-month tours were 'dry'. The idea was that we could relax and unwind in the evening and then have the following day off and do some shopping in Lisbon before going back on duty for the next shift. It all sounded great and I was looking forward to it.

As expected, on our night off we had a particularly heavy session. There were eleven Paratroopers and our boss in the bar, none of us had had a drink for three months and we were getting completely mullered. I was really on one, drinking everything on offer, and even snorting vodkas along with a few of the other lads. It was clearly not a good idea. After all the guys and the boss had eventually gone to bed, Rab and I were left chewing the fat, putting the world to rights and finishing off any alcohol that was left. For whatever reason, I apparently decided it would be a good idea if we threw a few things at the bar and suddenly I was smashing things up. It wasn't pent up anger or violence, just drunken stupidity. I honestly have no recollection at all, of actually doing it. I did not even know that I had until the journey back to the base when I was getting flash backs and when we eventually arrived back at the camp the next day after our shopping trip in Lisbon, some eighteen hours later. I had ended up destroying the bar and the ramifications affected all around me as I handled the entire incident very badly. When the new Commanding Officer (CO), who had only taken the battalion over a few months before the tour and did not know me at all, found out about it, he wanted to make an example of me and there was no warning or fine this time. I was demoted and sent to A Company based in Dungannon, County Tyrone. That was too much for me to handle. I knew I had messed up big time and was so embarrassed and angry with myself for being such an idiot. I was only two weeks away from going on my Section Commanders Battle Course (SCBC) at Brecon, and I decided in a moment of impetuousness, that I needed to leave the army and make my way in civvy street. A clean break was required, I needed to sort my life out and find a new challenge. It was an opportunity and necessity to grow up and control my drinking, which had got out of hand and was destroying everything around me.

I handed in my notice, which had to be a one-year period, shortly after joining my new company. The OC of A company was great and told me to take a few weeks to think it over, and most of the senior NCOs tried to persuade me to consider what I was doing and change my mind. It appeared to be a knee jerk reaction as my pride had been dented, which was of course true. I was absolutely gutted about what had happened and from what I could see at the time, my career lay in tatters. That was certainly how it looked and felt from my perspective. However, once I make up my mind, nothing can change it. Throughout the year, I could have reversed my decision at any time. I could have done the twelve months and would most probably have been made back up again afterwards. Most people were sure that I would change my mind, but there was no way. As time went on, my plan for getting out and onto the private security circuit became clearer in my mind and my excitement for this new challenge and era of my life was growing.

Telling Caroline what had happened wasn't easy. I had caused this misfortune by my own stupid actions, under the influence of alcohol, which of course had a detrimental effect on my family as well as me. However, she was so supportive and stood by me, even when I had been such a dick. She is an amazing woman and an absolutely fantastic mother and remained supportive even when I caused my family such issues and this was not the first drama I had brought upon her due to my liking and inability to control the poisonous nectar. I had been fined for getting RTU'd (Returned to Unit) from a search course due to a stupid night out, (Shifty also got bust due to this, apologies mate!), spent time in army jail, a night in civvy nick, was arrested and jailed for assaulting some RMPs in front of her in Aldershot – the list went on.

Over our time together, I wasn't a good husband. I realised quite early on, that I was still single at heart and that what I wanted most was to be a paratrooper and to spend time with my mates, and I went out with them more and more. We had a daughter together, Chelsea, who I adore and is the one constant good thing in my life, to this day. Chelsea, who is near on twenty-five as I write this book, has all the good parts of me and luckily none of the bad; she is a thoughtful, sensitive girl with her head screwed on properly, and I am so very proud of her. She gives me the motivation every day to be a good father and become a better person and I love her with every ounce of my body. However, I do regret hurting her mother, turning her world upside down, causing the breakup of our marriage and consequently losing the ability to live with and bring up my daughter on a daily basis. I am very happy Caroline and I still get on so well today and that she allowed me to build a very good relationship with my daughter. It would have been so easy for her to turn Chelsea against me, which is what happened to so many of the other guys who got married and then consequently divorced after the Palace Barracks tour.

Caroline and I split up a few months before I was due to leave the army and she moved back to Bangor with Chelsea. We closed our house down in Aldershot, handed it back to the army and they arranged for Caroline and my daughter to move back to Ireland. This was the saddest moment of my life, but in reality, I was not ready to be married and knew that the path I was about to embark on was not the life for them.

CHAPTER 7

BREAKING AWAY

The year notice period was finally up and I left 1 Para at the end of August 1998, ten years after joining the army as a junior leader. In that final year, I took full advantage of the military resettlement system which allowed me around five thousand pounds to spend on civilian run training courses. I chose to do the Task Close Protection (CP) Training Course that was four weeks long and took place in Maidenhead. At that time, it was considered the best and most respected course on the market. I knew this course was important to my long-term aim and would help me if I wanted to achieve my next goal of working in the secretive world of private security.

The private security industry was still relatively low key at this time, a lot of cloak and dagger stuff. After 9/11, the world changed dramatically; the Afghan and Iraq wars followed soon after, along with a huge wind of disruption blowing through the Middle East and North Africa with the Arab Spring. Security work was about to explode into big business, but for me back in 1998 getting work on the security circuit was still very difficult. I had seen several guys over the previous few years get out and go onto what was known as 'The Circuit', fail to get a foot hold and join back up within a couple of years.

I was determined to achieve my goals and not let this happen to me. I used the dread of having to sign back up as my incentive to stay positive when the going got tough. I would not give those individuals, who would take great joy in my failure, the satisfaction of seeing me come back through the gates of 1 Para with my tail tucked between my legs.

The Circuit was a lot smaller in the late nineties; it was really a case of who you knew and not so much about what you knew, and therefore very difficult to break into. Most of the work was carried out by older, retired Special Forces operators and it involved close protection for private families, high-net-worth individuals, celebrities, and a small amount of work in Africa working as security managers for oil companies. There was no easy access to the Internet to browse for companies recruiting and no easy online application forms like there are today.

The military did help by offering short courses on how to write cover letters and put together a CV. I used the computer in the barracks to write a cover letter and put together what I thought at the time was a good CV, but in reality, I didn't possess any skills to make me stand out from any other paratrooper or marine leaving the forces. I had no real experience with regards to security skill sets, but I did manage to find some names and addresses of people who ran and owned security companies. I posted my well-presented covering letter and CV printed on quality paper in A4 envelopes with the hope that this would get some sort of response.

I walked out of 1 Para barracks in North Camp, Aldershot with one bag of belongings and about five hundred quid to my name. Caroline and our daughter, Chelsea had already moved back to Ireland and I was on my own, starting again. Despite the nature of the job and the strict discipline, being in the army gives you a feeling of being safe and secure, and that you are part of one big family. I had been fed, watered, given a bed and surrounded by people my whole life. In the army, there was structure to each day and a paycheck at the end of every month. Walking out into civilian life when I had been used to the army environment since I was sixteen was daunting, but I was up for the challenge. I was excited about what lay ahead, and it was definitely time to grow up and sort out my drinking.

An old school friend of mine, Mark, who worked for British Airways, had a flat in West Drayton, close to Heathrow with easy access to central London and he kindly said that I could kip on his sofa for a while. I remember arriving there and thinking 'What the hell am I doing?' I was clear in my mind about what I hoped to achieve but I wasn't sure how I was going to make it happen, particularly when replies to my letters started to come back. I slowly unfolded the letters and immediately saw the words 'unfortunately not recruiting at this time' or words to that effect and had that sinking feeling in my stomach. This continued for a while and I felt like I was banging my head against a brick wall. However, I was not going to be deterred and I continued to research new points of contact in the security companies and kept on sending out my letters. If I am nothing else in this world, I am persistent and I won't give in.

In the meantime, I needed to earn some money. Lee, from the Staffordshire Regiment, who I became good friends with on the Task CP course had also come out of the army at the same time as me and was also trying to get on The Circuit, so we stuck together and got into door work. We were basically bouncers at various pubs and clubs in West London. It was hard work but also great fun. We both got jobs at a notorious pub in Hounslow used by the local hoods and drug dealers. We had a decent door team, some ex-military guys and a couple of civilians and we had to deal with a lot of trouble and some difficult characters who frequented the bar. Fights broke out regularly, knives and other concealed weapons were commonplace, it was hard and risky work at times, covering each other's back. The pay was pretty crap, but the main thing was we were earning, and we had a good social life and all got on well.

I also worked at another club in Ealing Broadway, which was even worse. It was an underground basement club like a rabbit warren with numerous passageways leading into different bar areas. We all had radio mikes and earpieces to keep us in touch with each other and when something kicked off in a certain area, I had to quickly push my way through crowds of drunken people in dimly lit corridors to where it was happening. I wasn't big as far as bouncers go, but I was strong, fit and pretty fearless, and I knew I had to prove myself with these other guys who were built like brick shit houses and had been working together for some time.

One night, the message came through that something was going off in the cellar bar and I ran, pushing and shoving my way through the mass of drunken, dancing bodies in the subdued lights of flickering colours. I reached the area and I could just make out a pile of bodies beating hell out of one another on the floor. It reminded me of a scene from the Bash Street Kids in The Beano with elbows, knees and legs sticking out at all angles. I pulled one guy off and threw him out of the way, and then I dived back in, grabbed another geezer who seemed to be the main protagonist and was on top of a young lad, I put him in a choke hold and dragged him out of the melee. Once I released him, he kicked off again and in the heat of battle one of my punches missed its intended target and landed on the top of the head of my fellow bouncer who was also trying to take this huge guy down. He glared at me and then we both turned back to sorting out the brawl. Afterwards, we had a good laugh about it and it turned out to be a good bonding session. Even though I had got the wrong guy, they knew I was willing to get stuck into any trouble. We always had a drink together after work and became a close-knit crew. It was completely different to the Paras, but it was still a good team environment.

I worked as many hours as I could to earn as much money as possible at the clubs for a few months, still staying on Mark's couch. It was a great bolt hole but depressing not having my own bed and I eventually got enough cash together to rent a tiny box room a couple of streets away. The whole time, I continued to send out letters to prospective employers to get a job I really wanted.

I finally got a job working security at Selsdon Park Hotel in Croydon. Initially, I went for a week's work but ended up staying a couple of months providing security for the whole hotel. The security team stayed in the hotel rooms and ate in the staff canteen, so that was a lot more comfortable than my lodgings at Mark's place. I was earning a decent day rate and not spending anything. I had a good time with the guys I was living down there with, got myself a Danish girlfriend who also worked at the hotel and became team leader reporting direct to the firm based in Wembley.

My first real break came from a security company called Remedy; they were a top-notch firm highly respected on The Circuit. I knew a lot of guys who had tried to get in with them in the past but failed, so when I got a reply letter from Remedy, I wasn't expecting much. The letter was from PB, who, although I didn't know it at the time, was going to become a big influence on me, and my career development, in the future. He was an ex Squadron Sergeant Major in the SAS and now the Operations Director of Remedy. He was asking me to come for an interview. This was great news; I was really pleased and full of hope when I went to the office in Kensington to meet him.

PB offered me a one-day job working on the Getty estate in Stokenchurch. The vast and beautiful buildings and grounds were permanently protected by a team from Remedy made up of mainly ex Special Forces guys. The grounds included a cricket pitch and he was holding a charity match with famous celebrities playing for the Getty eleven against the West Indies team who were about to start a tour of England. It was a great opportunity and I was incredibly excited.

I didn't know where the estate was located, I had never heard of it, but I got my road map out, worked out how to get there, and how long it would take me. Being a soldier, punctuality was built into my DNA, and I was totally prepared to get there well before time, ready to start at nine. I woke up that morning with a jolt, looked at my alarm clock and it was eight-thirty; the alarm had not gone off! I could not believe that I had overslept. I threw on a suit and drove at the speed of a thousand gazelles to get there as quickly as possible but knowing I would be late one way or another. I had to meet a guy called Jimmy, the ex SAS team leader for the Getty job. When I eventually got there, I apologised profusely to him. He was really good about it and briefed me on what I needed to do. I got straight on with the job, but the whole time I was kicking myself, thinking I had blown any chance of further work with Remedy.

The West Indies' team was sporting a certain, in-form, Brian Lara, who I watched smash one hundred in the match without breaking a sweat. I had the most fantastic day but finished with the terrible feeling that I would never hear from Remedy again: to be late in the military is an absolute no no. I hadn't even been drinking the night before and I could not believe that it had happened. Every time I thought about it, my stomach turned over.

PB called me into his office the following week and I was sure I would get a bollocking, but instead he told me that he'd received good reports about me and that there was a job coming up with the Sultan of Oman. I was totally relieved and amazed that I had got away with the late start. To this day, I am sure he knew that I was late and for whatever reason decided to give me another chance.

The Sultan of Oman came over to the UK every two years for a month-long visit with his own security and an entourage of local Omani people. There was a strong link between the British military and the Sultan and he loved Remedy. He knew most of the ex SAS guys who worked there from their days of operating in Oman and was very close friends with the owner of the company. A twelve-man team was required to provide security while he was staying in his Park Lane town house in London. I became part of the security team and we moved into the house much to the upset of the house staff and butler who bitterly resented the presence of so-called hired guns.

Our job was to protect the residence during the Sultan's stay and to provide extra mobile security when he went out and about on official meetings. It was fascinating work and I met some very interesting people. At the end of the month-long contract, I went back to the office and PB gave me an envelope containing one thousand pounds in crisp fifty-pound notes. It was a gift from the Sultan and a huge bonus on top of my pay. I was really proud of myself; I knew a lot of guys who had been out of the army for two or three years without finding work like this. I have always had a massive drive to succeed and I enjoy pushing myself forward, grabbing any opportunities that come my way and working hard to do them well.

It was around this time that I met my second wife, Jo. One of the guys working with me for the Sultan of Oman, knowing that I was single, told me that his wife had a good-looking sister and put us in touch. We began writing and calling and I eventually went to Hereford to meet her once the job was over and I had a couple of days off. I presumed that when I arrived in Hereford, I would be able to book into a B&B, but when I got there, they were all full due to some event that was on that weekend. I told Jo and I could tell that she didn't believe me. She very reluctantly said that I could kip on her couch. She was a very attractive girl, a few years younger than me and we went out and got on really well. I didn't sleep on the couch; we started seeing each other and had a great time. We eventually ended up buying a house together in Hereford, and that is where I began to spend my time when I was off work.

My next Remedy job was working for the Saudi royal family, protecting the princesses when they came over to London on their summer shopping trips, which took up most of the day, every day. They were staying in Claridges Hotel, so that is where we stayed too, ready for two to three weeks of looking after the ladies while they shopped. They went out with vast amounts of cash and just spent, spent, spent. Shopping with your own wife is one thing, but this was another. I never knew shopping could be such hard work, but the ladies were lovely and it was also a lot of fun.

Unfortunately, after five days, they had to suddenly return to Saudi due to a family bereavement. I was gutted and really worried about what I was going to do next. I used to keep a diary to record how many days of work I had done and how much I earned, and I was always determined to keep increasing the amount month upon month. I got another five-hundred-pound bonus from the Saudis, which helped, but it was a blow to my plans.

More work was coming up though. PB called me in again and told me that there was a vacancy on the permanent Getty security team, working two weeks on and two weeks off. They had been impressed with how I worked and were looking to inject some young blood into the team. It was a no brainer for me; as a member of a permanent team like that with a monthly salary, the cards were really starting to fall my way.

I was very happy and now knew that leaving the Paras was the correct decision. Sometimes things happen for a reason and finally the bar incident in NI and consequent demotion was starting to fade into the past. There were four men on each two-week shift. Each team worked for two weeks before being replaced by the other team. In the two weeks off you could do what you liked, even take on other work within reason. I headed back to Hereford to see Jo for a few days and usually did a little work for a friend's company who transported high value microchips from a bonded warehouse at Heathrow to Glasgow or Ireland. These short tasks lasted just a couple of days at a time and were a great way of earning extra cash on top of my salary.

On the Getty task, we stayed in a little cottage on the estate and our job was to secure the residence. We had a high-tech operations room with numerous cameras, infrared beams and electric gates. We were also taught how to work with guard dogs. We patrolled the grounds with these dogs and had to look after them. I knew the grounds were massive with a cricket pitch, pavilion and a stunning walled garden, but now I was to find out the full extent of the Wormsley estate.

Set in two thousand, seven hundred acres of rolling countryside in the Chiltern Hills, it is famous for one of the finest collections of books and manuscripts in the world. I remember seeing a copy of Canterbury Tales in a sealed glass cabinet with special ventilation to preserve the pages. There is a working farm as well as the cricket pitch and of course, the main house which is more of a castle. Our job was to protect the inner sanctum of the main residence and offer close protection when John Paul Getty II left the house. He wasn't in good health and didn't often leave, but when he did, two of us, a driver and CP, accompanied him. The older members of the team preferred to stay in the grounds; it was an idyllic life where they could run and bike around the estate and just chill out in the cottage. The other young guy, Scott and I tended to do all the movements; we liked going out and doing the job for real.

I got to know John Paul Getty II quite well; he was a highly intelligent and lovely man who had become a recluse in the 70s and 80s and was now a philanthropist. He had dealt with the terrible tragedy of his son John Paul Getty III who was kidnapped at the age of sixteen. JPG III was the grandson of American oil tycoon J Paul Getty I, who was once the richest man in the world. While living in Rome in 1973, JPG III was kidnapped for a seventeen-million-dollar ransom. His grandfather was reluctant to pay, as he felt that it could have put his other grandchildren in danger. After a newspaper received the severed ear of JPG III, a deal was done, and Getty was released. Unfortunately, JPG lll never got over his ordeal and developed a drug and alcohol addiction, which eventually led to a stroke that left him severely disabled for the rest of his life.

Due to the kidnapping, JPG II was now very tight on security and turned to Remedy for this service. He had an affiliation with the SAS, and donated the Mappa of Mundi, a medieval map of the known world dating back to circa 1300, to the cathedral in Hereford. He was a sponsor of the new camp at Credenhill and flew in by helicopter for its opening ceremony. I also got to know the lady of the house, Victoria Handsworth, known to us as Lady Getty or Ma'am. She was his second wife, very beautiful, posh and charming.

I continued to work on the Getty team for nearly two years as it was interesting work and great for my CV at this point in my career. You need to show loyalty in this business and not get a reputation as someone who jumps ship at every opportunity. To be honest though, it was starting to become a little boring and when PB came to see me one day when I was on duty up at the estate and said that they had another CP job working in France for the Aga Khan which would be a lot more active, I was ready for a change. A lot of younger guys were now starting to get into the business and the opportunity to go to France was a good one. It was another level up when it came to the task and responsibility involved, so I decided to take the job.

I moved to the Aga Khan's estate in Chantilly, just outside Paris and started to learn more about him, his love of horses, and his work as head of the Ismaili population. A dispersed people living in over twenty-five countries around the world, there are an estimated ten to fifteen million adherents of Ismaili who make up around ten to twelve percent of the world's Shia Muslim population.

The Aga Khan is a business magnate as well as a racehorse owner and breeder and the founder and chairman of the Aga Khan Development Network, one of the largest private development networks in the world. In 1957, at the age of twenty, he succeeded his grandfather, and became Imam, under the title of Aga Khan IV. It is believed that the Aga Khan is a direct lineal descendant of the Islamic prophet Muhammad. He is one of the world's ten richest royals but is unique because he does not rule over a geographic territory.

He went on tours to visit his people with an armed protection team provided by Remedy. My primary job at the time was to look after Aly, his two year old son and heir apparent. I was in charge of looking after Aly wherever he needed to go. He also had a dedicated French driver and two nannies who worked back to back, one of whom was German and the other British, so Aly got the chance to learn both languages. The Aga Khan was an extremely hard working and pleasant man, very laid back and kind, but his wife, the 'Begum', as we had to call her, was a very difficult woman. She had previously been married to a German Prince and had a daughter who also lived in Chantilly. I sometimes looked after the daughter and assisted on extra trips abroad on my time off.

I once took her to visit her father in Germany. We flew by private jet to Dusseldorf, where the Prince's staff met us and took us up into the mountains to his iconic castle overlooking the dam. I was introduced to her father, a real gentleman who spoke perfect English, who clearly appreciated that his daughter was so well looked after when over in France with us. He was keen to make sure I had a weapon when at the castle in Germany and he took me to his office and opened his gun cabinet, which contained a number of different pistols. I wasn't going to argue, but was worried that he might give me an old German Luger. Luckily, he took a new model Glock pistol from his safe and handed it to me. He also gave me the use of a beautiful Mercedes to drive around in so I could get to learn the local area. I had a wonderful time driving along the winding roads and through this typical German mountain town with the castle up above. I was there for a week and made sure I gave father and daughter plenty of space to spend some quality time together. Part of the job is making sure that you are providing protection without actually being seen to do so.

I thoroughly enjoyed the work with the Aga Khan, and during my stint there, I was still going back to Hereford, but Jo and I hit a sticky patch and split up. I was called into PB's office once again and this time he had two jobs on offer for me. He believed in allowing progression for determined and ambitious young men and I was getting good reports for my work.

The first job was a highly sought-after role on a contract known as 'Protector'. An ambassador to the United States based in Washington with his family had a close protection team. Unlike Getty and the Aga Khan who lived reasonably private lives, this client enjoyed a very high-profile existence. It was well-known within Remedy that the guys who worked on Protector were paid well by the firm and also received bonuses from the client, as well as gifts such as very expensive watches. PB offered me the chance to go over for a trial after which it would be up to the Protector management team to decide whether they liked me and wanted to offer me a more permanent position, or not.

Paul went on to talk about the second opportunity; this one was in Kabul, Afghanistan working for the European Commission. The first part of the team had been out there for two months already and they were in the process of up scaling the team from three to four. I knew that this was a fantastic chance to work on a properly armed task in a hostile and live environment. This was the first job of its kind and well ahead of the curve on what was to come in the future on The Circuit.

I had left the Paras before the Balkan, Sierra Leone, and Afghan conflicts had broken out, so I had a burning desire to, in some way, make up for what I had inadvertently missed out on. This is what I had been trained to do and it is what every trained soldier worth his salt desires. The golden opportunity of getting onto the Protector team was amazing and is what I had been quietly working towards and hoping would come my way since I started at Remedy. Now I had the Afghan opportunity on the table in front of me, and on top of that, my old friend Chris was calling me from Kabul and telling me how much he was enjoying the task and the excellent opportunity it provided. He knew that I was going to be offered the job as it had been discussed when PB was last over in Kabul. This was my chance to take my career on The Circuit to a whole new level, something I had only dreamed about when leaving the Paras three years earlier. PB told me to go away and think about it, but I knew I had already made up my mind.

CHAPTER 8

KABUL BOMBING

I went back to PB the following day and told him what he already knew; that I wanted to go to Afghanistan and join the European Commission (EC) Security Team. He had already put things in motion with a replacement ready to take over my role in France with the Aga Khan and a start date for me to go to Kabul in less than two weeks' time. Just the practicalities of applying for a visa and booking flights needed to be arranged over the next few days.

I immediately started mentally preparing myself and finding out as much as I could about what was going on in Afghanistan. After the September 11th attacks in 2001, the Americans had been quick to put in motion a search for those responsible and they knew that Osama bin Laden, leader of Al Qaeda and others were hiding out somewhere in Afghanistan. The administration of George W. Bush demanded that the Taliban, who controlled ninety percent of Afghanistan, deliver the leaders of Al Qaeda to the US. When they refused, plans were put in place for war, with the aim of ousting the Taliban and dismantling Al Qaeda.

The initial invasion began with UK and US Special Forces going into the country at the end of September 2001. They were joined by Afghani troops working with the anti-Taliban forces of the Northern Alliance and by 6th December 2001, the Taliban had been driven out of power and effectively defeated. Of course, this proved to be a very naïve understanding of the nature of Afghani people and the resilience of the Taliban and Al Qaeda. The Taliban had merely retreated into the mountains and border region of Pakistan to regroup or were lying low in the cities and villages awaiting instruction. I was going over in early 2002 when most of the fighting had ceased and the main purpose of Westerners' presence was to help rebuild the country and provide humanitarian aid.

I spoke to Chris, who was a former member of Two Squadron RAF Regiment and one of the best hands-on medics I have ever met. Chris had also worked his way up the ranks of Remedy just like me and was now the designated medic on the EC team. He told me about the kit I needed to bring with me. The rotation in Afghanistan was three months on and one month off, this made us tax free in the UK, which was an added bonus. The salary was great at the time and near on double anything I had ever earned before. I went on a shopping spree to kit myself out with the right clothing. Obviously, the idea of close protection work is that you are fairly low key and blend into the environment. This wasn't really possible in somewhere like Afghanistan where the few westerners there stood out like sore thumbs and you were driving around in conspicuous vehicles. The clothing became a bit of a uniform in itself as we all tended to wear similar gear: beige combat trousers, outdoor walking shirts, fishing jackets and even baseball caps and sunglasses. I would have preferred to wear clothing that was more normal, but a fishing jacket is very useful with all its pockets for carrying your kit.

Having split up with Jo, I was now in London staying in Kensington, close to the Remedy office in one of their team houses. I had a relaxing couple of weeks off catching up with friends, seeing my daughter over in Belfast and getting my visa done. Finally, the morning arrived, and I was ready to go. I headed off to Heathrow airport for my next adventure.

My first flight stopped in Dubai, the first of many visits and the beginning of a love affair with the city, which still lasts today. I stayed in a transit hotel and the following day I went to Terminal 2 for my flight to Kabul. In complete contrast to the very swish and modern Terminals 1 and 3 at Dubai airport, Terminal 2 in those days was a shock to the system.

Most flights operating from there were for the 'Stan' countries and it was packed with workers from these regions wearing dirty, long shirts, baggy trousers and sporting long, flowing beards. There were rows and rows of scruffy, grimy bodies sleeping throughout the terminal, the hole in the floor toilets made you wretch they were so disgusting and there was nowhere to get anything to eat.

The airline was the Afghan airline Ariana, which was appropriately nicknamed 'Scaryana'. The seats were terrible, the food inedible, and overhead lockers kept falling open. The only other Westerners on the flight were what we called 'tree huggers', members of various non-government organisations (NGOs) going over to offer aid to the people of Afghanistan. Coming into Kabul airport, the view from the airplane window was shocking. All I could see was the devastation of burned out planes, armoured vehicles and tanks everywhere. It was like a scrapyard for military vehicles and the runway was literally a strip of ground cleared to allow planes to land. I knew that I had arrived in a war zone, even though the war against the Taliban and Al Qaeda was officially over. From the plane, we had a four hundred-metre walk to the temporary terminal that was more like a tin shack.

Stepping into the Wormsley estate had been like walking through the wardrobe into a magical world. It was vast and beautiful and although I took my job very seriously, I was living surrounded by wealth and luxury. Patrolling the grounds with the guard dog or going for a run through the deer park and by the lake was relaxing and peaceful. With the Aga Khan it was the same, the Chantilly Chateau is perched in the middle of a large moat; it houses a museum and a library with masterpieces of original art and literature. The grounds are expansive and picturesque with the fabulous Great Stables, probably the grandest and most luxurious stables ever built. I had a privileged glimpse into the lives of the rich and famous, actually lived on the same premises and travelled around in style. I had walked through a very different door this time from a fairy tale castle into a dubious war-ravaged land.

Chris was coming to meet me, but I had no means of communication and I was caught up in a melee of shoving and pushing human bodies. There was no concept of queueing and it was just a scrummage trying to get to the makeshift box with a bit of glass in it, which was the passport control desk. Armed soldiers were all around, it was hot, sweaty and stinking and I'd never experienced anything like it. Thank God it was still springtime and the temperatures were cool. All I could do was start pushing myself forward along with the rest of them. I was caught up in it for over an hour and I was well out of my comfort zone, thinking, 'What is going on?'

Eventually, I got to present my passport and visa to the official. I was asked a few questions in broken English, got stamped in, and went through to the baggage collection area. There weren't any conveyor belts, let alone duty-free shops. I went into a big room with a hole in the wall. The hole led directly to the outside area and bags were literally being thrown through the hole and across the floor. I was there for about half an hour just trying to work out how I could find my bag. There was one man in the centre of it all, a little man with a huge head and little legs; his bright henna dyed beard was longer than his body. He was driving around in a small tractor-like vehicle, super busy moving bags around in a haphazard way. I still couldn't see how I was meant to find my bag, which contained everything I needed plus some essentials that I'd brought over for the team. I was beginning to worry when I spotted Chris with his distinctive ginger hair and broad, booming Bristol accent. He came over, gave me a massive hug and said, 'Good to see you mucker,' and I was filled with a sense of euphoria. I was so relieved to see someone I knew. He had come with a local Afghani man who could speak Farsi; we found my bag and headed outside.

The drive from the airport into Kabul was fascinating. Off the main roads were dirt tracks thronged with people, donkeys and trucks. They were sights that I have since seen a million times in various places around the world, but at the time, it was a complete culture shock. It looked and felt exactly as I imagined a post war city. There were people wearing military gear, people carrying weapons, crumbling walls defaced by bullets. There were signs of fighting but in fact, the city was not destroyed in the war; it was just a tired shabby place. There were lots of small restaurants with white plastic chairs and tables outside, slums and shanty towns. Some rich Afghanis lived in plush villas but, overall, the place was poor, smelly and dirty. Even the Intercon Hotel, which was at the time the number one hotel in the city, was a dingy place in need of total renovation. It was a crazy experience seeing all of it, but I felt excited. This was what I wanted to be doing. I didn't want to be wearing an expensive Armani suit strolling around Paris or Washington with some high-net-worth, pretentious client, struggling to justify why I was there. I wanted to be on the front line of whatever was happening and experiencing the true conditions and risks that came with operating in places such as this.

We drove through the city and eventually into an area called Wazir Akbar Khan, one of the wealthiest and most affluent areas of Kabul with many of the embassy buildings and large villas. We headed to our compound that consisted of a large six-bedroom villa with a big courtyard, a garden and some outhouses surrounded by a ten-foot-high brick wall with a double gate just wide enough for our vehicles to get through. At the end of the yard was a prefabricated building with a kitchen in it that consisted of a decrepit old cooker attached to a gas bottle that had the potential to burst into flames at any moment. It was a dirty, miserable place with a few more of the ubiquitous white plastic chairs and a table. There were two breeze block single floor rooms comprising of two bedrooms in each on either side of the gate where the security team slept. When I arrived, the team leader, Dickie had gone on leave a few days earlier and Phil, another ex SAS guy and team second in command (2ic), was running the show.

Phil arrived, shook my hand with his huge, Hampshire hammer hand and said, 'Hi Jase, good to meet you. I hear you are ex-Para Reg. Chris speaks very highly of you and that's all I give a fuck about.' It was a brief introduction that I discovered was typical of him. Phil had served fourteen years in the military and five of those in the SAS; he had a huge amount of experience and was one of the members of the team who carried out the hostage rescue mission in Sierra Leone.

Operation Barras, as it was known, took place on 10th September 2000, during the late stages of their civil war. The operation's aim was to release the five British soldiers of the Royal Irish Regiment and their Sierra Leone Army liaison officer, who were being held by the 'West Side Boys'. The soldiers had been held for over a fortnight and fearing they may be killed or moved, the British government authorised an assault on the West Side Boys' base, to take place at dawn the following day.

D Squadron, 22 Special Air Service, Phil's old unit, conducted the ground operation. They assaulted Gberi Bana in a bid to extract the Royal Irish. Elements of A Company, 1 Para, my old unit, launched a diversionary assault on Magbeni, which was the other side of the river. The operation freed the five soldiers as well as twenty-one Sierra Leonean civilians who had been held prisoner by the West Side Boys. The capture of the Royal Irish patrol had damaged the reputation of British Forces operating in Sierra Leone and this operation went a long way to restoring confidence. The successful use of 1 Para in Operation Barras also influenced the creation of the Special Forces Support Group (SFSG), a permanent unit, initially built around 1 Para, whose role is to act as a backup force for British Special Forces on large or more difficult operations.

I got on well with Phil, he was loyal, totally fearless and a great wing man; you knew with great certainty that if the shit hit the fan, Phil would have your back. We became good friends over the next few years, and because of knowing Chris, I very quickly fitted in with the team and we all got on great.

Unbeknown to me, there had just been a major drama with one of the team members; an ex-foreign legion guy, who had got drunk a couple of nights earlier, had gone a bit crazy and although Chris and Phil had put him to bed, he had got up and fired a round off in his room. The EC contract was a dry job i.e. no alcohol, but as the guys had been working so hard for two months, they had decided, as Dickie wasn't there, to have a few well-earned beers and to unwind a little. A few turned into a lot and the idiot had ended up drunk as a skunk. It reinforced why Dickie was a stickler for his no alcohol rule.

Phil had phoned PB in London to ask what he should do and the solution was to just get rid of him, get him out of there. They couldn't find a flight, so they were going to put him on a bus on a route to Jalalabad, and on through the border up the Khyber Pass into Pakistan. Phil had actually taken him to the bus station when the London office decided that it wasn't a good idea because it was too dangerous. They got him back and managed to book him on a flight. Phil took him to the airport and made sure he got on the plane. I arrived to join a team that was one man down.

When the team had first arrived in Kabul, they had spent a few weeks sourcing weapons locally while they waited for the EC weapons and equipment shipment to arrive. They didn't have anything. It took time for vehicles and everything they needed to be shipped across and in the two months they had been there, they had had to find their own and buy locally. Chris was very excited because they had finally received a delivery of weapons the week before. He took me into his room and pulled out a massive black, padlocked box from under his bed. He opened it and revealed that it was full of weapons. They had purchased AK47s locally for use on field trips or if the situation got really out of hand, but now they also had Glock 17s (thirty round machine gun pistols that fire on fully automatic, which I had never come across before) and MP5s that the SAS used for Close Quarter Battle (CQB). The weapons of choice were the pistols, which were easy to carry and conceal as well as the MP5s that fold down neatly into a day sack and go on your back or in the vehicle next to you. State of the art weapons had finally arrived along with extra medical equipment for Chris, which was good news for the team.

Glock 17s and MP5s were the perfect weapons for a CP task such as this and I needed training on how to use them, effectively and safely. I had used the MP5 back in my days in the COP in Northern Ireland but had never even seen a Glock 17 before. Chris spent some time bringing me up to speed on them both, going over stripping them down, cleaning, maintaining them and of course how to actually load, handle and use them. I wasn't going to risk going out on the ground in Kabul in a dangerous and hostile environment not comfortable with the weapon I was carrying. With the team now one man down, I was straight into it and no time to mess around.

A commercial contract such as ours was completely different to a military organised security team. The American or British Embassy typically had equipment, vehicles and men flown in on a large transport plane. Specialist teams who have trained together and ongoing supplies of whatever they needed were the norm. In complete contrast, we were employed by a private security company who in turn were contracted by the European Commission; they didn't have their own army or capabilities such as this and we were viewed by many as mercenaries or at best highly paid guns for hire. In fact, we were the team responsible for the protection of the EC Ambassador and his staff and we had to make do with whatever we could get our hands on. We had to be flexible and adapt to whatever cards we were dealt. We also had to be highly disciplined, vigilant and fully prepared, as there was no one to call in for back up if things got sticky.

We were the only commercial team on the ground at that time. The other security teams such as the British, American, Dutch, German and Spanish, all of whom we met and got to know well, were fully geared up and serving members of their respective nation's army or police units. In some ways, I was lucky to be joining at that time because the guys had built up their own supply and now a consignment had arrived, we were much better equipped. However, we were still one man down and it was going to be full on until Remedy could get another guy out to us.

Life fell into an absolutely manic routine. We sat down for 'prayers' every evening, which was basically where Phil went over the itinerary for the following day. We tried to plan as far ahead as possible but usually you couldn't do much more than a few days ahead at most, unless there was a field trip coming up, which we would start to discuss.

I was introduced to the ambassador, referred to as 'The Boss', who was a very tall and highly experienced Dane of few words, but I got to know him really well; he was a great character and a huge support to the team. He had a staff of different European nationalities many of whom were French and quite cold towards us from the start and, for whatever reason, against having a security team. They didn't like us whatsoever and we were the last people to get anything as they held the purse strings for most local purchases. We had a small expenses float from Remedy, but were told to use it sparingly, plus we never wanted to run it down in case it was required in an emergency. We needed a decent kitchen, living area, training equipment, and better food, but the money just wasn't forthcoming. A French guy, Jules, who was the communications officer for the EC, was also responsible for the cash. He was clearly anti-English and anti-security and made it clear that he didn't see a need for any protection detail in Kabul. There was a general feeling of animosity towards us from some of the staff, but luckily not from the ambassador.

The ambassador loved a drink on Thursday evenings, which was the start of the Arabic weekend, and often asked us to take him to the Danish embassy so that he could socialise with his compatriots. We took him and sat for hours waiting for him to finish. He stumbled out afterwards and said he wanted to drive the vehicle, which of course did not happen. At other times, he invited his friends to the villa and entertained them. He relied upon us to source the beer, which you could buy, but illegally. He was a lovely guy, he'd been around the block and he believed that this was his last posting: he wasn't going to live like a hermit.

We were in this crazy routine trying to cover the movements of all the staff and we still needed an extra man. We eventually had a guy called Rick join us but Phil really didn't take to him. He was a bit of a Walter Mitty character that we just couldn't work out. None of us could get down to the truth of what experience he had or what his military background was. He seemed to have a chequered past and none of us really liked him that much. Phil was at a point where he really wanted to know who we were getting, particularly after the experience with the ex-French Legionnaire guy. However, we just had to get on with who PB was sending us. Rick actually stayed with us for quite a long time and to be fair, he turned out to be a competent operator.

More EC Diplomats were starting to arrive, including some female members of staff. Some were given permission to live in another villa compound down the road, as the villa in our compound was nearly full. We were responsible for their safety as well. The security situation in Kabul seemed reasonably stable on the face of it; the war was officially over and the Taliban had been defeated for the time being at least. However, that didn't mean that things weren't going on under the surface and military operations were still on going in other parts of the country. We put plans in place for how we were moving people around and what we would do in case certain situations occurred. We had an emergency evacuation plan, which entailed the use of burqas, which would cover us from head to toe, and a local taxi. This would be used if we were the last ones left in the country and there was no other way out. These plans were reviewed and modified on a regular basis as slowly but surely, the insurgent activity was beginning to grow.

More and more members of staff were now arriving and the EC decided that it needed another location to act as their official office away from the main accommodation compound. Up to this point, the villa was also doubling up as the embassy, but then the ambassador decided he wanted another location that would be his place of work for meeting people. We didn't have enough vehicles to cover the movement of all the different people to and from the different locations.

We trained up local people to guard the gates of the new embassy building, which was used during the day, but nobody slept there. Every day we needed to get the staff to the embassy to open it up and to get them home again. We had two vehicles, but Jules decided that one of the vehicles, which really should have been considered a pool car, was his personal vehicle and constantly said that he needed to go here, there and everywhere. Sometimes he just took a driver and went out without telling us. Often, I actually walked to the embassy just to open it up. This meant packing my day sack with an MP5 stepping out into the main street and walking for twenty minutes along streets bustling with traffic and people, across a completely open square full of stall holders selling fruit and vegetables, drinks, snacks and plastic toys under faded umbrellas and awnings. In the distance, I glimpsed the ridges of the snowcapped mountains surrounding the city. I was poised with my hand ready to pull my weapon at any moment. There was nothing obvious to cause a problem but being out in the open felt very uncomfortable and to be quite honest, very exhilarating. You just never knew who was around, who might be watching. It was a bizarre situation and just not how you would ideally want to operate. As I said, nothing was actually happening to threaten us at this particular time, but you could sense that things were not as calm as they appeared on the surface. As things transpired, the dangers were all there and the insurgents were in a phase of regrouping and planning for their next attacks.

I got to the embassy building, opened up and called the villa to say it was safe. We didn't even have radios to keep in communication with each other. They sent us out some equipment, but it wasn't fit for purpose. We just had handheld VHF radios, which in built up areas didn't work properly and had limited range. We waited months for the proper equipment to be set up with re-broadcasting units at each of our main locations, which boosted the range of our radio transmissions.

There were lots of little things that made life and work very difficult. The ambassador had his own personal chef, but we didn't really have enough food to eat of the quality we required. The argument was that our company should pay for our food and not the embassy. There were no cash machines, so it was difficult for the company to send us money. Each time one of us flew out, we'd come back in with thousands of USD in cash, but that wasn't enough for everything we needed. We became scroungers and it actually became good fun and a challenge seeing what we could get and from where.

Using the contacts we were making and force of personality we managed to get by very well. We went up to Camp Souter which had become a British Army base and had a troop of the SAS based up there. Kabul was reasonably quiet for them at this time, but they were still heavily involved in the continued search for Osama bin Laden and keeping an eye on other pockets of resistance across Afghanistan. Phil knew the guy in charge and we wanted to acquire some ammunition from them. Phil knew very well that they had more than enough. We had just about enough ammo for a firefight as long as it didn't last too long, but we didn't have enough to do any range practice. We all needed to train; I definitely did. There were things Phil wanted to show us and although we'd done lots of dry training, it wasn't the same as actually getting on the range and doing our drills and live firing all our weapon systems in conjunction with the use of the vehicles. Sure enough, we came away with enough spare ammo to serve our purpose and offered them any favours we could do in return. It was comforting to know that the Regiment was just up the road and we now had a direct number for them if worse came to worst.

On another occasion, we went onto the camp where the main British army contingent was based. Chris and I were in one of the vehicles and Phil had gone up on his motorbike. He was a complete lunatic on it, and he was spinning the bike around in the camp square, messing about doing donuts when this British Army Colour Sergeant came running out. He started shouting at Phil and moved aggressively towards him. I geared myself up ready, when suddenly, they recognised each other and the next moment they were hugging and slapping each other on the back. It turned out that he was an ex Hampshire from Phil's old battalion. Before we knew it, he was taking us into the store and asking us what we needed. Needless to say, we were not shy when it came to our wish list of kit.

In general, the guys at the camp were great with us, but the Royal Military Police (RMPs), who had taken over the British Embassy close protection duties now that the SAS had handed it over, didn't like us at all. We were a commercial unit and they thought we were earning a lot more money than they were, so there was a certain amount of resentment. The truth was, we were earning far more than they were, but that did not help when it came to getting by in Afghanistan without any logistical or operational support. The rations given to us by the EC were the bare minimum and we were often short of necessities such as good bottled drinking water. The RMPs were supplied with absolutely everything they required, and they had the necessary back up for any operations they had to carry out.

The RMPs tried to ban us from the camp; it was quite unbelievable really in an environment like this where we were all British serving or former soldiers. Luckily, because we had made some great contacts and friends in the camp we always managed to get in there and scrounge whatever we needed. We got to know the chefs in the cookhouse, reversed our vehicle up to the back door and loaded up what we could. We stocked up on essentials we were finding hard to acquire in the city like bread, milk, eggs and water. For weeks and weeks, we went up there on a regular basis. Never knowing how long it might last, we gathered ammunition and stockpiled food and water as well as British army ration packs which would be handy on field trips or if we were ever locked down in the compound and unable to get out for fresh supplies.

We garnered whatever we could from wherever we could and it became fun, a contest to see who could source the best things. We had a per diem rate for our daily expenses and in the end, we were saving most of that. Of course, it couldn't last. As time went on, the situation changed and a lot of the personnel on the camp changed. There were new people coming in and we managed to get around some of them, but it gradually came to a point where the chefs told us that they had been told not to give us anything anymore. They would still give us something to go away with and we kept on going up there for a while but the amounts we were given got smaller and smaller. Luckily, by then we had stockpiled brilliantly.

In the meantime, we also got to know people from the different embassies. The guys at the British Embassy clearly hated us. They never offered us any assistance, but we went up to the Spanish Embassy and literally knocked on the door, told them we were with the European Commission and they invited us in for lunch and asked us if we needed anything. It was the same with the

Italians, the Germans, and the Dutch; I still have great Dutch friends from that time. We could tell them we had a trip coming up and they helped us out with anything we needed; they were quality operators and absolute gentlemen.

Apart from the scrounging, we still had our daily tasks to complete. Taking the ambassador wherever he wanted to go was our primary duty. It might be visits to other embassies to discuss diplomatic matters with other ambassadors or meetings with NGOs and local aid organisations. I once had to take The Boss to a function at the Palace in Kabul to meet President Hamid Karzai. Karzai had a huge amount of security around him at all times because the risk to his life and the fragile interim government was huge. When we first arrived in Kabul, the US Navy Seals' Team had been providing his security, however when things settled down, DynCorp who were a US private security company had taken it over. There were American armed security guys everywhere, all wearing baseball caps and dark glasses with thousand-yard stares. It seemed a little over the top if you ask me, but that was how they operated and to be fair what Karzai expected. It was interesting to actually see Karzai up close and to hear him talk to our Ambassador. The DynCorp guys, once I introduced myself, were very accommodating and pleasant towards us and allowed me to do my job without any undue interference.

We took The Boss to his new office to meet various people; he always wanted to be there for whoever might need to speak to him. Often people just turned up to see him; the NGOs knew that they could go to him if they needed help with anything. Then of course, there were the other members of staff to move to the embassy and other meetings around the city every day plus the manning of the residence compound and any security related meetings we needed to attend ourselves in the city.

It sounds fairly straight forward, but we took our roles very seriously and it was very important to us that we planned meticulously and didn't make any mistakes such as using the same route at the same time each day. There were no direct threats against us at this time, but we didn't know who might be watching our movements and we didn't want to make ourselves easy targets. This proved to be a battle with the staff that couldn't see the possible dangers and sometimes had meetings that they needed to get to at a certain time. We tried to change our routes and vehicle types constantly, but again, there were only a few variations available. We were super professional at all times and of course, when it came to field trips out of Kabul, the planning had to be even more diligent.

An English man called Julian was second in charge of the EC embassy and when the ambassador went on leave, Julian effectively took over his role. For all intents and purposes, he was the EC Ambassador while The Boss was away. In turn, he was allotted all the support and perks that came with this position, including the personal security detail. He was very good company and often came over to our area in the villa compound to sit and talk to us. One night, when Dickie was still in charge of the security team, Julian wanted to go and play squash at the UN compound, just as he did most weeks when not in the ambassador's chair, and I was designated as his Personal Protection Officer (PPO) for the evening.

The UN compound was about twenty minutes' drive away. I put him in the back of the armoured Mercedes G-wagon, jumped into the front passenger seat alongside the local driver with my weapons close to hand and we headed across town to get to the compound.

The sprawling city of Kabul had been quiet since the official end of the war against the Taliban, but insurgent activity was bubbling away under the surface. On high alert inside our armoured Mercedes G-wagon, with my MP5 down the side of my leg, we made our way along the roads between the embassy villa and the UN compound where Julian wanted to play his weekly game of squash. In the side streets, old, clapped out cars, trucks and mopeds made their way along the same streets as donkeys and carts. Women fully covered in burkas, men in loose, baggy trousers and shirts with jerkins over the top made their way along the dusty, dirty sidewalks. People carrying their belongings on their heads weaved in and out of street stalls and avoided men and boys on bicycles as they passed shabby buildings riddled with bullet holes, a stark reminder of the recent hostilities.

In the dying day, the mountains surrounding the capital city loomed in the background, their giant forms silhouetting on the horizon as we reached our destination without incident. I went into the squash courts with Julian and watched for a while as he and his playing partner smashed balls and themselves into the echoing walls. After a while, I wandered outside to the empty square in front of the main building and sat down on the low wall surrounding a flowing fountain. The air was warm and pleasant as I looked up at the starry night sky. I was vaguely aware of the hum of traffic and the tooting of horns beyond the compound walls; the noise muffled by the constant, soothing flow of water from the fountain. Looking up at the clear, star-filled sky, I lit a cigarette and drew in deeply.

The explosion split the air and rocked the walls. A violent blast of hot air lifted my whole body and threw me like a rag doll across the fountain, smashing me against the small stone wall to the rear, cracking the top of my head open. Blood ran out of the wound and streamed down the side of my face. I must have blacked out briefly but when I opened my eyes, I was half in half out of the fountain. A surge of adrenalin shot through me. I leapt up and looked over at the squash courts. The windows and door had been shattered by the blast and I could see smoke. I rushed into the building where I could hear Julian talking to his playing partner saying, 'Just stay down on the floor, my security will be here in a minute.' As I burst through the door, Julian looked up and stared at me. He said, 'You're covered in blood Jase and you're soaking wet!' I hadn't even noticed.

I quickly took Julian outside, across the square and into the middle of the main hard standing building which I thought gave us the best cover in case of any sort of follow up attack, which was common place with Al Qaeda and other terrorist groups. The UN staffers were running about in a state of panic and all of them rushed outside to gather on the other side of the square for a roll call. I sat Julian down and told him I had to make a call. I contacted Phil and gave him a quick update on what had happened, what I had done about it, where I was and what I needed from him. Phil asked if we were all okay, I said Julian was fine, just a little shaken up and I just had a few bumps and bruises. He told me to stay where I was; he was sending Chris our medic and the Quick Reaction Team (QRF) to my location to pick us up, and to be ready to arrange a safe pickup point on their arrival away from the main gate area where the bomb had gone off.

I was very concerned about the UN staff's decision to go outside and have their roll call. I remembered a terrible incident in Northern Ireland years ago where a small explosive device had gone off and everyone had run to a clearing down the road to set up an Incident Control Point (ICP). Not long afterwards, when many people had gathered, another device went off at the meeting point killing an even larger number of people who had gathered there for safety and control.

I explained to Julian my thoughts on this matter and told him the story about NI and possible follow up attacks. I told him that was why I was staying put inside with him and monitoring the situation with a cool and calm head. He said he had never considered that, but now that he had, he couldn't believe the way the UN staff were acting. It just showed how little they actually understood about the real threats or what security is all about.

The blast had gone off just to the side of the main gate into the UN compound. It was luckily a small device or had not detonated properly because it had not destroyed the outer wall. If it had blown through the wall it would have turned the debris of the wall into shrapnel that would have caused way more damage and probably would have killed me and any others in that area at the time. I was very wary about whether it was just a small device that was not particularly effective, or the first of two planned attacks.

Julian wanted a drink and I said, 'No way! I can't drink on duty.' He insisted that he needed a drink and that I drank with him. I wanted to keep him calm and relaxed, so I had a beer with him whilst waiting. Finally, I received a call from Chris to say that he was at the east side gate. We went out to meet him and he drove us back to the EC compound.

On return and after Chris had cleaned me up, Dickie took me to one side to ask me what had happened. I told him very simply what had occurred and what actions I had carried out to get Julian away from any danger. Apparently, Julian had told him his version and had highly praised my actions and cool head.

Dickie talked to all of us about the incident that night. In the fridge in our dingy kitchen, there was one can of Heineken. It had been there for ages and nobody touched it. It was a bit of an ongoing joke that the one beer stayed there as a reminder of what we were missing. Julian came over to our kitchen with a can of beer in his hand to say thanks and just generally have a chat with us all. Dickie talked through what happened and as always, after any incident, made it a 'hot' debrief. He praised my actions and calmness under pressure and then suddenly he said, 'Why don't you have the beer that's in the fridge, Jase? You have earned it tonight.' As tempted as I was to sup it straight down, I said, 'I couldn't possibly have a drink, Dickie. It is a non-drinking job and I don't want to break that long standing rule.' I don't know if he knew that I had already had a drink with Julian up in the UN building. I looked at Julian, he winked at me, and we both smirked.

Needless to say, this incident had a positive impact on us as the security team and proved to those within the EC who were not fans of us that there were real-time threats to them in the whole of Afghanistan. The incident drilled it home that this risk was also in Kabul, which they were all starting to think was immune to what was going on in the rest of the country. It also showed them the true worth of the security team. Julian was now, of course, on side with us big time and the ambassador confirmed that stance on his return.

Julian sent a full report to the head of the EC in Brussels on what had happened that night and I got a message from Remedy thanking me for my actions and inviting me to visit them at the London office when I was next home on leave. A few weeks later when I turned up, I was invited up to the top floor to have dinner with all the directors at the Remedy head office. DW, BN and PB were all present and they were very complimentary about what had happened. They stated that they had received a letter of thanks for the team's actions that night in Kabul from the head of the EC. Even though it was what we were there to do, and what was expected of us, they were pleased and proud of my actions and said that it had gone a long way to enhancing Remedy's reputation with the EC and to cementing the Afghanistan contract.

Later, I received a letter from the European Commission and a personal letter from DW thanking me for my actions that night. I became reasonably untouchable for a short while and my position in Remedy was sealed. However, when I look back at this incident, I realise just how lucky I was to survive with only a couple of bumps and scratches. It was lucky escape number one. I didn't do anything that any of my colleagues wouldn't have done in that exact position. It just went to show the true worth of having a well drilled security team in an environment such as this. When the average civilian person such as Julian flapped around and stressed out, we would calmly take control of these situations. We would keep our heads firmly on our shoulders when all those around us were losing theirs.

CHAPTER 9

AFGHANISTAN FIELD TRIPS

Between organising the staff and taking them on their daily journeys, we needed to train to keep our fitness and our skills up to a high standard. Ever since the bomb at the UN compound, the job had become a lot more real for all concerned. Kabul is built inside a mountain range and at the back of our district was a feature known as Observation Hill. At the very top of the hill was a massive, empty swimming pool covered with bullet holes. The pool had been attached to a large, beautiful villa but that had long since gone; just a few ruins remained. The pool was where the Taliban used to take prisoners and execute them a group at a time. The place had become infamous for the Taliban's barbaric crimes and now had an Afghani National Army Observation Post (OP) at the top.

We used to run up the hill early in the morning while most people were still asleep to maintain our fitness levels. It was a little risky, but we needed to exercise. Every morning, before anyone else was around and before our duties started, two stayed in the compound and the other two ran up the hill, pistols covertly carried in bum bags around the waist. We ran fast through the streets and then zig-zagged up this incredibly steep hill. It was hard work and really kept me fit. The climate in Kabul didn't help; it ranged from boiling hot temperatures in the summer to freezing cold and snow in the winter. We arranged for local Afghani tradesmen to bring us steel poles that were concreted into the yard to create pull-up and dips bars, we got a punch bag and we'd go through self-defense exercises. We were highly motivated to keep ourselves in peak physical condition at all times. Out by the tank graveyard was an area that was perfect to use as a live firing range. We got some targets from the camp that we placed all around, we drove the vehicles onto the range to practice our debus and embus drills i.e. getting in and out of the vehicles, and created some really good exercises for ourselves. We re-created scenarios that might occur, using our MP5s when we first came under contact and then changing over to pistols when the magazine ran out of ammo. Grabbing hold of each other, one or two of us acted as clients and we practised how to safely extract them under fire whilst providing body cover. Phil ran most of these training drills and it was great for me being trained by someone who had only just left the SAS and was up to date on all of their CP contact drills. Dickie was there, but he left all the training up to the much younger and more up to date Phil. We even took the ambassador up to the range one day and used him in one of our live firing vehicle exercises so he could have a better understanding of what it would actually be like with live rounds flying over his head, what we would do in these situations and how we wanted him to behave. This was great training for all concerned, and only reinforced the confidence and close bond the Boss had with the security team.

This was our life. We trained hard, took care of the embassy staff and the rest of the time was spent planning and scrounging. Getting out in Kabul, making contacts, finding things, reconnaissance and acquisition of whatever we could get our hands on from other expats was the aim. We got to know the locals as well. Phil established a great relationship with the owner of the local corner shop who he called Ronnie Barker, as he genuinely was open all hours. He didn't speak a word of English, but he gave us whatever we wanted when we were passing by, and we went back at some point in the week and paid him what we owed.

It was really good fun most of the time; I loved it, just living by the seat of my pants. However, there was a sticking point with our position there. All the other security teams in Kabul and the expats in the EC were classed as diplomats and had diplomatic immunity, but we didn't. This left us in a very difficult position. We didn't know where we stood if the worst-case scenario occurred and we had to use our weapons in the line of duty to protect those we had been charged with keeping safe, and killed someone. Would we just be left rotting in some Afghani jail? We talked about it a lot. When we asked the bosses in London, they weren't too sure either and said they were working on it. Therefore, we created our own Standard Operational Procedure (SOP): if someone had a contact and injured or killed someone, we would get that person out of Afghanistan immediately. The others would stay, but the actual person responsible, the one who fired the shots, would be taken straight to the airport and flown out to the nearest and safest country available at that time. That was our drill because we really didn't know what the consequences might be and did not want to find out the hard way.

I was working three months on, one month off and although I was really enjoying my new contract in Kabul, I had begun to really miss Jo. We had split up a few months back and both of us had gone our separate ways. I knew that she was seeing someone new and it started to play on my mind. I couldn't call her from Afghanistan, but I managed to send her a voice message telling her that I missed her and still loved her and asked her if she'd like to meet up when I was home on leave. A week or so later I received a message back and to my surprise she was saying that she felt the same and we reconnected on my next leave period. Jo and I had a crazy on off relationship with lots of ups and as many downs. We ended up getting married a couple of years later and moving to Torquay to begin a side venture in property development.

Back in Afghanistan, an exciting and interesting part of my job was when the ambassador or other members of the EC delegation needed to travel outside Kabul. Field trips, as they were known. The first trip I was involved with was when The Boss needed to go to Jalalabad to meet with a local dignitary.

The Kabul – Jalalabad Road, also known as National Highway One, is a highly dangerous road running between the Afghani cities of Kabul and Jalalabad, the largest city in eastern Afghanistan and capital of Nangarhar Province. A portion of the road runs through the Tang-e Gharu gorge. It's not just the threat of insurgency that makes Highway One so perilous, it's also the narrow, winding lanes that climb up to six hundred metres through the gorge with steep, barely protected drops off the side of the road. It is a busy route and because of the many traffic accidents, this road is considered one of the most dangerous in the world. Phil and Chris had had some issues with vehicles on the last field trip to Jalalabad, before I arrived, and Phil was keen not to have a repeat of that this time.

Jalalabad was about four hours east of Kabul on a good clear run and not far from the Pakistani border. Just beyond Jalalabad is the route to the border and the Khyber Pass. We took time planning the safest way to get the ambassador there. We had an armoured Mercedes G Wagon that the ambassador used all the time in Kabul, an old, white Land Rover Discovery, a soft skin Pajero, which Jules had decided was for his own personal use, and a Nissan Patrol armoured vehicle that was so old and heavy it felt like it was going to break down at any time.

We decided to take the two soft skinned vehicles and to leave the armoured vehicles for use in Kabul. Chris and I were tasked with this trip, leaving the rest of the team in Kabul with Phil covering the remaining EC staff. Assisting us with nearly everything the European Commission did was an Afghani named Hamid. He was an extraordinary guy and had become invaluable to us. He was in his late sixties, highly intelligent, educated abroad and super well connected throughout Afghanistan. He had returned to his homeland after the war to do what he could to help the country rebuild. He had been put onto us by a trusted source and was every bit what he claimed to be. He seemed to know everyone in the country and spoke many different dialects. Wherever we went, he knew people and he knew his way around like the back of his hand. We always took him with us as check navigator and to make introductions in different places. He was the ambassador's chief advisor, confidant and a true Afghani Elder.

Ideally, we would have had three vehicles on a field trip like this with the Boss. One would be used as a scout car and we would have the capability in case of a breakdown to easily cross deck all our people from the broken down vehicle into the other vehicles and keep moving with enough capacity to complete the task safely. However, with the vehicles we had at our disposal we had to make do with two. There was no way we would risk going in one; if it broke down, we would be completely stuck and vulnerable to any potential threats around us. There was a thin line between being inhibitors and enablers in this business. Whilst our job was to protect the EC staff, we still had to work within the boundaries of what we had at our disposal and do our damnedest to make sure the trips and meetings the EC required to attend in and out of Kabul happened. Otherwise, all we would do is stifle the client's ability to operate and ultimately see ourselves out of a job.

The roads on the whole were not good in Afghanistan. We set off from the city along the road that varied between reasonably suspect surface with a few potholes to really bad and slow going. It was mainly a tarmac road but about two thirds of the way to Jalalabad this came to a sudden end. The Taliban had never got around to finishing it and the tarmac literally turned into a gravel and dirt track for the rest of the way into Jalalabad. It was horrendous driving on this surface, we all bounced around inside the cars and even driving slowly was wrecking the vehicles. Despite the slow, tortuous drive, the journey was unbelievably spectacular. We deviated off route a couple of times to visit certain locations that Hamid wanted The Boss to see and I have never seen such beautiful views anywhere else in the world. Afghanistan is a truly, breathtakingly stunning country. We reached the top of ridges and the views into the valleys below and the mountains in the distance revealed craggy rocks, vast open valleys and areas of lush greenery. If Afghanistan could ever sort itself out, then it would be a wonderful place to visit on holiday.

We left very early in the morning to ensure that we had time to get to Jalalabad before sundown. Hamid took us along numerous tracks and paths and we passed through many local villages. The people stared at us as if we were freaks with two heads; some had obviously never seen a white man before. Hamid was greeted with respect as an Elder wherever he went, and he talked to everyone. It was unnerving waiting for him while he chatted away. We didn't know where we were or if the people were really kindly-disposed towards us. Stories were starting to spread about the Taliban growing in support again. They definitely had eyes in Kabul now and were responsible for the bomb at the UN compound, and you just didn't know whom you might be dealing with as you travelled around.

We arrived at the Jalalabad Guest House, where we were staying, just before last light, and were welcomed in and presented with a wonderful spread of local food by our host and his family. Chris and I were starving and we tucked in heartily. We first checked our local surroundings, made sure we knew exactly where the ambassador would be sleeping and where we would be staying close by. We split the night into two halves with one of us staying awake and keeping a close eye on what was going on throughout the night. It's difficult to explain how I felt during these kinds of trips. Outwardly, there was a sense of calm, the people were kind and welcoming, but I never felt completely comfortable. It was partly because of our set up; normally there would be a whole team involved, someone would have already been up ahead to do a recce on where we were going, where we would be staying and who would be here on our arrival. Our lack of men and resources meant that we were just turning up at places on trust. We were completely dependent on Hamid (who to be fair never let us down) but it was as though I could sense the rumblings of things to come and I always slept with one eye open and my weapon close at hand.

We went on another field trip with the ambassador and spent a night in a tiny village in the Panjshir region. This was the home of the late Ahmad Shah Massoud, a national hero and one of the greatest guerilla leaders ever. He earned himself the nickname of 'The Lion of Panjshir' as a Mujahideen insurgent leader against the Soviets. In the post-communist state, he became Minister of Defense and Military Commander and later Vice President. He tried to make improvements in health, infrastructure and education, led battles against militias and warlords and eventually the Taliban. He did not share the ideology of the Taliban and did everything he could to fight against them. As they gained power, he was forced to flee to the Panjshir region and became leader of the Northern Alliance controlling less than ten percent of the country. He had been to the European Parliament and pleaded with them to give aid to the people being terrorised by the Taliban and to put pressure on Pakistan to stop their support of the Taliban.

Months before the 9/11 attack on the Twin Towers he warned of a terrible terrorist attack taking place if the West did not take notice of what was happening in Afghanistan. On the instigation of Bin Laden and the Taliban two suicide attackers from Morocco managed to get into Afghanistan posing as Belgian journalists and gained an interview with Massoud on 9/9/2001, two days before the planned 9/11 attacks. The timing was imperative for Osama bin Laden, as he knew that Massoud would be against him and his group seeking refuge with the Taliban in Afghanistan after the attack on the Twin Towers. With a camera loaded with explosives and a battery packed belt the two men succeeded in assassinating Massoud. Al Qaeda effectively 'cut off the head of the lion' in the hope of protecting themselves and the Taliban. After the attacks, of course, they succeeded in rearing the head of a much bigger lion; the US aligned with other western countries including the UK and the Northern Alliance to defeat the Taliban and drive them into hiding.

Ahmad Shah Massoud became a martyr and was buried in his hometown of Bazarak, Panjshir. His supporters built an impressive tomb and shrine on the edge of the mountain in his honour. We went up to visit the shrine and I was filled with a sense of awe and deep feeling for the country and what it had been through in recent years. From the mountain, I looked down the craggy slopes into the green valley with the Panjshir River weaving its way peacefully across the picturesque landscape. It was hard to imagine the troubles that had been before and would soon come again.

Back down in the village, Hamid had prepared the people for our visit and we were welcomed in and offered food and drink. They were kind and friendly but as I looked into their eyes, I could see the hard lives that they led, and I just couldn't tell what they were really thinking. My pistol was hidden but I was always alert to anything happening at any moment.

On another field trip, this time with Jules, Hamid took us to a remote villa that we reached after driving along countless rough tracks with Hamid on the satellite phone receiving guidance from the other end. Finally, we reached a fertile area full of olive trees in a deep valley and entered through a gate into the grounds of a small but lovely villa. There was only room for Jules to stay inside the villa but outside they had set up camp beds, like bivouacs on comfortable mattresses for the rest of us to sleep on.

The light was dimming, and the twilight created an eerie feeling of shadows and silhouettes. Again, the people were very hospitable, and they were preparing food as we sat around outside. Hamid was having a conversation with the host who had just come off the phone and I saw the expression on Hamid's face change to reveal deep concern. He tried to hide it as he announced that we were being joined by some of the local Mujahideen. These are hardened warriors from various tribes. He explained that they were not Taliban and advised me to keep my weapons hidden, which they generally always were. However, I wasn't going to discard my weapon; I would rather die in a firefight than end up kidnapped by these guys. However, at that moment all I could do was stay cool and keep my wits about me.

Suddenly, they were there. It was as if they had emerged out of the shadows in the garden unseen and unheard until they were among us. Clad in their robes with impressive turbans and an even more impressive array of weapons they sat down in a protective cordon around us with the leaders joining Hamid, Jules and the host for dinner. My MP5 was in my day sack; just one quick pull and the weapon would be free. My pistol was hidden in my quick release bum bag around my waist as I sat on my bivouac observing the proceedings. They seemed really friendly, and the group was laughing and chatting in French and Farsi. A banquet was served, and I was brought food as I sat there wishing they would just go.

I was way out of my comfort zone. I was a former British soldier and I didn't know how they would view me. They only needed to have had a bad experience with the British or US army and I would become the ideal point of retaliation. If they were Taliban, I was dead. What if they decided to kidnap

Jules? All these thoughts were running through my head in the strange light created by glowing lamps. I could see the dark, hard eyes of these men armed to the teeth. They had lived lives that I couldn't even imagine; the vast landscape, the mountains and caves were their home where they ate and slept and fought.

Suddenly Hamid came over to me and told me to relax. The leader of the Mujahideen had decided that he and his men were staying the night to protect us. The leader thought that we were too vulnerable in the valley and after some words and gestures his men formed a ring of steel around us facing up to the mountains and into the darkness beyond the villa. Perhaps I should have felt safe, there was no one better you could want to protect you in that environment, but I did not sleep well. In the morning, they left with hugs and fond farewells and I breathed a sigh of relief.

In late 2003, we flew up to Mazar-i-Sharif on a UN plane with the ambassador to meet the famous Warlord, Dostum. During the Soviet–Afghan War in the 1980s, Abdul Rashid Dostum was part of the Afghanistan National Army and the regional commander of the country's north, commanding about twenty thousand soldiers participating in battles against Mujahideen rebels. He subsequently became the de facto leader of a proto-state, controlling the country's northern provinces and Mazar-i-Sharif with an army of up to forty thousand men with tanks and jets supplied by Uzbekistan and Russia. In 1998, he fled the country when the Taliban overran the city and massacred many of the inhabitants. Dostum returned to Afghanistan in 2001, joined the Northern Alliance after the US invasion, participated in the retaking of Mazar-i-Sharif from the Taliban and became part of Hamid Karzai's administration. Situated in a large plain in the North of the country, the city is home to the beautiful Blue Mosque or Shrine of Ali, believed by some to hold the remains of the Prophet Mohammed's son-in-law.

As head of the European Commission, the Ambassador's role in the country was to look into projects that required aid funding. These could be anything from huge dams to small requests for help with schools or health facilities in tiny remote villages. Sometimes we didn't even know where we were going. The limitations of a commercial security team meant that although we were highly diligent in planning and preparing the security plan we had limited intel and we were rarely able to send anyone ahead to check out locations before we arrived due to lack of manpower. We accompanied the ambassador on these trips to remote villages maintaining our vigilance while at the same time not encroaching on his space to allow him to connect more comfortably with the locals.

Everywhere we went, the people were lovely, really friendly, and I could appreciate what difficult lives the majority of them led. We saw poppy fields on our travels, and I have a fantastic photograph of a little girl standing next to one of the fields, but the poppy industry was not part of the ambassador's remit. The EC was concerned with humanitarian projects and didn't get involved in politics. I found out from other people there that the US had been trying all kinds of ways to persuade the local farmers to stop growing poppies for the opium trade. At one point, they were air-dropping wooden pallets full of US dollars that were picked up by covert operatives on the ground and paid to the farmers in return for them destroying their poppy fields. Of course, the money ended up going to the Taliban and so in effect the US were funding the resurgence of the Taliban and this would come back to bite them in the future.

Dickie was replaced by a strange character who we nicknamed, 'The Prince of Mince'. He was in his late fifties and had a very impressive background; he had been in the Paras and the SAS and an officer in the Omani army, but there was something very camp about him. He had a very high-pitched voice and instead of saying, 'hello' he would shout, 'Coooeee,' when trying to get the locals' attention. He wore a satchel, like a schoolchild, and kept his pistol in it. I'm not sure how he thought he would access it in an emergency. The ambassador didn't take to him and he didn't last long. When he left, Phil was put in charge. Chris had left the job by this point so he could spend more time with his family back in the UK, but the team was now up to five and I became Phil's 2ic (second in charge).

There were a lot of NGOs based in Kabul by this time and the United Nations had a large footprint across the country with organisations that had come over to do what they could to assist and support the Afghani people. In fact, the Aga Khan established his own development agency and invested in a new mobile phone network for Afghanistan, as the current one was not reliable. Due to my previous experience of working with the Aga Khan, PB asked me to assist the Development Network local management team in its first few weeks whilst he recruited a new full-time security manager to take on the running going forward. I, of course, had a deep affiliation with and respect for the Aga Khan and his team and was very happy to get involved. Initially, I assisted in the recruiting and training of the first armed guards they took on and went around to all the proposed cell tower sites to check that these locations were suitable for use from a security perspective. I handed all this over to the new guy, Neil, once he arrived a couple of weeks later.

One night in mid-2003, we received a call in the early hours of the morning telling us that the EC embassy compound where The Boss and the diplomats worked during the day had been broken into. At first, we were unsure about what our response should be; was it wise to leave it to the morning, call in the Afghani police, who to be honest were near on useless, or go down to investigate? Phil made the call for four of us to head down immediately and take a look, leaving one man back at base to manage the guard force and coordinate communications.

We drove down in two vehicles and on arrival, I could see that the main gate had been forced open. I headed in with one other guy to clear the compound and establish what had occurred. After confirming that the compound was empty and no threat existed, the remainder of the team entered and we spoke to the guards to find out exactly what had happened. It turned out that one of the local Afghani militias had raided the compound and arrested our primary Afghani driver, who we fondly called Brian. It turned out that Brian had no reason to be there and had apparently been taking a local woman to the location in order to 'get it on with her'. This is of course a massive 'no no' in the Afghani culture and reflected badly on the EC.

Phil decided that he wanted to confirm the validity of the story and at least check on the welfare of Brian. He headed up the side street alone in the dark. We warned him of the risks of following this decision, but he was adamant that it was the right thing to do. I could not let him go alone so I went halfway up the street behind him and got into a fire position where I could cover him with my MP5 if required. Phil continued up the dark, poorly lit street until the militia guards challenged him outside the villa they occupied. I could see Phil put his hands up and gesture that he wanted to approach and talk with them using his basic grasp of the local dialect. He then disappeared into the villa. I was very concerned at that point, especially as the consensus of the team was to wait until the morning before reacting to an incident such as this.

I waited anxiously outside; I was really worried that we were completely off the grid here and on the verge of a possible diplomatic incident. If things went badly for Phil inside, what would my next move be? After a very tense and seemingly long thirty minutes, Phil re-appeared to my extreme relief and headed down to brief us on what he had found. Apparently, Brian was being held inside on sexual charges and Phil had been given assurances by the militia that they would treat him well until the morning. He already had the marks of taking a beating, as we expected. They also said that they would not go back near our embassy compound, saying that they did not realise it was a diplomatic building. This entire incident had the potential to go really badly for all concerned. Brian was up to no good in the embassy grounds and the militia had entered the embassy grounds without permission. In a more normal environment, it could easily have caused a huge diplomatic incident.

We informed the ambassador what had happened on our return and went down the following morning to investigate the previous night's incident more thoroughly to see what, if anything, could be done to resolve it. The Boss liked Brian, as he had been his driver since arriving in Kabul. Brian was consequently charged by the Afghani police and was last seen being taken off to the local jail. None of us ever really knew what became of him after that and the ambassador, quite rightly, had to distance himself from it.

When Dickie had been in charge, there was a strict no-drinking policy but later on, things did change. Kabul was starting to move forward again, a few restaurants opened up for expats and alcohol could be found if you knew where to look. Every Thursday night became party night in the city at one of the villas of the NGO workers. We became friendly with Jack, a former British Marine who now worked for the UN demining agency, he would pick us up and take us to a party somewhere in the city. Jack knew everyone in town and if there was a party with beer then he found out about it.

As security operators, we were not exactly on the same page as the NGOs, and were certainly not their ideal house guests, so we kept a low profile and certainly did not mention what we did for a living. Least said, the better in these situations, but if cornered, we just came out with some cock and bull story of how we were there working on an EC aid project. These parties were a lot of fun; there was music and, more importantly, dustbins full of cold beer. At some point, Jack, Phil and I started self-defense classes in Jack's compound for all the expat women working as reporters, NGOs or for the United Nations and then we all went to a party afterwards. We had some great times. The work was full on and we took it very seriously but there were some good times to be had as well. When you are in a place like that for three months at a time, you need to relax and unwind at times to keep the mind and body going. Work hard, play hard, as they say.

During my time in Afghanistan, I met a guy called Francis. He was a true businessman and entrepreneur and was over in Kabul in 2003 promoting and selling his force protection products. Francis was a charming fellow and a natural salesman who was introduced to me by Jack. I listened to Francis and learned a lot from him, it fuelled a fire deep inside me to one day have my own business. At the end of my time in Afghanistan, we heard about an opportunity to bid for the security contract in support of the new Afghani ring road project. Jack, Phil and I decided we wanted to give it a go with Francis as our partner. I went over to his west London office during some time off to work on setting up a company, registering a name and creating a logo for our new company which we named 'Barhadar' (brave and courageous in Farsi). We never really had any chance of winning this contract, but it was a great learning curve for me and cemented what was to be a long-lasting relationship with Francis. He became a great friend and mentor over the coming years and we embarked on some interesting adventures together.

In 2003, the second Gulf War against Iraq took place and I proudly watched on as a spectator as my old regiment in the Paras crossed over into Iraq and did their thing. If I'm honest, I felt a hint of jealousy. By late 2003 the war was over, the reconstruction phase had started, and the private security industry was starting to move into Baghdad. I felt my job was done in Afghanistan and I needed a new challenge. The time had come for me to move on. I handed in my notice to PB giving the statutory one month's notice period. PB thanked me for all the years of service I had given Remedy and told me I was always welcome back. I thanked him for giving me the opportunity to work for Remedy on all the great contracts I had the pleasure to be part of and that I would always be personally grateful to him for his faith in me.

A year later, I heard from Chris, who had gone back to the contract as team leader, that the villa compound was attacked, and they had to evacuate the ambassador and his team under fire to a safe location. Luckily, everyone got away safely and uninjured, but it just showed that the security climate in Afghanistan had changed again and was set to get a lot worse over the coming years.

CHAPTER 10

IRAQ MAYHEM

Afghanistan was an incredible experience and a great learning curve; I enjoyed my time there, but I was getting itchy feet and I was ready for a change. It was September 2003 and the US led invasion of Iraq had taken place earlier in the year. In less than four weeks, Baghdad had fallen, and Saddam Hussein had gone into hiding.

Large, mostly American and European, companies had won huge contracts to move into Iraq to begin the reconstruction programme of what was now a very unstable and turbulent country with insurgency on the rise. Looting, bomb attacks, shootings, organised crime and the emergence of local militias were becoming the norm across the major cities. Iraq was the new Wild West and actually made Afghanistan seem reasonably normal and safe in comparison. Regardless of the politics involved, what this meant for me was new opportunities with a boom in security contracts to protect contractors, government embassies, and news' teams covering the unfolding events. New firms were popping up all over the place. It was early doors when I went over, and it was only going to get bigger. This was the beginning of a new era in security work; 'The Circuit' was up and running and was going to increase exponentially, unfortunately attracting some dangerous cowboys along the way.

My plan was to leave Afghanistan in early November and have some time at home with Jo in Torquay before looking for another job in the New Year.

I was home for just a few days when a call came out of nowhere from a guy called Andy who I had never met. I didn't know it then, but Andy and I were to become great friends and we are still the best of pals today. A tall, strong, charismatic bloke, ex Special Boat Service (SBS), a superb rugby player and athlete, he is one of those guys that just annoys the hell out of you as he is so good at everything he does and never gets in a flap. He told me that his company, Elea had won a contract in Iraq and that Chris Morris, who I worked with in Afghanistan, had recommended me to him. The job was on a healthy day rate, way above what I had been on in Afghanistan. The only proviso was that I needed to be in Baghdad within the next seventy-two hours.

Andy's company was predominantly made up of ex SBS guys from his former unit, so his main source of contacts for guys to work with him came from the UK Special Forces. I was the first Para to work for him. I had gained a good reputation and more importantly, my experience in Afghanistan stood me in good stead. My CV stood out and I was given the six-week contract in support of an international communications company. I was really pleased and excited to be getting involved with a new fledgling company in a country like Iraq, which was at the start of its own transition period.

Jo was of course not happy when I told her. She had been looking forward to having me home for Christmas, but she knew that I would go, whatever she said, as it was an opportunity too good to turn down. I promised that I would be back for New Year, and off I went.

There were no flights directly into Baghdad, so I flew to Amman, the capital of Jordan where I met up with another guy, Mike an ex New Zealand SAS guy, also joining the Elea team. In the early hours of the next morning, we set off by road from Amman with two other guys from Elea who had come to Amman from Baghdad on an admin run and to collect us. We drove to the Jordan/Iraqi border where there were long queues of traffic and absolute mayhem caused by people using this route to get into Iraq because it was unsafe to fly into the country. There were also huge numbers of Iraqis attempting to go the other way and get out of the country. We eventually got through immigration and over the border where some local Iraqi guys from the company met us. They had two more cars and plenty of weapons, which they handed out to us.

In the three cars, we then set off on the six-hundred-mile journey through the desert with the aim of getting into Baghdad before sundown. The road was extremely smooth and in remarkably good condition sweeping through miles and miles of barren, sandy landscape. After about an hour, with no one else around us, the cars stopped at the side of the road, and the local guys took us towards an area in the sand dunes where we could test fire the AK47s they had given us earlier. They were using the desert as a live firing range to test out the weapons and I was amazed that this was how things were done. The weather was hot but comfortable enough, unlike in the summer months when it could reach forty-five to fifty degrees Celsius. There was nothing except sand as far as the eye could see in every direction and I pulled my shemagh up around my nose and mouth as the wind picked up and blew sharp, stinging grains of sand into my face. The weapons cracked and thumped into the emptiness as we all satisfied ourselves that they were working properly. We then got back into the cars to continue our journey to Baghdad.

We flew down the highway at high speed in our three-vehicle convoy and it was fascinating for me to see such a vast expanse of real desert for the first time. For hours, we drove with the unchanging view and no signs of civilization, but we weren't going to slow down for anything. The road was renowned for bandits and we were constantly on the lookout for cars that might pop up out of nowhere with the intention of causing us harm. Nearing the outskirts of Baghdad, the scenery became greener as we approached Ramadi and Fallujah, small towns on the banks of the Euphrates just off the highway. The view may have been prettier, but the facts were not. These towns were known hot spots for attacks, and it was where the insurgents made their main bases. Cars on route into the city were attacked and robbed by gunmen from these areas on a regular basis. The towns became the sites of many battles and horrific incidents to come. A few months later, in a well-documented incident, an American security team drove into Fallujah and was attacked by the local insurgents. The men were pulled from their vehicles, beaten, killed, burned and hanged from a bridge crossing the Euphrates.

This route into Baghdad, with no viable alternatives available, took us straight past these towns in the infamous Sunni Triangle. This is a densely populated region to the northwest of Baghdad inhabited by Sunni Muslim Arabs, who were largely supporters of the former regime. It was a hotbed of armed opposition to the coalition forces. Further south was what was known as the 'Triangle of Death', also inhabited by Sunni hardliners, which would become the focal point of some major combat activity in November and December 2004. This is depicted in the 2016 film 'War Dogs' based on a true story of some American arms dealers running guns through the area.

When we drove through the Sunni Triangle and the Triangle of Death, banditry was the biggest threat. We were warned to be on the lookout for fast moving Mercedes and BMWs with blacked out windows that often targeted and attacked western vehicles making the journey to Baghdad. Several other teams had been attacked on this road in the last couple of weeks and had had to fight their way out of trouble. Mike and I were on high alert and cautious about what we were to expect in this war-torn land. Unlike Afghanistan, I was now in a country where insurgents were far from quiet. We passed through without incident, just a few dodgy looking vehicles sped by taking a good look at us and then deciding to leave us be. We arrived at our office in Baghdad at about eight in the evening and I met Andy for the first time.

He was slightly younger than I expected, and he welcomed us and took us inside for a quick chat. Andy handed me an old archaic Makarov pistol saying that he hoped to get some better pistols over the next few days. He told me that I would start work the following day by taking one of the client teams to work at Baghdad International Airport (BIAP). Then he announced that it was Thursday night and that we were going to a party. Much as I like a party and a few drinks, I was totally taken aback. I was expecting to have a chance to settle in, get a full briefing on everything that was going on in the country and what exactly my job entailed. But no. Andy said that we would go through everything in the morning, but tonight was party night when the guys let off a bit of steam and relaxed for a few hours. Off we went to a party in a private villa where Mike and I remained quite restrained, had a few beers, chatted to a few of the guys and then left on the first transport back to the Mount Lebanon hotel, where we were staying. We had not got our bearings yet and we were unsure about where we were and what was happening around us. In addition, we had to start work in the morning and needed to get a good kip after the day's long journey.

My new job was to provide security for a six-man team of telecommunication engineers working for a French communications company who were setting up a telephone switch, a means of directing one call to another as part of the mobile telephone system. The switch was located inside the perimeter of Baghdad International Airport (BIAP) and we had to get them to work each morning, stay with them throughout the day and bring them back safely in the evening. Getting into the airport was not easy due to the extreme risk and chaotic manner in which it was run, but Andy had a contact that lived within the perimeter. This was an American private contractor called Barry, who was running logistics for the US army; he lived in an outbuilding within the airport. On my first day, I called him up and introduced myself, and he came out and fast tracked my entrance through the long, sprawling queue waiting to get inside. He was a real character and living on BIAP, he knew everybody and every short cut, so he was very useful to know. Just like in Afghanistan, our currency of choice was alcohol, which was reasonably easy to obtain, especially for the army and government contractors who were confined to the BIAP and the Green Zone. Andy let me know what Barry's favourite tipple was, and I arranged the purchase of a bottle for him to show my gratitude for his support, knowing very well that I was going to need a lot more favours from him over the next few months.

Barry had access to the airport terminal that was still closed and guarded by the US military and a private security firm called Custer Battles. He took me down there one day so that I could have a look around and then through to the only restaurant, which was open at that time, which happened to serve one of the best steaks I've ever had. I have no idea where they acquired such good quality meat. It was fascinating walking around the empty terminal. It seemed huge with no one there, and I was particularly impressed by the splendour of the terminal roof, the height and decadence. Columns and arches created the effect of corridors of palm trees and I tried to imagine what it had been like bustling with local and international passengers before the war and the fall of the former regime.

During my first stint in Iraq, the hunt for Saddam Hussein was still going on. When Baghdad fell to the US led coalition forces, he had gone into hiding and over the six months that ensued, a massive manhunt had been underway with many false leads as to his whereabouts. On the 13th December 2003, a US Special Forces team finally found him hiding in a small hole, beneath ground, at the back of a tiny shack in Ad Dawr near to his hometown of Tikrit. I was at the airport when the news came through that he had been found and driving back that evening was the most incredible sight. Every household in Iraq at that time owned at least one AK47 and it was as if every single person in the whole of Baghdad had gone outside into the streets or onto their roofs after hearing the news and they were all dancing, cheering, and shooting their weapons up into the sky in celebration. It was like Bonfire Night on super steroids, an incredibly momentous day for the people of Iraq. Of course, we had to be careful as it was all very well firing these bullets into the air, but what goes up has to come down. We understood this theory and the risks it brought, but sadly, the Iraqis did not get it and there were multiple injuries and fatalities reported the following morning from bullets hitting innocent bystanders.

There were calls for Saddam Hussein to be sent to the International Court of Justice in the Hague, but the Iraqi interim government refused to give him up and after a lengthy and drawn out two year trial, he was eventually found guilty and hanged in Baghdad. Videos of his execution leaked out on the Internet and this event brought some closure for the Iraqi people and entire world to see.

The coalition hoped that arresting Saddam Hussein would be the end of the fighting and that Iraq would move smoothly into a new democratic era. They did not foresee the rise of insurgency and the various terrorist groups with militant Islamic connections who began a series of attacks against coalition targets and ethnic Iraqi groups in the major cities and outlying towns. It was only the beginning of hostilities and violent assaults that would last for many years to come.

A sure sign of where things were heading and proof of the level of chaos that ruled at this time in Baghdad occurred at our client offices on a weekday in December 2003. The offices were in a villa within a walled compound in the al Mansour district. This was a very rich and affluent area of Baghdad a few miles outside the Green Zone. Many of the big international commercial companies had bases that they used during the day for office work and meetings in this area. A group of local Iraqi guys, that we had trained, guarded our compound. For some reason or another, a dispute had arisen between our guys and a militia group from a neighbouring area. The argument had been simmering between them for ages and boiled over on this particular day with our client office being drawn into the dispute. A large number of militia turned up at the gates to the villa compound and the argument quickly escalated into weapons being drawn with rounds fired into the air, which then turned into a full-on OK Corral gunfight between the two rival groups.

The militia outside, who heavily outnumbered our guys, began firing at our villa with bullets slamming into the gates and up into the second floor of the building. Two of our quick thinking Elea security guys inside the villa managed to get the client personnel down on the floor or into safer parts of the downstairs area as best they could and continued to provide support to them throughout the incident. There was a huge amount of firing going on, with bullets raining down. I was away from the compound at the time, just dropping my clients off at their hotel when I got a call from the guys inside informing me about the incident and requesting support. As I headed back to the compound, I quickly made some calls for assistance to a couple of so-called quick response units who covered the local area including the US military and even spoke to some friends who worked as security advisors for one of the US news teams.

A crazy former Greek Special Forces guy, Alexandros, who worked for us at the time and who was mainly responsible for most of the Jordanian border runs, was luckily, just returning from one of these trips while this firefight was underway. Arriving back into the area, he came in on a side road and saw all these militia firing at the villa. Without being briefed on the situation at all and seeing that our clients were in imminent danger, he jumped out of his vehicle and intervened. It took a few moments for the attacking militia to realise what was actually happening and that they had lost the initiative, but once they did, they quickly began to retreat. Our friends from the news' security team also arrived around the same time and provided more support that finally led to the attackers dispersing and heading away. The American military finally arrived and closed down the area about half an hour after I got back. My team arrived to find a couple of our guards had been injured and provided them with some medical support. The top floor of our villa looked like a well-worn shooting gallery. However, considering the number of rounds fired and the time it had been going on, the death toll and injuries were minimal. It was lucky that Iraqis are such bad shots or else it would have been real carnage.

Alexandros certainly had some balls on him, but the event obviously shook the clients up and was a big wake-up call for all of us to the very real threats that were out there, how quickly situations like this could get out of control, and the increasing lawlessness that was spreading throughout Baghdad and Iraq as whole.

There was a strong military presence in what was known as the Green Zone. The Green Zone was the common name for the International Zone (IZ), a ten square kilometre area in central Baghdad that housed the Coalition Provisional Authority (CPA). The CPA headed up by Paul Bremer, an American diplomat who assumed the title of Interim President of Iraq, was established in May 2003 and held executive, legislative, and judicial authority over the Iraqi government until its dissolution on 28 June 2004. The Green Zone was home for many of the foreign embassies including the US and British as well as several other international and Iraqi organisations. It was heavily fortified and guarded by a mixture of Iraqi and American troops.

We were able to get into the Green Zone without too many problems using the identification cards we had acquired. We visited the US embassy building, which housed the CPA, again using ID we had acquired or made ourselves. It was a little scary how easy it was to bluff your way into places such as this in those days! The embassy was situated in one of Saddam's favourite old palaces. The splendour of the palace was incredible. We wandered along vast marble corridors with domed roofs and giant chandeliers. There were elaborate decorations and ornaments along with sumptuous furniture, golden thrones and stairways. We even managed to get ourselves through the back to chill out and have a quick swim in Saddam's swimming pool. It felt good and it was an amazing feeling to be in such a place at this time in history; the luxury that Saddam had lived in was all around us. Whilst there, we always made a point of eating. Just like everywhere the Americans go, they always put on a good spread plus it was free, and we all love a freebee.

The Red Zone referred to anywhere outside this protected central area and was the normal Baghdad city. We were staying at the Mount Lebanon, a small basic hotel that was in the Red Zone and was popular with international journalists and western contractors. The first contract I was on finished and I did get home for New Year. However, Andy asked me to carry on working for him and I went back to work on the main contract he had at that time which was for another large mobile phone communications company. When I returned to Baghdad in February 2004, we all moved into a different, larger hotel down the road. On the evening of 17th March, a huge suicide car bomb rocked the city and destroyed the Mount Lebanon hotel. A number of people were killed, including one of Andy's best friends, a civilian who had come over to see about some work opportunities. It was shocking and sad, and I called it lucky escape number two for me.

Brian, a former SBS soldier with a fantastic reputation had arrived back in Baghdad from a stint down south in Basra. When I left, he took over my position. He was a phenomenal character, old school SF who had climbed Everest on several occasions and was a bit of a legend. Brian had been the one to put Andy in touch with the client, so when he asked for a job, Andy was happy to make room for him.

Brian got into a relationship with an Iraqi woman who lived in Saydia, a particularly dangerous part of southern Baghdad, but somewhere he would visit on occasion. Rather than travel to the UK on leave, Brian opted to remain in Baghdad and spend some time with his girlfriend. Insurgents found out about these visits and one night posing as policemen they raided her home. Once inside, they began shooting and although by all reports, Brian put up a hell of a fight and nearly managed to escape, the insurgents caught him while he was climbing over a high wall. The insurgents killed him and most of the women in the villa, but one managed to escape and tell what happened. Andy had her put in a private witness protection program until the court case against the Iraqi Police who were identified as the suspects. It was horrifying, a very sad and real wake up call for us all again.

The incident was just another sign of the rising dangers from insurgents. There were so many different factions in the country vying for power with one another and all against the military and western interests. The Shi'ites, the Sunnis, Al Zarqawi and his section of Al Qaeda were all attacking anything western. The need for security was huge. Over the time that I worked there, it became increasingly dangerous and a number of my friends working for other security firms were killed and injured. Everyone had their own stories of contacts and fights with militia or insurgents. Every single night American and British Special Forces were banging down doors searching for insurgents and trying to find Al Zarqawi.

As time went on, kidnappings and consequent beheadings filmed and shown on the Internet became commonplace. Where I was now staying on this new job in al-Mansour was close to where Ken Bigley was living. Ken was a British civil engineer working on reconstruction programmes who shared a house with two American colleagues. The men were aware of the danger of staying where they were and knew that insurgents were watching their movements. Their Iraqi house guard told them that he had been threatened for working for them and quit his job, but the men decided to remain in the house. They were all kidnapped on 16th September and the Tawhid and Jihad Islamic extremist group, led by Jordanian Abu Musab al-Zarqawi, released a video of the three men kneeling in front of a Tawhid and Jihad banner. The kidnappers announced that they would spare their lives if the coalition forces released a number of Iraqi women prisoners. Their demands were of course not met, and all three men were subsequently beheaded. The kidnappers posted horrific videos of the killings on the Internet. It was a shocking and troubling time and made us all look again at our personal security in Baghdad and how we operated. We all devised and agreed upon action plans. If we were ever to find ourselves in a difficult position, we would not allow ourselves to be taken alive.

There was so much going on in Iraq and the security was becoming intense. There were new firms popping up all over the place; some were very good and well run and others not so much. It was like a combination of the Wild West and the California Gold Rush and because of this, some people were managing to pick up contracts and operate in Iraq who would not normally manage to get into or survive on the security circuit. The times we did go to the Green Zone or down to the airport there were some real sights to see. There was one group of American guys who were carrying out convoy work between the various cities and towns. All had Mohican haircuts and carried large knives and swords; they were using pickup trucks which had large plates of armour welded onto the sides with heavy calibre machine guns pointing out of holes everywhere. It was a scene straight out of a Mad Max movie.

Another, South African, company employed Boers who looked like they were out on safari with their ginger beards and rugby shorts. These types had no real idea what they were doing and had no care for the local Iraqi community amongst whom we lived and worked. They saw all Iraqis as the enemy, which was far from the truth as the majority of Iraqis were good guys with families attempting to live normal lives amongst the mayhem going on around them. It was a crazy time and probably won't ever be seen again; the requirement for guys to work on the ground actually far outweighed what was available, so of course all sorts were able to get in and make a living at this time. It wouldn't last and these guys were making the best of it and living out their wildest fantasies. As funny as it was to see, these guys were dangerous and they posed a real threat to us moving around in our low-profile vehicles. They just did not understand the environment they were in and I believe they were genuinely scared and in many cases out of their depth. They became trigger happy and did not think twice about shooting at innocent Iraqis who got in their way or just came too close to their vehicles. This is exactly what happened on 16th September 2007 when employees of a US private military company shot at Iraqi civilians, killing seventeen and injuring twenty in Nisour Square, Baghdad, while escorting a U.S embassy convoy. The killings outraged Iraqis and strained relations between Iraq and the United States. In 2014, four Blackwater employees were tried in a U.S. federal court; one was convicted of murder, and the other three of manslaughter and firearms charges. We could easily be mistaken for locals the way we operated in our low-profile vehicles and these rogue operators were a real danger to us as we moved around the city.

My contract began to wind down and I headed off for some time at home. While I was back in the UK, I went to see businessman Francis, who I had met in Afghanistan. He was an expert in the force protection side of the business, providing cutting edge technology for organisations looking to protect high profile buildings or compounds with bullet proof windows and towers. I went to his office in Fulham for a meeting and after some discussion, he suggested that I set up a security consultancy and close protection business as an extra side to his existing company.

Francis gave me the use of a flat in Fulham and I split my time between London and Torquay as I started to set up 'Explorer Security' as a branch of his existing business. I had my own area in his office and a free reign to set it up as I saw fit. I really got into the whole thing putting together brochures, sorting out the registration and creating a website. It was my job to win the clients and then organise and run the tasks. I realised that I didn't have a clue where to start with the business development side of the plan. I felt a bit lost and began to lose momentum. Then Francis came to me and asked if I would accompany him as his security advisor on an eight-week tour of the Middle East to garner business. We started by going to Dubai and went on to visit Jordan, Afghanistan, Iraq and then Israel, where a lot of his clients and suppliers were based. In each country, we met with his business associates to sort out problems, met new interesting people in the likes of the UN and other US government organisations and attempted to win new contracts.

Francis took me with him for security but also so that I could keep him company, learn about the business, and take any opportunities to push the new 'Explorer Security' brand. We travelled together for two months and got on great; it was very interesting and informative for me. We stayed in some great five-star hotels and met so many different people. In Afghanistan, I was able to help him out with my knowledge of the country and my local contacts. He had a problem in Kabul with an Australian guy who was working as his country manager at the time, a weasel of a man who was totally untrustworthy. We found out that he had got into bed with the local Afghani partner and they were stealing a lot of the business for themselves, rather than pushing it through Francis' company. Francis confronted him in a meeting, but the Australian was very abrupt and rude to Francis and denied any involvement, which was clearly a lie. I wasn't having that, so I arranged to meet the guy privately the next day and told him, in no uncertain terms, that he needed to stop what he was up to or there would be some severe consequences. From what we could tell, he did stop but I advised Francis to sack him at the next opportunity. I hated to see people taking advantage of Francis' very generous and trusting nature and became very protective of him.

I was there to learn and to build my side of the business but I also proved very useful when we were in Iraq as I had made contacts with guys in the large American camps where Francis was trying to win lucrative contracts to supply protective walls and ballistic towers. I also used my local knowledge to decide where was suitable and safe for us to stay, and to source reliable local transportation and drivers.

We drove from Amman to Israel via the King Hussein Bridge, an iconic border crossing which links Jordan with Israel. In Tel Aviv we met his local partner who took us out to a kibbutz to check out the armoured vehicles they were making there. The communal way of life was fascinating, with everyone working towards a common goal and not making money for themselves. We went up to the Golan Heights to the area where the missiles fired from Syria into Israel tended to land on an alarmingly regular basis. Every single Israeli building within range, including houses, schools and restaurants, had special hardened rooms built which the people could use when the attack alarm sounded. Using super high-level technology, they provided protection from missiles, that you couldn't even see. They were so advanced in their designs because they had been living with these attacks and threats for so many years.

Although I had a great time and loved Francis' company, I realised that I was missing the work – being on the coalface so to speak. I felt that I really didn't have the skills to move the business forward at this particular time of my career and I was earning a lot less than when I was on the ground in Iraq. When I was in Afghanistan and Iraq with Francis and saw the guys doing the work, it made me realise that that was what I wanted to be doing again and I missed it. It was definitely a mistake in many ways, as I had been given a huge opportunity and was on a massive learning curve with Francis who had become somewhat of a mentor to me. He could see the potential in me to run a business, but the time was just not quite right, my feet were itchy, and I began to look for work in Baghdad again. The time for my own business would come again in the future and Francis would remain a key influence in my life.

By this time, there was a huge number of new security companies and all of them were recruiting because there was so much demand in Iraq. I wrote off to a few of them and got interviews with Control Risk Group, one of the largest security firms in the UK that had a contract with the British Embassy in Baghdad. I also heard from one of the directors at Olive Group who said he had heard good things about me and wanted me to go for an interview with his company.

Early one morning in London, I had a meeting with Olive Group, which was very interesting and tempting and then I headed over for an interview with Control Risk in the Union Jack Club that afternoon. My CV was solid, and I knew that I was super-employable but when I arrived at the hotel, there were about twenty other guys there. All of them had just left the army and were there in their demob suits clutching their newly written CVs, all as green as grass. I knew straight away that it was not where I wanted to be but having travelled there, I decided to go through the process. To begin with, we were all shown into a room together and briefed as a group. A couple of company representatives from CRG gave us an overview on what was happening in Iraq and what they were looking to achieve. As I listened, I realised that a lot of what they were saying was incorrect and complete bullshit in parts. Neither of the speakers had been to Iraq. I kept my powder dry and said nothing. We had a tea break, followed by short individual interviews.

My interviewer had worked on a security team for John Paul Getty III and had visited us up on the John Paul Getty II team when I was working there. He was now high up in Control Risk and for some reason did not acknowledge that he knew me. He was a very experienced guy and could be quite temperamental. In the interview, despite knowing my background, knowing me and having my CV in front of him, he asked me about when I'd left the army, what rank I was when I left and showed no interest in my security industry experience or even the last few months I had just spent in Baghdad, which I found bizarre. It was very frustrating and annoying.

After the interviews, they wanted everyone to go into the next room and provide copies of their passports and to sign some forms that would confirm we were ready for deployment if selected. By then, I had really had enough so I left without doing any of the paperwork or finishing the interview process. I was on the train going home when I got a call from someone at Control Risks offering me the job. I couldn't believe it. I had walked out, hadn't even signed their forms or given them a copy of my passport and they were still offering me a job. I politely turned them down. Within a few hours, I received another call from Olive Group. I had really liked the guy who interviewed me from Olive, but after thinking long and hard about it, I decided to turn them down as well. I realised after that day that I didn't want to work for a large numbers-based company.

Control Risk and Olive at that point were large successful companies and a lot of people were attracted to the bigger companies because they got military and government support, proper ID cards for the Green Zone, licensed and high end weapons were flown in and they were generally much better organised. However, I definitely preferred working for the smaller, niche type companies, because they were generally more selective in who they recruited. I felt more in control of decision making on the ground and generally reported directly to just one or two people. They paid well, treated you with a level of respect, and we all worked together towards a mutual goal.

A couple of days later, I got a call from JD at Minthis who had a new contract in Baghdad. I met JD the following day down in Windsor and he offered me an interesting position as team leader for another new mobile phone company working in Baghdad. This was the job for me; I was heading back to Iraq.

CHAPTER 11

BAGHDAD AMMO DUMP

My new contract was for six-weeks protecting two British engineers who were coming into the country. We set up in porta cabins (with living areas and bedrooms) in BIAP where Minthis had yet another telecommunications company. I had to recruit and train eight local Iraqi guys as our drivers and security guards who would sit in the front of our four vehicles when we moved about the city. The guys from the other contract helped me find some suitable local candidates. I trained them up along with three other English guys who flew in from the UK to make up the twelve-man team. None of the guys from England had been in Iraq before, so I briefed them all on everything they needed to know and all the drills we would be carrying out on this contract. We trained hard to make sure we were ready for when the clients arrived and nothing was left to chance as we carried out vehicle and contact drills, live firing on the range and polished up our medical skills.

One of the new English guys was an ex-foreign legionnaire, who had been earmarked as my second in charge by head office, a skinny lad who, unfortunately, was absolutely useless in every way. After a week of training, one of our clients arrived and our job was to move him from the airport to various locations around Baghdad. I soon found out that the ex-legionnaire was going behind my back and telling the client that the journey was too dangerous and that he shouldn't be doing it. This of course is an absolute 'no no' in our industry; this sort of lack of professionalism scares the client and shows conflict within his own security team which puts the contract in total jeopardy.

Of course, in some ways, he was correct to be wary; but that didn't justify his cowardice or unprofessional manner. The road between the airport and the city was risky and eventually became known as the most dangerous road in the whole world in the months and certainly years to come, but right then it was workable. Code-named Route Irish by the American military, the road was a ten kilometre stretch from the Green Zone to Baghdad International Airport that was a magnet for insurgents because they knew that coalition forces as well as private security companies protecting international business and embassy staff were using it on a regular basis to get to and from the airport as there were no other viable options.

The insurgents used the slip roads, which had very little security controlling them, to get onto the main highway in cars containing Vehicle Bourne Improvised Explosive Devices (VBIEDs). They drove alongside obvious looking western transport in these mobile bombs and detonated themselves as suicide bombers. The road was not in a great state of repair due to these attacks; it was full of craters and burned out vehicles and these made it easy for insurgents to hide more IEDs. The whole route was perilous but workable if you had the correct training and drills in place, and of course, a bit of luck.

In April 2005, a British security company with a three-vehicle low profile team working in support of the Election Commission of Iraq came under contact on Route Irish. They had been stationary on the road due to an incident going on further up ahead towards the airport and had decided to separate themselves from the rest of the traffic queue. This, however, drew unwanted attention to them and gave the insurgents, who were clearly on the lookout for targets, the time to mount an attack that sadly killed three members of the team.

It was dangerous work for sure, but it was why we were there; it was achievable and it was our job. As long as we followed all the drills we had in place, remained low profile and professional at all times, we could make the journey without incident. The legionnaire guy basically had no balls for the job and should never have been out there with us in the first place. When I heard that he had been talking in this way to the client, I disarmed him and sacked him on the spot. I told him that I would not work with people like him. I then moved him into an empty porta cabin and phoned the company. He was taken off the job and a replacement was brought in. My issue was not that he pointed out the dangers, as that was fair and up for discussion. It was the way he did it behind my back and spoke to the client. He clearly had no intention of leaving the base from the day he arrived, but was happy to take the job and the money that came with it. We subsequently ran the gauntlet safely and successfully and carried out the contract with no problems.

A few weeks later, near the end of the task, JD called me to say that someone was leaving the other team and that a place on the full-time contract was available if I wanted to take it. I had already met and worked with most of the team, so I was very pleased with the offer.

I took the new job and found myself working with my old friend Trevor Rhys-Jones. Trev used to work for the Al Fayed family; he was the guy who survived the crash that very sadly killed Princess Diana, Dodi Fayed and their driver, Henri Paul. We had been in the Paras and served together in the COP and were good friends. At the time of the devastating car crash we were not in touch and I was in Northern Ireland when it happened. I can remember someone coming in, telling me the terrible news, and then saying that Trev had been in the car. We all said at the time, 'Only a Para could survive a crash like that.' Afterwards, he couldn't remember anything, and to this day, he has no memory of the accident. He refused to say what Al Fayed wanted him to say about it being a government conspiracy, because he didn't believe it was true. The Al Fayed family abandoned him after that and stopped paying for his medical fees. Trev is an extremely honourable and stand-up guy and he refused to be turned for money or manipulated by Al Fayed. Due to this attitude, after he recovered from his serious injuries, he was able to get back on The Circuit and create a new and very successful career for himself in the corporate security side of the industry, which is still going strong today.

After a few months on the new team, I got a call from Andy who told me that he had won a contract for Elea with a German electrical company, which was a one to two-year contract working six weeks on and six weeks off. It was really good money, I wasn't that content where I was by this point and really wanted to be back with Elea if the opportunity was there, so I decided to take it. Trev left soon afterwards as well, but we would work together again in the future.

I was now back with Elea, which was where I really wanted to be; I loved the relaxed, fun but professional way they worked and stayed with them for the rest of my time in Iraq. This new contract was a four-man team, working with 'Ollie' Ollerton from the TV Series SAS *Who Dares Wins*. Ollie was a former member of the SBS and one of the best security operators I have ever worked with on The Circuit. Unfortunately, he was also fighting some personal battles with alcohol, drug addiction, anxiety, and depression at that time, which has now been well documented in his own books and TV series. For me, Ollie was a great guy to work with, switched on and a lot of fun on our down time. There was also Marcus, an ex-Grenadier Guardsman and vet of the first Gulf War with a lot of experience in the private sector; Marcus was the straight bloke out of us all and a really diligent and professional operator, who was a great guy to be around and excellent with the local national teams. Then there was Carl (Mr. Beer as the Iraqis affectionately came to call him), another guy who became a great friend and my first business partner further down the line. Carl was one of life's real characters, a bit of a living legend and another SBS guy who had been pretty well involved in most conflicts and wars the British have had over the last couple of decades and with the medals to prove it, as he would say. Carl was a super star, a real joy to work with; he had a great sense of humour and was a massive wind up merchant. We all bonded very quickly, got on great and soon worked out how to bring the best out of each other and knew where our own individual strengths and weaknesses lay. The four of us made a great team and operated on a rotation so that we all worked with one another at some point, with two of us in Baghdad at all times.

We lived in a villa in the Red Zone, which was even more dangerous by this time with insurgents everywhere. We were the only people from the company in country at the time, there was no real dedicated management team to oversee the running of the villa as Andy was having some problems with his business partner and was pre-occupied with obtaining a clean break away from him. We were pretty well running everything ourselves by this time and because there were problems getting money into us we had to become businessmen and entrepreneurs. We recruited an ex-colonel from the Iraqi army called Ammar who came highly recommended, and he sat downstairs and controlled all the local staff we employed.

After a few incidents in town and the issue at our own villa a few months before, the guys had moved into another villa in al Mansour where the rest of the company were then based. Carl and I were now tasked to reopen the old villa and get the new electrical client contract up and running. Cash was in short supply at this time, with clients owing the company a substantial amount of money as well as the difficulty of just getting sufficient cash into country to pay the locals.

On the second evening of our return to the old villa, I opened up the safe that had been left there during our absence. I was going to give it a clean out and get it back into use once we received some cash that Andy was trying to arrange for us. Whilst tinkering around with it in our newly designed office, I felt something rattle in the top of the safe and discovered a secret compartment. I managed to pull it out and to my complete astonishment and absolute joy the drawer was full of US dollars. I could not believe my eyes. My first thought was that it must be a test of my integrity and looked for the hidden cameras, but I quickly realised that this was not the case and it had just been left there a few months earlier. It was unbelievable really, but a very welcome find, taking into consideration the pressure we were under to pay the local wages on time. I called Carl in to show him what I had discovered, and his face was a picture. We counted it up and there was near on twenty thousand dollars that would cover the local payroll that month. We sat down and had a few beers to celebrate our good fortune. You have to ask yourself how twenty thousand dollars could have been misplaced, especially at a time like that when we were short on cash. This was typical of life in Iraq with Elea, the ups and downs of the journey we found ourselves on, but I would not have swapped it for any other job in any other company.

We soon realized that we needed to make our own villa a lot safer than it was, so we brought in a steel man to reinforce the whole place. He basically built a steel cage around the villa and reinforced all access points to the upstairs where we worked and lived so we could control entry properly and sleep with an element of peace at night. At the top of the stairs, we placed a table that had a few spare weapons and grenades on it. This was there in case the insurgents tried to attack our villa and gained entry up the stairs and through the steel works; our drill was to move to this table and repel them from this point with everything we had, whilst hoping that the US Army or some other friendly forces came to our aid. Otherwise, the plan was to make it to the roof with our own personal weapons and hot tail it over to one of the neighbour's villas where we could lay up and wait for support or alternatively, move down to the street and make our own way to another friendly location by foot. There were so many attacks going on at this time in Baghdad that as a matter of routine we all carried pistols with us at all times even when in the villa moving from room to room and slept with them close by or under the pillow at night. Our grab bags were always ready to go, just in case. It was a stressful life, more so than we actually realised at the time it was happening.

We trained up a lot of local Iraqi guys whom Ammar recruited. There was of course a huge element of trust involved with these guys as you never truly knew where their allegiances lay or, even more worrying, who could get to them or their families and force them to give up info on us. We made sure that the information and timings of all the movements we made around Baghdad with the local guys were never passed on to them in advance so at least this way they were unable to pass info on us to the insurgents if they were ever put into this awkward position. To be fair to the Iraqi guys we had working with us, they were great, never let us down, and were a fiercely loyal, hard-working crew under very difficult circumstances for themselves.

Most of the other larger international security companies worked in a high-profile manner, but we didn't like this style and preferred to be as low profile as possible. We tended to use old model, discreetly armoured Mercedes and BMWs as well as just bog standard soft skinned saloon cars for moving around the city. Due to our requirement to raise enough cash in country to pay the local wages each month, which was pretty damn important as our lives were in their hands, we started to rent our armoured vehicles out to some of the international news' teams who we knew and who, like us, much preferred the low profile way of moving around. As there were not many of these vehicles around at the time, they were in great demand and made us some good money each month. The trouble was the vehicles were so old and badly maintained due to the lack of servicing capability in Baghdad that they tended to break down every now and again. We took turns heading out in the evenings with our Iraqi teams to drop off the vehicles with the clients and then manning the phone during the rental period. We always hoped that the phone would not go off until the rental period was over, otherwise we ended up taking calls from guys we knew well, saying that our shitty vehicle had just broken down in the city centre or even worse, on Route Irish and that we needed to get out there to recover it. It was all part of the fun and games of working for a small company at this time in Iraq.

Some of the more maverick, larger style international security companies moved around in great big, up-armoured trucks or otherwise in brand new B6 armoured Land Cruisers. Either way, they were high profile, blatantly armed to the teeth, and the teams wore uniforms, so they were obvious targets to the insurgents. Their philosophy was that they would not hide, but would attempt to outgun any attackers instead. We were the opposite and employed the Northern Ireland and British Special Forces style of low-profile operating techniques. Most of our guys were highly trained, experienced and most importantly, comfortable working in this manner. If worse did come to worst and we were compromised, we had trained well and we had excellent drills in place to hopefully get out of any situation in which we found ourselves.

These drills were put to the test one afternoon. We had a short-term task on the go and we had brought in a couple of guys from the UK to carry it out. They were driving back to our villa through the streets of Baghdad with a client when they realised that a suspicious looking car was following them. Our driver put his foot down and moved off the main road and down a side street in a bid to get away from it and to confirm if they were being followed or not. The car followed and they found themselves boxed in at the end of a street. Iraqis wearing militia type clothing with scarves wrapped around their heads got out of their vehicles holding AKs and approached our team's vehicle with their weapons raised in an aggressive manner. Our team had inadvertently found themselves in a situation with a client on board who they were responsible for and they had no choice but to make a split decision. Our security team opened fire at the approaching assailants through the windscreen of their own vehicle. One of gunmen was hit and the others dispersed enough for our driver to accelerate past them and get away safely.

We worked with local Iraqis around us at all times and we dressed like them as much as possible. This sometimes caused problems with other security companies thinking we were hostiles and trying to run us off the road or firing warning shots at us if we got too close to their convoys. We tried to avoid this whenever we could, as we all knew that the level of training and experience of some of the guys working for these companies and manning heavy machine guns on these convoys was not good and could at times be just as dangerous to us as the insurgents themselves.

An example of how dangerous it was at this time in Baghdad and why we preferred a low profile approach, was with an old friend of mine from 1 Para, John Dolman, a veteran of the Balkans and Iraq wars and a well-respected hard-core northern lad, nicknamed 'the Dolmanator' by his mates. John was taking clients to the airport in two high profile armoured Land Cruisers. They came out of the Green Zone and made their way up onto the flyover. A suicide bomber drove up alongside them, got as close as he could and detonated his car bomb. John's vehicle had no chance and was blown off the flyover. It flew over the edge, crashed down below and exploded, killing him and everyone inside instantly. This incident hit me hard, I had only been talking to John at the US embassy a couple of weeks earlier after a chance meeting and it really brought the dangers of this job home to me. There were numerous similar stories on Route Irish and a number of people I knew were seriously injured or killed during this time.

The contract for the electric company turned out to be very easy as clients from the company rarely came over to Iraq. We went to survey their sub-stations and sent regular reports to them and we were always on standby for any client personnel to arrive, but they didn't come very often. Apart from the weekly meeting with the prime-contractor, we were left with loads of spare time to organise our new armoured vehicle letting business and carry out any other ad-hoc short-term tasks that Andy could send our way. It was a real team effort and Andy made sure we all benefitted.

We were tasked to oversee a convoy of equipment that was being brought down from Kurdistan and we received a call to say that the convoy had come under attack. We were told that one of the Peshmerga (Kurdish) soldiers had a serious facial injury and would require immediate medical support as soon as they got to Baghdad. I was working with Denny at the time, another of the company lads. We met the vehicle carrying the casualty just outside the IZ check point 12, cross decked him into our vehicle and then headed to the IZ for treatment at the US Combat Support Hospital (CAS). Denny was driving our vehicle, a low profile armoured Mercedes. I quickly assessed the soldier's situation and realised he had been hit in the head and half his face had become partially detached; he was in a very bad way. It was touch and go whether he would make it or not and time was clearly of the essence. I added another field dressing on top of the one already there and held his head steady and together the best I could. As we raced to the hospital, I constantly reassured him that everything was going to be okay. Denny approached CP 12 with a Union Jack Flag clearly up for the US guards to see, but we were ordered to halt over the loudspeaker and they signalled for us to move back. Denny jumped out and bravely identified himself. He walked towards the nearest soldier and explained the situation, but they were reluctant to let us pass. Eventually, after a lot of frustrating discussion and persuasion, we were allowed entry and quickly made our way to the CAS. The injured soldier was met on arrival by a doctor and taken straight in for assessment and then emergency surgery. I went back that evening to see if he had made it and to my great relief, I was told that he was okay. He was under sedation in the recovery unit and someone from his unit was coming down in the morning. That night Denny and I had a few beers and toasted that brave soldier's health.

We had a great social life in our villa, back to the work hard, play hard philosophy and, to be brutally honest, we needed to unwind in the evenings and take the edge off the stress we were constantly under with a few beers and some good old fashioned military banter at which the guys have always been so good. Most evenings we ate a lot of crappy takeaway food, washed it down with a few bottles of Corona, or maybe a box depending on which night of the week it was, and the odd bottle of whiskey, and smoked some cheap Iraqi fags. We were definitely drinking too much, and it did get out of hand at times, which we knew ourselves, but it was keeping us going. I think all four of us only really realised how bad we had become and what stress we had actually been carrying around with us when we left and got back into the swing of normal life in the UK, which was never that easy to adapt to after living like that for so long.

It was a great couple of years, living by the seat of our pants to get what we needed and avoiding trouble. Most of the other companies were based in the Green Zone and had huge support and back up structures. We were on our own in the Red Zone gathering whatever we could from wherever we could. We had picked up a bit of a reputation and become known as being like Deals on Wheels, secondhand car dealers, although I like to think we were far more successful and operated with great skill and thought. We had built some excellent client relationships, some of which would come back around in the future. We knew other guys would love to have joined the company, but nobody ever left and when we did need to recruit, we did so from within and only brought in guys who fitted the exact profile of what we required. We were paid well, treated with respect, left to our own devices and got on great with each other. It was dangerous work; there is no doubt about it, but we understood the risks and were always well prepared to deal with anything that came along. In our opinion, the high-profile guys earning half what we earned were at much greater risk running those dangerous convoys day in, day out. The four of us held the whole thing together with great spirit, a few beers and a lot of fun.

I could see that the Baghdad electric company contract was coming to an end sometime soon and sure enough, eventually they gave Andy notice and he confirmed a finishing date. Then he pulled a rabbit out of his hat, which he had the knack of doing each time one of our main contracts got close to finishing, and won a contract in South Baghdad providing a security team for the rebuild of a major electrical sub-station. The contract was with a large international power generation company for a security manager and team to design and plan the protection of the power station and the staff they would be sending in that was located next to a large American Forward Operating Base (FOB).

I decided to take the bull by the horns and spoke to Andy one evening in the villa and made it clear that I was interested in becoming the Project Manager for the new contract, which he was pleased to hear. I was reluctant to leave the Baghdad villa set up, but I couldn't risk not having another job in Iraq and could also clearly see the potential and change of pace this new project could offer. Carl didn't see it to begin with, but after we chatted, he soon recognised the opportunity in front of us and wasted no time in getting his name on it with me. The electric company contract finished and while Ollie and Marcus found themselves in transition, Carl and I moved seamlessly onto the new project which we code named Eagle.

The first phase was for Carl and I to get down to Eagle to meet the US military that ran the camp adjacent to the power station and to get everything set up before any clients arrived. This in itself took a few months and involved a lot of planning and hard work. We were totally responsible for devising and implementing a robust security plan which delivered a workable blueprint for the power station project and kept the US camp leadership team happy that the safety of their camp was not being compromised. Carl and I knew from the outset that the relationship we formed with the US military was key to the success of this project and if handled correctly could help us out massively and make our lives much easier in the long run.

We had to find a viable way of bringing a lot of the local Iraqi workers in to work on the power station site on a daily basis. We decided to set up a checkpoint just off the main road where we could process them all in and then arrange to ship them up on buses to the power station area, one group at a time. This way, we could maintain complete control of them at all times under the beady eyes of the American military manning their towers and watching our every move with keen interest.

We needed a barrier, a chicane and a guardhouse as well as some blast proof walls so that we could safely control who came in and provide ourselves with the necessary level of protection from any insurgents wanting to take a pop at us from the surrounding area. The road then went all the way up, adjacent to the military camp, until it reached the entrance to the power station site. We required another checkpoint at the entry to the power station and a camp inside for the permanent members of the project team to live.

The Americans were happy with our plan as they did not want any nonsense going on so near to their camp and made it clear that we should have complete control of all the local workers at all times. They were very worried about who these locals were and whether they could cause a potential threat to the camp. We got very close to the Americans to make sure we had a good working relationship with them and shared our ideas and plans so that they could be sure we were going to run it well and conform to the required standard. If they did not buy into our plan then they would close us down, simple as that.

They were quite amazed because they had never met anyone like us before – ex-British soldiers setting up a camp outside the wire as they called it. They thought we were nuts and could not get their heads around our willingness to live and work outside the camp amongst Iraqis. Many of them, who did not understand the dynamics of the country like us, simply deemed all Iraqis as hostiles. We used all of our people skills to form good relationships with them because we had absolutely nothing and needed their full support. They provided us with a porta cabin inside their grounds to live in, and the use of all the camp facilities. This included being able to help ourselves in the US army dining facility (DEFAC), which had a fantastic array of food. We began eating far more healthily than we had in our Baghdad villa.

We started looking around their camp, which was about three-square kilometers in size, to see what we could find that would be of use to us. There were some old concrete T-walls in one part of the camp which were perfect for providing a screen and blast protection at our new checkpoint. We asked if anyone was using them and when they said no, we started arranging for their removal. We managed to get the use of a crane and a truck and moved the T-walls through the camp and out into the area of our new checkpoint so that we could then start to build our chicane and control point.

Lying around in another area, we found a load of Hesco, which is primarily used for military fortifications. It is made of a collapsible wire mesh container and heavy-duty fabric liner and is used as a temporary to semi-permanent blast wall against explosions or small arms fire. The US soldiers laughed at us from their armoured guard towers as we stood outside in our t-shirts in the scorching heat orchestrating the building of our two checkpoints outside the wire, next to the main road using the materials we had scrounged from their camp.

We were becoming proper Del Boys now, but with results that were definitely far more successful than the Trotters. In the grounds of the power station, there was an old villa and we needed to renovate it and make it habitable for use by the three English site security managers who we would be bringing in at the start of the project. We got the electrics back on, installed a water pump on the roof, and made it more comfortable for them with a few pieces of basic furniture and beds, all acquired from the local markets. There was a gate between the military camp and the power station grounds that the Americans kept locked. We persuaded them to open it at times, in order to allow us easier access to the camp from the power station.

By now, Carl and I were working back to back and living on the camp as full-time liaison officers with the US military leadership team. We ate in the military canteen and got on very well with the Americans. We had contacts outside the camp who could get beers and whisky and we used this to give to the commanders and anyone else we thought might be helpful. They appreciated this and we got on really well with them. The camp commander known as the Mayor was an awkward character and said, 'Who the hell are you guys?' when he first met us, but in the end he chilled out and gave us pretty much anything we required. We told them that it was all part of the reconstruction of Iraq programme and that we were working for an international power generation company who would bring better power to the local area when the project was completed. This would reflect well on the US military as well. They decided that we were doing a good job and that they would support this excellent initiative. It was mostly bullshit of course, as we were there to make money first and foremost, but there was an underlying truth to it and a win-win for everyone, including the Iraqi people.

Whilst clearing the site, we found a stack of old black cables lying around, which no one had any use for, but we discovered that they had copper in them, and copper was valuable in Iraq at this time. We soon had that all collected.

We had more than one hundred Iraqi guys working for us now and we provided them all with uniforms, trained them on how to safely use the weapons, perform basic first aid and carry out the search techniques properly at the checkpoint. In effect, we created our own little army and built a safe and well protected complex to support the rebuild project of the power station.

Once we had the villa up and running at the power station, we began a new tradition. Every Thursday, a team from Baghdad came down with any supplies we required and of course, some booze. We sneaked a few of our American friends from the camp in and had what we called 'Helmet' parties i.e. A gathering of men drinking alcohol and talking crap. We went up onto the roof of the villa, made a fire in an old oil drum and then drank, chatted and generally took the piss out of each other all through the night. Friday was a day off, so we went around most of that day with terrible hangovers hoping that nothing major happened.

Andy supplied us with a few second hand, four by four vehicles and buses that kept breaking down. KBR (Kellogg, Brown & Root) had an encampment inside the military site and they had a garage that we took the vehicles to in order to repair them. A German guy called Herbert, who we quickly renamed 'Herman', for some strange reason, and a couple of Americans who were real hillbilly type characters were running this garage. The only thing they couldn't get was beer, so we came to a mutually beneficial agreement whereby we supplied them with booze and they kept our vehicles on the road. Sometimes, they came to the Helmet parties on a Thursday, stayed all night, crashed on the floor and we then smuggled them back into the camp at some point on Friday.

Camp Eagle came under attack on a regular basis. It was in a very dangerous area of Baghdad with pockets of insurgents all around and became notorious for how many times it was attacked. The insurgents generally fired mortars and rockets into the camp during the evenings and nighttime hours; it was easier for them to get away with it at those times of day when there were fewer military patrols on the ground. The alarm would go off when the first rockets or mortars were heard coming in or landed in the camp; it was a bit of a lottery and you just had to hope that your name was not written on one of them. There were what are called duck and dive bunkers scattered around the camp. These were just concrete horseshoes with sometimes sandbags filling in the empty sides – very basic shelters, but better than nothing. Our villa in the power station had some protection with a flat concrete roof and most of the American military camp was built with some sort of overhead mesh and sand protection designed to absorb any hits. However, our porta cabin was not protected at all, and Carl and I lived in this area with a couple of Filipino chefs and an old American engineer who had fought in Vietnam and was now working with the US Corps of Engineers.

I think Carl had had too many close shaves in his military career and he didn't take any chances anymore. We were doing a hand over one night and heard the rockets coming in. One landed what seemed very close to our cabin shaking the paper thin walls and roof and whilst I decided to casually get under the desk, Carl burst out of the door and ran across the open ground towards the nearest duck and dive shelter. At the same time, a second rocket came in and this time landed right next to where he was running. It was so close, I feared for Carl and was relieved when I heard that he had made it safely to the shelter.

The following morning, we went out to see where the second rocket had actually landed. It had struck about thirty metres away from our cabin leaving a sizeable crater in the ground, but what was really amazing was that all around there were shrapnel marks on the walls thrown up from the rocket. Carl had run out of the cabin literally in the direction of where the rocket had landed. He had run past it as it came down and dived into the shelter in the nick of time. How he wasn't hit, I do not know; he was a lucky lad and definitely used one of his nine lives that night. It was like this all the time in Eagle, with the camp under constant attack. It is amazing what you can get used to in an environment such as this. When the evening lottery began, it was definitely not the place for the faint hearted.

On the military side of the camp was a huge ammunition dump providing ammo for the whole sector. I was in the porta cabin chilling out on my own and the other guys were up at the power station villa. The camp came under attack as usual but this time there was a direct hit on the ammunition dump and the whole lot went up. The rocket had somehow penetrated the layer of overhead protection and exploded inside, the chances of this happening were a thousand to one. I heard the terrifying noise of the first few explosions going off and quickly realizing that this was not the normal rocket or mortar attack, I ran to the duck and dive shelter. Inside already were the two Filipinos and the old US engineer. The explosions got louder and louder and hot shrapnel was now flying over our heads and in all directions.

I lost radio contact with my team in the villa and the phone signal had gone down as the ammunition went up and up with massive explosions and resounding booms; smoke and flames burst upwards in huge mushrooms. The noise and heat was incredible and fires broke out all around the base. The KBR section on the opposite side of the camp, which was also in porta cabins with no real overhead protection, caught fire and the whole lot burned to the ground within an hour. We hunkered down in our feeble little shelter unable to move anywhere safer through the whole night as explosions continued to blast out all around us. The Filipinos had resorted to praying and over in the power station house Paul, Ems, Geoff and Lee were watching the show from their roof wondering what the hell had happened to me. They knew that I lived in the area that they could see was now being completely destroyed. They couldn't get any closer and they were concerned for my safety. To be honest I have never experienced anything like it and would not want to go through it again; there was nothing I could do at all apart from just hope I was going to be lucky, again.

By first light, the ammo dump had blown itself out and the explosions were finally over. I managed to get radio contact with the guys in the villa, much to everyone's relief, and we all started to look around at the aftermath. They told me the attack was all over the international news and headlining on the BBC so I gave Jo a quick call to let her know I was okay. The whole of the KBR camp had gone, scattered all over the place were pieces of shrapnel that had flown through the air over our heads, some had gone as far as a kilometre to the power station which was now covered in Un-Exploded Ordnance (UXO) and full of holes. It was a good job they hadn't started the main phase of rebuilding it yet. It took weeks to clear the area of the UXO and to this day, I have no idea how we were not hit in our small flimsy shelter, or how our porta cabins didn't burn down around us; it didn't make any sense. Lucky escape number three for me, for sure.

Once the contract ended at Eagle, Andy asked me to go back to run the villa in Baghdad as Country Manager. He was looking to move the company on and to inject some new blood into it. I moved back into the old villa and completely re-organized it, which was another great learning curve for me. It got to the end of 2007 and all sorts were going on. Insurgency was still on the rise; attacks were just getting worse and I decided I had finally had enough of Iraq and had become bored with it all. It was time for a new challenge in a different and demanding environment, away from all the mavericks that Iraq had now attracted. I decided that I wanted to work in Africa as a security consultant, challenge my mental skills more and move my career on to the next stage.

CHAPTER 12

TIME TO MOVE ON

I was the country manager in Iraq, based in Baghdad. I had operational oversight of all our client contracts and the responsibility of making sure we had the supplies and procedures in place to run everything as smoothly and as safely as possible; a lot of responsibility and pressure lay on my shoulders, but I felt the need for change again and wanted a new challenge. More and more commercial and security workers were piling into the country as the demand for security rose. The situation across Iraq was not improving as militia groups and insurgents grew in power and levels of violence increased. The Iraqi government was starting to make life difficult for us to operate with a new law obligating low profile vehicles to have markings on the side identifying who they were; more and more bureaucracy was blocking our way. I had spent over four years in Iraq and had had my fill. I handed in my notice to Andy and thanked him for his support. I left in December and went home to spend Christmas with Jo in Torquay with the plan to start applying for new challenges after the New Year.

I had spent the last six years in both Afghanistan and Iraq and watched them both change over that time. I also grew in myself. I had had incredible learning experiences, survived dangerous incidents in both countries, and had developed my own personal abilities as an operator and as a manager.

I now wanted to find something more niche and challenging, to get away from the guns and bullets and put my brain to real use with what was now becoming a considerable amount of commercial experience. I felt that I had to stay one step ahead of the tidal wave that was engulfing the security circuit and spreading across the Middle East. I had heard that there were some well-paid contracts in Algeria, Nigeria and other parts of Africa working as a security consultant or as an advisor for international oil and gas firms, and this was what I was interested in exploring.

This time, I actually did take a rest and felt fully refreshed when I began looking for new opportunities. I wasn't going to rush into the first thing that came up and I was going to take my time. However, work in Africa, especially Algeria, as I found out, was still run in a very old school fashion with a lot of the contracts held by the older generation of former SAS guys who had set up companies and were getting the work. They weren't that interested in guys who had been in Iraq and Afghanistan because in their view they hadn't been doing anything more than sitting on the back of vehicles with a gun in their hands and living in the Green Zone. They couldn't really differentiate between someone like me and guys who had been little more than a lookout or a hired gun on the back of a vehicle as they described it. I had been living outside the safe areas, using my own initiative and more importantly had set up entire security operations dealing with clients on a daily basis, but with just a quick glance at my CV, they weren't getting the whole picture.

I met up with JD again who had hired me in Iraq a few years earlier. He had set up a new company with a contract coming up in the south of Sudan (this was 2008 before it split into Sudan and South Sudan). The job sounded really exciting and I found out that "Big Phil Campion" who I had worked with when I first went to Afghanistan was also going to be working with me as my back to back. The job was for a French drilling company who the Sudanese National Oil Company had sub-contracted to operate their drilling rig in the White Nile area of the country. This area of the White Nile was in the swamps with temperatures ranging from pretty hot to scorching hot followed by monsoon rainfall with all the nasty little insects which came with this sort of sticky environment. We lived in containers stacked up on a barge in the middle of the swamp. It was hard core living, none of the usual oil and gas industry luxuries out there, that is for sure.

Our job entailed putting in place a feasible security protocol and writing up an evacuation plan in support of the French drilling company workers stationed on the rig. In previous years, companies had pulled out of the region after attacks from local tribes that had resulted in a number of workers being kidnapped, injured or even killed.

The remit sounded fairly straightforward, but there was one slight problem. The main Sudanese National Oil Company (NOC) was totally against any foreign security personnel in any shape or form and so the French drilling company was not officially allowed to employ us. JD had presented the French with the solution that Phil and I would go over officially as Health & Safety (HSE) officers.

A few years earlier, I had completed a week's course in Health and Safety that amounted to the equivalent of going on a creative writing course and learning to write, 'Once upon a time'. The amount of health and safety knowledge and experience that either of us actually had at this point could be easily written on the back of a postage stamp in bold capital letters with a thick black marker pen. I was going over as the company's on-site Health and Safety manager; it was going to be an interesting challenge. Phil was in the same boat as me and was first man in; I would follow him at the end of his first month's shift.

The plan was that we create a defensive protocol but not tell anyone that we were there for this reason. The only people who knew that we were not actually HSE managers or really even qualified in this particular skill at all, was the French company Drilling Manager based in Khartoum and the Tool Pusher as he was known, who ran the actual drilling rig in the swamp. The other workers could not know who we really were and so they judged us purely on our abilities and knowledge of Health and Safety. They must have thought we were absolute idiots. Not only did we not know that much about our supposed role, but also the main Sudanese contractor had sent out its best HSE man. He was clearly keen, professional and very switched on, far more than I expected him to be. It was typical of my luck that I had the keenest HSE guy in all of Africa on my tail, when usually, in my experience, the Africans paid little or no attention to HSE at all. One day he asked me to prepare a power point presentation on how we should be using the 'boom'. This, I quickly learned, is something that extends around the rig in the water to make sure any oil spills do not leak out into the water area and affect the local people and wildlife. I had absolutely no idea what he was talking about when he asked me and just bluffed my way through it. He spoke perfect English, which was really annoying; I couldn't even blame the breakdown in communication between us on my inability to understand his bad grasp of the English language – shit!

After that, I spent my whole time trying my best to avoid him. If he came into a room, I tried to slip out of the back door and pretend that I was needed or busy in another area of the rig. It was a joke, but it kind of worked. Phil and I worked there for six months on back-to-back shifts of one month on and one month off. The only guy we could really talk to about work was the tool pusher and he used to laugh and say that he did not want to be in our shoes. He was constantly getting complaints about the useless HSE guys. Over time, of course, I did actually learn quite a lot about Health and Safety and even managed to implement a half decent HSE protocol on the rig. I am proud to say that there were no HSE incidents of note; not that I knew about anyway!

The French struggled to get staff to stay on the rig because the conditions were so terrible. The climate of the swamp combined with the fact that the food was awful meant a high turnover of workers. The French chef pulled his hair out when supplies arrived by barge days late and he found that half the contents in the food containers had gone off and were ruined. The French workers were used to eating well, this is embedded in the French culture, and when their food and wine supply is interrupted, they are not happy teddy bears. For me as a former soldier, I was used to getting by on minimal rations, eating whatever was available or whatever I could get my hands on at the time. I was quite happy living in our container accommodation stacked on top of the barge in the insect infested swamp, navigating the waterways to the rig each day on a power boat and despite the embarrassment of my pretend HSE role, preparing and writing up the evacuation plan and making contacts within all the relevant authorities and friendly forces around us.

The drilling company knew why we were there and wanted us to stay because they didn't trust that the Sudanese authorities would protect the French workers or get them out of country if an incident was to occur. Sure enough, a few years later, there was a revolution and without the evacuation plans in place, companies such as ours would have been stuck.

Late 2008 saw intense fighting break out between northern and southern forces in the disputed oil-rich town of Abyei. In the end, the International Criminal Court in The Hague issued an arrest warrant for President Bashir on charges of war crimes and crimes against humanity in Darfur. In December 2009, Leaders of the north and south reached a deal on the terms of the independence referendum, which was finally implemented in 2011. Sudan and South Sudan were created.

The job and the living conditions in Sudan provided me with a completely new working environment, nothing like the life in Iraq. On the whole, it was fun and interesting whilst very different and arduous work. One problem that we faced was with the local Dinka tribe and a militia group that splintered off from them. I had been told by Phil that they often visited the barge and so I was prepared for them, or at least I thought I was.

One night, I was out on the top deck with a few others, smoking a cigarette and taking in the evening music kindly laid on by the insect orchestra when I heard the noise of a gentle swish of oars nearing our accommodation barge. Looking out into the dark water, I couldn't see anything at first and then I made out the shape of the long, low boat filled with black bodies. They pulled alongside, tied up to the barge and as they climbed silently onto the deck, I took a step back. They were the tallest men I have ever seen in my life; it was like the Harlem Globe Trotters basketball team turning up except that these guys were armed with long, sharp machetes.

They all looked about seven-foot-tall to me and they arrived in the middle of the night on a fairly regular basis demanding money, food or whatever else they could lay their hands on. It was a very intimidating sight witnessing these massively tall men with their machete blades glinting in the moonlight. If they had turned aggressive, there was nothing I could have done to protect the team, apart from try to de-escalate the situation. They would have chopped us up and thrown the pieces into the swamp never to be seen again without a second thought.

I briefed the French workers to be submissive and as friendly as they could with these guys if confronted by them and not to inflame any situations that occurred, even if pushed or provoked. We also relied on the local Sudanese crew who worked with us to try to deal with the situation, as they knew these guys best. However, in truth, they were shit scared of them and hid away downstairs whenever the giant tribesmen came on board the barge.

There was little we could do apart from give the tribesmen what they wanted. One night, the chief of the local tribe came to visit and said that we should employ some of his guys. The rig manager did not want to argue and took them on as roustabouts (general labourers) and, as the HSE officer, it was my job to kit them out in the proper safety clothing and at least try to brief them on the health and safety protocols of the rig. The French company had a container full of gear – coveralls, hard hats and safety boots – that everyone had to wear. However, trying to find overalls and boots to fit giants like these with size fourteen feet was virtually impossible. The shorter ones amongst them, just six foot four, managed to squeeze themselves into the longest coveralls we had, which ended up just about covering their knees and some managed to squeeze their feet into the largest boots, but the rest went about quite happily, but totally against all health and safety regulations, in their flip flops and shorts. They didn't want to work; it was really the local chief's way of making sure that they were all well fed, and that he had some eyes and ears on our rig. What I can say for them is that they knew exactly when breakfast, lunch and dinner were served. They were first in and they devoured practically the whole canteen.

Once the first phase of drilling was completed, the tribesmen marked the day by bringing all the local dignitaries and the Chief on board the rig along with one unsuspecting sheep. The sheep was then duly sacrificed over the drill head to bring luck to the new source of local income.

The French finally had enough and pulled out of the contract. Phil was there for the shut down and I was back in the UK looking for new work opportunities again. Carl, my good friend that I worked with in Iraq, had a job working for an ultra-high-net-worth family in America. A member of a radical group who had just been released from prison had some old claims to some land that the client family had acquired many years previously and he had issued some serious death threats to the clients. The FBI knew who the man was, but he somehow managed to disappear into the underground network, and they were searching for him. The company security officer for the family preferred to use British rather than American security teams at this time and had used his English contacts to put together a team to go over to provide an extra layer of security for the family. Carl, three others and I flew over to a state in middle America expecting to be there for about a week to ten days while the FBI found the man in question. We ended up being there for four months.

We flew over in BA business class, which was nice and were paid an excellent day rate. We set up and stayed in the family's summerhouse next to the client's beautiful main residence. It was a far cry from the mosquito-infected swamps of Sudan and just the sort of job I fancied at this time. We set up our surveillance equipment around the house and grounds and monitored anyone coming into or around the house.

Each day, we took it in turns to escort the primary client to his office. He didn't want us in the same car as him so we had to follow as discreetly as possible and as closely as we could in another vehicle. We were provided with brand new Remington pump action shotguns with sporting licenses so that we could legally carry them on the private grounds, but according to the law when outside they had to be in a zip bag with a plastic tie. The ammunition had to be in a separate bag, also with a tie on it, and they had to be kept in the boot of the car. If anything happened, we were in a very difficult position to react quickly and bring the weapons into use.

I remember one night when Carl discreetly followed one of the other clients to an engagement he had at a house on a private residential street in town. He parked up just down the road and watched the client go into the house. For whatever reason, Carl must have accidentally hit a switch in the car that set off the car alarm. He could not get it to stop, no matter what he tried. He rang us in the summerhouse in a bit of a flap and said to get over to where he was asap to take the vehicle away and give him one of our vehicles. While this intense call was going on, I could hear the car alarm going off in the background and that was making me laugh. Carl was mildly worried, to say the least, that a neighbour would hear what was going on, call the police, and want to know why some strange English guy was sitting in their road with a pump action shot gun in his car. The trouble was we had no idea where he actually was, and his explanation was far from clear. I told the guy with me, Scott not to worry too much, there was no point in going out and leaving our own task when we really had no idea where he was and I was sure he would sort it out eventually. Sure enough, the next call came five minutes later; he seemed a lot calmer now and had worked out how to turn the alarm off and was luckily not yet in some hillbilly jail with his back to the wall all night or a new boyfriend for company!

A couple of weeks into the job, it was decided that the brother of the main client and his family based up in New York now required protection and so I went up to New York with one of our team, TC. We met the brother, a tall imposing man with a ferocious business reputation. I did get to know him well in the end and he turned out to be a really nice guy, but at the first meeting I could sense that he was very sceptical about what we could actually do for him and his family.

Once we arrived at his Manhattan apartment, he took TC and me into his private library and introduced us to his current bodyguard, Jim. Jim was an ex-New York policeman who could legally carry a pistol on his person and really did not understand why we were there or what we could offer that he was not already providing. The brother put us on the spot and asked us to explain what value we believed we could bring to his current security set up, bearing in mind that we couldn't be legally armed in New York and he had Jim who was.

We sat in his library and laid out our experience of carrying out similar roles in the past with the various high net-worth clients for whom we had worked. He asked us about our time in Afghanistan and Iraq, which he seemed very interested in. We explained what our strategy was for keeping the family as low profile as possible over the next few weeks; breaking up any routines his family had in place, which a possible assailant might be able to ascertain and link into, and generally adding an extra layer to his security whilst this current threat was still in play. We also spoke to Jim privately; he had his nose out of joint and we made it clear that we were not there to replace him or to steal his job, but to work with him while the threat remained.

We all stayed in New York and bonded over the Ryder Cup which was being held at the time. Then I flew down to Aspen with the brother and his wife in a private jet, whilst TC stayed in NY with Jim to look after the kids, who we deemed would be a soft target if any part of the family were to be targeted by the assailant's group. Whilst in their Aspen home, they mixed with the rich and famous, and generally relaxed a little away from their manic New York work routine.

Back in New York again we flew regularly by private helicopter from the edge of the Hudson River to the Hamptons for weekends, where we landed in the back garden of their Hampton house. It was a very enjoyable experience; we got on well with all the house staff and we taught Jim and their other security people a lot of useful tactics. We explained the more subtle style that the British use when carrying out security tasks. We told them that certain weapons, as useful as they are, were last resort, and if we found ourselves in a fire fight or rolling around on the floor with an assailant then we had failed in our job; it was all about avoidance at this level. The FBI eventually caught the man responsible for the threats and it was time to move on.

The next job is not one I remember particularly fondly. Around this time, the maritime industry was coming under increasing threat from Somali pirates. With no enforced rights protecting their own national waters, numerous intruders had overfished the seas around Somalia. Locals who relied on fishing for a living lost their work and became very poor and it is suspected that this led them into piracy. Added to this, Somalia was a lawless state run by warlords and terrorists and piracy was becoming a very lucrative business. Just as the maritime industry was about to explode, I agreed to take on a job protecting a super yacht that was being sailed from Salalah in Oman to Sharm El Sheikh in Egypt. The Gulf of Aden and the Horn of Africa were historically notorious for pirates but in recent times, there had been a resurgence of the activity and they were now getting bolder and more desperate than ever.

We didn't have any weapons when we boarded but what the yacht did have was a sound wave machine. A Long-Range Acoustic Device (LRAD) is an amazing device that emits painfully loud sound frequencies that can be concentrated in a narrow beam and aimed at the target. If you direct it at any hostile boats coming close to the yacht, it acts as a massive deterrent to them coming any closer.

The main problem for me was that I have never had very good sea legs but thought I would handle it fine and be okay. It was only a ten-day transit – what could possibly be so hard? My partner was an ex-marine and we were doing alternate twelve-hour shifts, and for the first few days, all was good and going well. I was enjoying the evenings sitting on the yacht, monitoring the water for other vessels, and generally chilling out. However, a few days into the passage, once we got further out, the sea state changed dramatically and became very choppy. My stomach turned upside down. I was so bad at one point that I was literally incapable of doing my job properly and the other guy had to cover a couple of my shifts as well as his own, which I felt bad about. This of course was embarrassing and got back to the company at home and I had to face a lot of piss taking on my return. I vowed to remember my own strengths and weaknesses in the future and never to take on a job like that again.

However, then the pirates started getting more organised and ambitious in their exploits. They began targeting and taking over large cargo ships and super tankers and were successful in taking a few of them over, diverting the vessels to Somalia and holding the crew hostage while they attempted to negotiate for millions of dollars in ransom money. In 2009, the well-known kidnapping of Captain Phillips, which was turned into a Hollywood film, was to take place. Armed guards were not the norm on board these ships at first so in this early stage of this new threat level the crew and security teams had to improvise and try their best to make the ships as impregnable as possible and hope that the pirates targeted other vessels that might be easier to take on.

I took on a job protecting some tankers in the knowledge that these huge vessels didn't rock and roll as much as smaller yachts! A team of four of us boarded the first of these huge ships in the port of Aden and it was up to us to devise ways to stop the pirates getting on board. The ship's captain had ordered masses of concertina barbed wire and as the ship was sailing through safe waters, with the help of the crew, we went about the task of putting the wire all around the edges and in vulnerable areas where the ship could be boarded by the Somali pirates. We worked hard to get it all complete prior to reaching the high-risk water areas.

Some ships had very low free boards making it easier for pirates to get on, so it was essential to protect these areas even more. We always felt better when we arrived and saw that the ship had a higher free board. We knew that the pirates were less likely to target it, and even if they did, their chances of success were far less. In case they still managed to get on, we also placed as many hurdles as possible in their way. Blocking stairways and putting grease on the handrails and bannisters would give us time to get the crew to a safe room in the ship. This was usually down in the engine room area that we called the citadel. From there, emergency calls for help could be made and sometimes the steering and power of the ship could be diverted there as well.

All of our ideas were complete improvisation in these early days; we were constantly implementing ideas to prevent pirates from getting onto the ships and ensuring that the vessel reached port safely. Once we reached a port, we were usually, as quickly as possible, sent by the company onto another ship going back the other way and sometimes even cross decked between two vessels, whilst still at sea, using a small boat. This was a challenging feat in itself, especially at night when both vessels were still moving, and could be very dangerous. Sadly, a security guy from another company was killed whilst attempting this procedure, which just highlighted the dangers of this work.

We took turns two at a time manning the two bridge wings, port and starboard, scanning the sea with binoculars and night viewing devices for potential pirate vessels. We saw many of them, usually in skiffs, which are small, nimble fishing boats. We saw them taking a good look at us and weighing us up as potential targets. Based on our advice, the captain usually challenged them over the international radio channel, which we knew they monitored, to identify themselves and then informed them that he had security on board the ship. We gambled that the pirates would leave us alone and wait for an easier, unprotected target to come along.

Later on, the maritime security teams started to be armed. This of course meant that if the pirates ignored all the warnings and decided to take the ship on, the security team could engage them from the bridge wings with high calibre rifles. To the best of my knowledge, no ship with armed security has ever been boarded and captured, which just proves the worth of the service to the shipping companies. The only incident of note that I experienced whilst working on one of these teams on a ship was when I received a call in my cabin from the captain to say that one of our own guys had managed to shoot himself in the face with a flare gun whilst demonstrating it to the crew on the ship's bridge. I grabbed the medical kit, rushed up with another member of our team to find the guy with blood dripping from his wound after somehow accidently firing it into his own face. I managed to clean his wound and put some stitches in him. A little embarrassing for him, but it could have been a lot worse and only his pride was seriously damaged!

Luckily, I didn't suffer from seasickness again, but I was reaching a point where I had had enough of being out on the water. There were only so many sea views and sunsets you can enjoy. Maritime security was not really my thing and I looked at it as more of a gap filler until something more suitable came along.

I received a call from Control Risk Group asking me if I would be interested in a job working for an oil company in Nigeria and the timing was perfect. I went for the interview in London and the job involved working on a drilling vessel that was permanently anchored to the seaboard where they were working. In the past, the ship had been boarded and taken over by Nigerian pirates and several members of the crew had been taken hostage. The company had been tasked with providing a security team and upgrading the physical security measures on the vessel.

I was excited to be getting into Nigeria where I had heard there were opportunities; it seemed to fit in with my recent past experience and was another step in the direction I wanted to take. I was under the impression that I would be a security advisor on this project, so I took the position. When I got there, it turned out that I was on night shift, patrolling the ship and watching over the radar for any suspicious vessels that might come into our exclusion area. Within days I was bored with the job which I felt was well below my ability and experience level and I let the company know what I thought. I got on with the other guys on the team and stayed for the month-long stint that I had signed up to do, but made it clear that I would not be coming back on this particular task. Then CRG called and said that they had another job, which might be more suitable, based in Port Harcourt working for a large, international oil services company security team, which sounded more interesting, so I decided to take it.

During this year, my relationship with Jo deteriorated again. We had moved from Torquay to Poole, a place where I had always wanted to live and Jo was very keen to move to as well. We first rented a place on the Sandbanks where we were both very happy. I had many friends there, but Jo didn't really know anyone and was having difficulties settling into the new environment. I was clearly spending too much time with my old pals, which she understandably disliked, and it caused issues between us. We had purchased a new property and got involved in a big renovation project that had not been going very well due to so many unforeseen problems with the property and mounting costs in a falling market. We began arguing, largely due to the stress this was putting us both under. I was still working away to make ends meet and eventually everything took its toll and we separated. This time Jo and I split up for good and were in the process of getting divorced. I was very sad that our marriage had gone wrong, I loved Jo very much, she was a great girl, but something had to give.

I flew back out to Lagos before travelling on a small light aircraft to Port Harcourt, the largest town in the Rivers State in the Niger Delta. The area is known for its history of kidnappings and violence. The staff of the oil companies based there live in highly secure, self-contained compounds under constant threat from terrorist attacks. I was responsible for one of the company's mobile security teams ensuring the safety of client personnel moving around the local area. We worked with the Nigerian Mobile Police Units known as (MOPOL) who were basically hired out to the oil and gas companies by the government and provided us with an armed escort everywhere we went.

Although this part of Nigeria was fraught with danger, life on the compound was really amazing. Within the walls it was like a small town; the accommodation was great, there was a bar, we could get pizza deliveries and play any number of sports in our time off, with a couple of clay tennis courts at the back of my villa. I worked a six weeks on, three weeks off rotation and I travelled all around the state. I stayed for about a year on this contract and had plenty of time to also work on the security networking events business that I had begun planning and it was starting to get some real traction. However, it was nearing the time when I felt I needed a change again, but this time the decision was made for me.

In our time off, we used to play football with the local Nigerians who worked for the company on a five-a-side pitch in the compound. They were excellent and skillful players who used to run rings around us. Fancying myself as a bit of a player and getting frustrated at being constantly beaten to every ball, I tried to take down a guy, who had been sliding past me all afternoon, with a wayward tackle. It didn't go as planned and, in the process, I managed to go over on my ankle. The pain was incredible and my ankle quickly swelled up like a balloon. I hoped that it was just a simple sprain, which would go down after a few days of rest, but it turned out that I had badly torn some ligaments and required a lengthy recovery period. I was sent home on sick leave to rest up and get some physio and luckily still received sick pay while I thought about what I wanted to do next.

Around the same time and whilst I was recovering from my injury, I began seeing an intriguing and beautiful lady called Dawn, who was a lawyer. I had first met her by chance many months before in a bar on a drunken night out with my mate, Des. I tracked her down through social media, and eventually asked her out on a date. At around the same time, Andy got in touch with me about a new job in Kurdistan. It sounded very interesting and I was up for the challenge. A group of investors who had heard that the Kurdistan region offered the potential for some substantial oil field discoveries had set up a brand-new exploration company. The area they had acquired was in a former war zone covered in mine fields and they needed a security team to check out the area, implement a security plan and protect the workers while they explored for oil over a projected eighteen to twenty-four-month period.

I handed in my notice to CRG, thanked them for the opportunity, and informed them that I would not be coming back. Once my ankle was healed, I agreed to go to Kurdistan for two months to set up the security required and get a back to back organised to come in once I had completed the initial set up phase. I had kept in touch with Trev Reese-Jones who had also been working in Nigeria for CRG and called him up to see if he would be interested in joining me over in Kurdistan as my back to back. He happily agreed and joined my team.

I flew over to Sulaymaniyah in Kurdistan a few weeks later to stay in a luxury villa with five floors that the company had rented for the duration of the contract inside a secure compound that was also used by all the other international oil & gas firms. It was top quality accommodation with our own personal chef. On arrival, I met up with Sig, who had arrived a couple of weeks before me and was the in-country manager, and we discussed how he wanted the plan to be implemented. The company was splashing out money in all directions at this time in an attempt to get set up quickly and to get things

Left: My first full time contract since leaving 1 Para. Wormsley Operations Room, working for John Paul Getty ll.

Below: Fulfilling the Close Protection Officer (CPO) role on the final exercise of my course when I left the military in 1998.

Right: Working with Francis to build some Hesco in Kabul, bit of hard graft is good for the soul, always enjoyed my time with this guy.

Top: European Commission Security Team with the Ambassador and Phil. Great team and Boss.

Middle: The Ambassador was invited along to a traditional Buzkashi, a pleasure to see the skills of these local tribesmen and made me think I was on the Rambo 3 film set.

Bottom: Field trip to the Panjshir Valley, stopped off to take in these amazing views and meet the locals.

Above: Main Supply Route (MSR) between Jordanian border and Baghdad, going past Fallujah.

Right: Another close shave, the crater left by an incoming mortar the previous night, which landed just feet from our portacabin.

Below: With our American landlords discussing the local security situation at Camp Eagle in South Baghdad, Iraq.

Jerusalem 2005

Left: South Sudan 2008.

Right: Kurdistan 2010 with Glenn.

Left: Nigeria 2009 with my driver Victor.

Right: Aspen USA 2009 CP task.

Top: Eating lunch with the Misrata Rebels on the front line with Gaddafi troops in May 2011.

Middle: My Libya Management & Operations Team in our Tripoli villa with the new company T-Shirts straight after the sale had gone through with JGO.

Bottom Right: Tripoli Street in Misrata just after the Rebels had pushed Gaddafi out of the city.

Above: It's not often you get most of your mates all in one place, all of whom I have served or worked with around the world over the last three decades. My Stag night in Cyprus 2015 with Andy E, Carl, Paul, TC, Nobby & Andy S. No need to black the eyes out on this one.

Below: On it in London, the night before we flew to Ibiza in 1992 with my best mates. Des & Stu, only ones missing from the above line up due to work commitments.

moving. We got the vehicles we needed and hired some local Kurdish former Peshmerga army guys who became my security team when moving down to and around the concession block. The area of the oil concession block was located near the Iraq/Iran border. I needed to get down there as soon as I could to check it out and learn the lie of the land. Most importantly, I needed to find out where the mine fields were and have them marked or cleared ready for the start of the seismic phase of the operation which was due to kick off in three months' time. This was when the large vibrator vehicles would fire x-ray beams into the ground in an effort to detect pockets of oil and pinpoint good locations to drill. The group we were working for was a Private Equity firm with a number of investors hopeful for healthy profits from the discovery of oil on this land that they had leased from the Kurdish Regional Government (KRG). It was a big gamble.

The journey to the oil field concession block from our accommodation in Sulaymaniyah took about three hours and so we often stayed in small villages nearby. In order to win the hearts and minds of the local people, the company agreed to fund and build a small medical centre and a road project in a bid to improve the lives of the people in the local area and of course to keep them on side.

It took about eight months of tests and planning before they could go into the drilling phase. They had to test the ground and decide where to drill and a lot of money was invested in the whole procedure. There was a massive sense of optimism and excitement as everyone waited for the first results with high expectations that they would deliver positive results. Word went around and people were buying shares in the company. The results came back from this first drill well and, to everyone's shock and dismay, they were negative.

Suddenly, the company was not so lavish with its spending and money was cut back drastically as the bubble burst. The company replaced Sig as the in-country manager with a cheaper Indian guy who had the remit to cut costs wherever he could. He sacked our medic on the team along with a new guy who was due to come out and join us. Trev and I were not happy; we could see the writing on the wall and decided to get out before things got any worse.

Trev was on a corporate path; his aim was to move up the ladder within large corporate organisations and this was a good stepping-stone towards his goal. I wanted to run my own company and had already laid the groundwork for this next move. We both handed in our notice to Andy who was of course upset as they took the contract away from him and gave it a to a cheaper, local company who promised the earth. As the saying goes, 'If you pay peanuts, you will get monkeys,' and that was quickly proven to be true. It worked out well in the end for us all because the company never found any oil and the whole thing fell apart leaving many people un-paid.

By this time, it was mid-2010 and I returned home to see Dawn in the house we now shared in The New Forest. I had been seeing Dawn on my time off and had fallen deeply in love with this bright, funny, sexy and intelligent woman; she had breathed new life into me, and all was rosy in our garden.

CHAPTER 13

SETTING UP A BUSINESS

During the time that I was working on the private security circuit, I was mostly on shift patterns of some kind with a certain amount of time working in the various locations around the world and a certain amount of time back home. I did various things on my time off including taking on other jobs to pull in some extra cash, as well as more ambitious projects like buying and renovating properties. These renovation projects gave me a huge amount of job satisfaction as they were hard work and I could truly appreciate the toil of my labour, especially at the sight of the finished product. However, I still had my dream of owning my own company. I had met so many interesting and inspiring people on my travels that I had learned so much from and who had lit the fire that was burning strong inside me. I had saved a bit of money and I decided that it was time to start turning my dream into reality.

To kill the hours between shifts whilst on the ship transits around the Gulf of Aden and the Red Sea, I spent a lot of time chatting to the other security guys as we crossed the vast open waters. There wasn't much to do, apart from sleep and eat the endless curries that the Indian chefs knocked up for us. I got to know one of my security team mates, JG, really well. He was a nice guy with a very different background to me; he had worked in the logistics and transport side of the military and he was now running an executive driver service based in London. JG and I began talking about the security world and the mystery still surrounding our business. We began discussing a venture whereby we could offer a greater insight into security work and all it involved.

Situations all across the world were increasing the demand for security personnel, but the reality of getting the work and what you could earn were shrouded in myth. Stories were going around about the vast sums of money you could earn on 'The Circuit' and they were enticing men and women to leave the military for this exciting and better paid work. It was also attracting people with no military training whatsoever. The truth was very different.

Most of the rumours came from guys who had already left telling their mates how successful they had been and how they were earning huge amounts of money when in fact most of them were not earning that much at all or were even struggling to find work. Military pride prevented them from admitting the truth to the guys back in their former units, so they exaggerated a little. The Chinese Whispers spread and guys were leaving the military in their droves in the hope of earning vast fortunes on these lucrative and sexy close protection contracts overseas. Even when I was still in the Paras, back in the late nineties, the rumour mill was in full flow. I remember hearing about one of the guys, who was hugely respected, leaving and earning massive amounts of money as a bodyguard. Allegedly, he was flying around the world on private jets with glamorous Hollywood clients but, when I met him a few years later, it turned out the stories had been hugely exaggerated. In fact, he had been struggling to make a living for a while and had been working on a lot of black-tie events in London on low hourly rates. He had now become disillusioned with the whole industry and was trying to get back into the Paras.

We wanted to help anyone thinking about moving into the security world to understand the pros and cons, to strip back the glamour and deliver the stark reality of this sometimes mysterious industry, warts and all, and answer some important questions for them. How much they could realistically expect to earn? On which of the many courses should they spend their resettlement grants or hard-earned cash? At the same time, we wanted to put them in front of the most reputable security company representatives who were genuinely interested in recruiting. We wanted to somehow let them know exactly what sort of person security companies looked for, what qualifications they required and what the work really involved.

Together, we came up with the idea of setting up a security networking events' company. JG said that he could register the company and manage all the marketing if I took responsibility for getting the speakers and exhibitors on board, and so the plan was hatched. We were eager to get back on dry land and get stuck into this new project and bring it to life.

We both got to work on our various roles and responsibilities and suddenly JG messaged me to say that the website was up and live. I excitedly logged on to check it out and discovered to my horror that there were adverts on there for the likes of hairdressers, shoe shops, tailors and car hire companies; products completely unrelated to the security industry and with no natural link or worth to what we were offering. To me it looked very Mickey Mouse and not what I had in mind, at all. I challenged JG on this, but he disagreed and just wanted to sell space on the site to anyone who would pay at low cost. We started to argue, and the main sticking point was about the style of the website. In my view, we needed to present ourselves as a top-end company, highly professional and clearly in the security industry. I began to get really worried; I had worked hard over the years to build what I hoped was a solid reputation and I felt I was in danger of being associated with something that could damage it forever.

After eliciting the advice of some friends and some very painful soul searching, I informed JG that I was 'out', explaining that I just wasn't comfortable with the direction it was heading. It was a hard decision because I really believed in the whole concept and I was bitterly disappointed. It had seemed like such a great idea with huge potential and I hoped JG would be the perfect partner for me. Sadly though, it was not to be.

The next time I was on leave, I got a call from my mates Carl and Paul saying that they had a business idea that they wanted to run past me. I met them in the local pub in Poole and they began to talk about their idea of setting up a networking event for guys looking to get into the security world. I couldn't believe what I was hearing and kept quiet with my best poker face on as they continued describing almost exactly what I had been trying to do. I was getting more and more wound up and eventually, I could stand it no longer. I burst out with my claim that it was something I had already been working on for ages. They said that they had no idea and continued discussing the idea as if they had just come up with it. After a while, they finally came clean and started laughing. They admitted that they had heard all about it beforehand and were deliberately winding me up; this was typical of both of them, especially Carl and I should have known better and not bitten so easily.

I told them that I had just pulled the plug with JG and explained what had happened. They agreed with my view of the company image, the brand I wanted to portray and how the website should look, and we began to talk seriously about how the idea could be taken forward and brought back to life. We quickly realised that we could work together to make it happen properly. Carl had some really good contacts in the industry and Paul was a natural networker. In the past, we had all worked together out in Iraq and had a real level of trust and friendship between us, plus we all lived in the same area of Bournemouth and Poole, so it was actually a much better fit. The added bonus was that we were all working shifts at this time so we could spend our time off concentrating on the events company, whilst still earning an income in the meantime. This alleviated the normal financial pressure people are under when they first start a new business.

We got going and formed the new company. Security Networking Events Ltd (SNE) was born and we brought in Andy for his business acumen, contacts, and a bit of seed funding. He said that he would be one of our speakers at the event and with his industry contacts, he could bring in some more high-end security business people as well.

We were building an excellent team and we then decided that we needed a chairman, someone of high standing and reputation to give us more credibility and open some doors, which may normally remain closed to us. Carl knew of a Rear Admiral who was already acting as Chairman for another company, but as we would be helpful to them rather than a competitor, we got permission to approach him.

We thought we ought to wine and dine the Admiral, so we took him to a posh wine bar in Fulham. We had a few drinks to calm the nerves at the bar and then sat down at a table with the Admiral at one end and me at the other. We ordered some wine and Carl began by introducing us all, saying that I was the one with the initial idea and the driving force behind the company and told me to take it from there.

I had made a few notes to make sure I covered everything I planned to say and set them down on the table. I was a little nervous and was unsure about how to start. I said, 'Right,' and swept my hand out across the table to get everyone's attention. My hand caught the side of my drink and the entire glass and contents flew down the table. I watched as the ink on my notes dissolved into a blurry, indecipherable splodge and everybody at the table jumped back from the flying wine. My opening words turned out to be, 'Oh shit, sorry!' It was a moment of disaster. However, once everyone got over the initial shock, it actually broke the ice and we all had a good laugh. I then started talking off the top of my head, quite naturally, about how we had got to this point and everything we were planning. The Admiral really liked the idea and he agreed to help us out and get involved as our chairman, which was great news and a huge step in the right direction. He subsequently introduced us to a few people in the city that were able to come along as keynote speakers or sponsors, which was a real boost.

Unfortunately, he was not able to attend our first event due to a clash in his diary, but he did put us in touch with another Rear Admiral, JR who was excellent and did a great job on this and all the subsequent events we held afterwards.

We really began to believe that we could actually pull this off and realised that we now needed to get our act together and fast. We worked hard on the website and got it looking sharp and professional, the way I originally envisaged it, booked The Union Jack Club next to Waterloo station for our venue and began putting our heart and soul into selling tickets and booking speakers and exhibitors.

I was renovating a house at the time with a large double garage that had been converted into an office, so we took that over as our base of operations. We put in a telephone line and bought a huge whiteboard that we used to jot down all our ideas. We created to do lists on the board and ticked them off when each task was completed.

In our search to find ways to contact as many guys from the armed services as possible, we came across the Career Transitional Partnership (CTP), which is a non-profit making organisation attached to the armed forces and aimed at helping those who are leaving to find work and in many cases, second careers. We contacted them and went up to Colchester to meet the man running it. We borrowed Dawn's car as my vehicle had fallen upon hard times and the road tax had expired. Carl realised it was an important meeting, so dressed accordingly. In his best black combat trousers and blue velvet game show jacket, he looked like a cross between Val Doonican and Leslie Crowther.

The CTP guy loved what we were doing and could really see the benefit to the serving men and women with aspirations of getting out of the forces and into the security industry. He even thought it might help with retention and keep a few in the forces once they heard the stark reality of what a hard, dangerous and unreliable living it actually was. Unfortunately, he just could not endorse us because we were a commercial enterprise and would be making some money from the venture, well we hoped we would anyway. This would have been so useful to us, it was very frustrating, but it was not to be.

In complete contrast, we came across a website which supposedly hosted a forum on all things to do with Close Protection (CP). There were lots of guys wanting to get into the industry who were not even from military or police backgrounds thinking they could just rock up, do a quick one week course, receive their certificates, be given an ear piece and a pistol and become Kevin Costner in *The Bodyguard*. There were also a lot of military personnel on the site asking what courses to do. They were being steered by some of the forum moderators towards expensive CP courses, which we knew were not that good and had bad reputations. At this time there were so many people thinking that if they could get out to Iraq or Afghanistan, they could earn their fortune and then retire to sunny Marbella, play golf, and live their days out in comfort. The subscribers were the sort of people we wanted to attract and help, so that we could destroy the myths and give them the reality.

We approached the guy running the forum, who turned out to be an ex-Military Policeman (RMP). These were not our favourite people at the best of times. I had personally had a few issues over the years with the RMPs and their investigative branch the SIB, especially during my time in the Paras, so I was very hesitant when it came to trusting him. He was very anti our company and it wasn't until just before the event that he finally agreed to give us a brief mention in return for a free ticket. On the day, we had organised professional name badges for all the attendees, but he turned up with his own company badge on a sign that was more like a placard across his chest than a professional name badge.

We could only laugh, take a deep breath and let him get on with it. He wasn't the only one taking advantage of those with a huge desire to get work in the so-called lucrative security circuit. We were beginners in the business world, we were learning fast and we were learning the hard way. However, we knew right from wrong, and all of us had great experience actually working in the industry and doing the job at the highest level, unlike these charlatans who are making their money from the vulnerable and ill-informed.

All in all, we had great fun throughout this process, but selling the tickets was very difficult and stressful; we were not natural salesmen and contacting people and trying to flog them tickets did not come easy to us. I sometimes spotted Carl in our office at the crack of dawn, beavering away on his laptop, determined to make some headway and shift those tickets. When he sold one, he was reinvigorated and celebrated. Paul was probably the best at selling, he had rhino thick skin and he sat in the chair leaning back to the point where it was about to topple over with the phone in his right hand, arm wrapped over his head and pushed against his left ear. How he did this I do not know, as he bellowed down the phone in his poshest Yorkshire accent, 'Do you want the ticket or not mate?'

It was tough going, but we got there in the end and through pure tenacity and pigheaded determination we sold over eighty percent of the tickets, which was a great result. Two hundred and forty of the three hundred capacity seats were now taken, a top draw guest speaker line up had been put together along with some quality exhibitors and sponsors coming on board. It was a big achievement, we were very proud of ourselves and rather relieved.

The night before the first event, all of us were on tenter hooks. We were down in the event hall and Carl was going over his opening speech that he was going to read. I don't think I have ever seen him more nervous. I had made notes for the closing words, but decided to just let it flow naturally because there was no way I could read out a prepared speech. I think all of us were out of our comfort zone; we would have been more relaxed through a rocket attack in Iraq than here in front of a crowd of our peers.

The day arrived and we were anxious but ready. The speakers were all highly professional and presented the truth of the industry and what they were looking for clearly and succinctly. Attractive event girls wearing company t-shirts helped with the smooth running of the day that included a morning and afternoon coffee break, a hot buffet lunch, a raffle and a bar that, to avoid any trouble, we didn't open until the end of the day.

Paul was in charge of the raffle and we couldn't have found a better man for that job; he is a natural performer and comedian. With the help of the event girls, it went down a treat, with some great prizes donated by some of the sponsors and exhibitors. We also managed to raise a few quid for our chosen charity, 'Help for Heroes'.

All in all, the first event went really well, actually far better than any of us actually expected. We received some really positive feedback on the day and some great messages afterwards thanking us for what we had done, some saying that after chatting to some of the guest speakers they had managed to get interviews lined up or found a suitable course to do for their resettlement. Positive feedback from our own peers was very important to us and made all the sweat and toil worthwhile.

However, financially it was not so successful. After we totted up all the hidden and unexpected costs and paid all our staff, it turned out that we had made a profit of just a few hundred pounds. We stuck it in our pockets and headed out on the town in London to celebrate. I think the cash lasted about four hours and the last I remember of that night was when the bouncer in the lap-dancing bar we found ourselves in, said that if our friend, being Carl, fell asleep again, he would have to leave. We decided to tie Carl's head up against the bannister using his own tie, where he stayed asleep and we had no more problems after that – not that I can remember anyway! If there had been any cash left over, which there was not, then that would have gone towards Paul's speeding fine on the way home, still a contentious subject today.

We held two more events, but by the end of that, as a collective we had run out of energy. After each event, we came out with a modest profit and it became tradition to spend it in one big night out on the lash. It certainly wasn't enough to live on and Carl and Paul realised that they couldn't put any more time and energy into organising these events. We had had great fun, been on a massive learning curve together, met some interesting people and widened our own personal networks that would come in handy in the future. Most importantly, we managed to actually provide a worthwhile service to our paying customers, which was our primary aim from the beginning. We had cut our teeth in the business world and this was only the start for us all. We went our own separate ways but happily always stayed the greatest of friends. Carl moved on to start a maritime security company of his own and Paul ended up running another maritime company's operations in Fujairah, UAE before starting his own Pest Control business back in the UK.

The following year, Dawn and I worked together, she brought some new energy and ideas to the table and we put on two more events. We changed the format to what we called a round table event. The whole thing was higher end and more niche with the aim of bringing a diverse group of people together from the security sector and giving them quality time at a table to chat and swap ideas. They would repeat this process throughout the evening on different tables with a bit of food and drink thrown in to lighten the atmosphere. These events went down well, but again, we did not make enough money from them to make it a really sustainable business. We learned a huge number of lessons about business during this process and now the time had really come to move on from the events and try to make some real money in the business world.

At the same time that I had been working on the events, I had been travelling back and fore from work in Nigeria and then Kurdistan. I sat down with Dawn to talk about going in a different direction. It made sense to go the whole hog and start working on my own full-time security company. I started to set it up in the UK and then, out of the blue, Dawn received a call from a lady offering her a job in a Dubai law firm. We realised that this was the perfect place for us to establish the new security company. SNE Special Projects was born, we began planning our move to Dubai, and things were about to get busy and very exciting as the next chapter in my life began.

CHAPTER 14

LIBYAN REVOLUTION

In the process of setting up my new business and moving to Dubai in 2011, I got a call from an old friend telling me about an opportunity to work in Libya. I knew that things had been kicking off in the region so I decided to do some research to find out what I would be getting myself into.

In December 2010, a trader in a Tunisian market set fire to himself in protest against the seizing of his stall by government officials. This single act marked the start of an uprising in Tunisia and saw President Ben Ali fly to Saudi Arabia for exile, which in turn sparked off a series of events now known as The Arab Spring. This spread to other countries and President Mubarak in Egypt became the second dictator to succumb to the movement, as the people rose up against repressive dictatorships across North Africa.

The next country was Libya where the protests against the leader, Colonel Muammar Gaddafi were first ignited on 15th February 2011 in Benghazi, capital of the eastern region of Cyrenaica. A human rights lawyer, who had been campaigning for justice for the families of the one thousand dissidents murdered by Gaddafi's men in the 1996 Abu Salim prison massacre, had been detained and crowds had gathered in protest. Benghazi had once been a thriving cosmopolitan city port of wealth and trade, but it had steadily declined under Gaddafi who neglected the city that he saw as a hot bed of his enemies. Two failed assassination attempts upon him had taken place in the region.

The trigger for the uprising in Libya was when security forces opened fire on the protesters, killing fourteen. The next day, a funeral procession for one of those killed passed the Katiba compound, a feared government stronghold in Benghazi, placed there by Gaddafi to keep control of the local population. Clashes between protestors and soldiers in the compound resulted in another twenty-four protestors losing their lives. Protestors subsequently captured two policemen who they deemed responsible for some of these deaths and hanged them in the streets and the police and army personnel withdrew after being overwhelmed. Several army personnel joined the protesters and helped them seize control of the local state-controlled radio station.

In al Bayda and Derna, towns even further east than Benghazi, local police and riot control units joined the protesters. Islamist gunmen, with the help of a defecting army colonel, stormed an arms depot in Derna, seizing weapons and an assortment of military vehicles. Gaddafi quickly lost control of the east, and the Libyan revolution was underway.

It was alleged that at this time, around three hundred mercenaries from southern Africa were flown into Benghazi and other towns in the east to help restore some sort of order, but rebel forces captured and executed many of them. The rebels commandeered bulldozers and armoured military vehicles and attempted to break into the Benghazi Katiba compound, throwing homemade bombs over the walls. Dozens were killed; many were cut down by high calibre anti-aircraft cannon fired directly into the crowd by Gaddafi loyalists. In response, a middle-aged businessman packed his car with gas cylinders and rammed it into the main gates of the Katiba, killing himself in the process of blasting the gates wide open. Hundreds of revolutionaries then stormed into the compound capturing and killing the government troops and essentially ending the hostilities inside Benghazi city limits. The battle for Benghazi was briefly over, but the war for Libya had just begun.

The revolutionary rebels quickly formed the NTC (National Transitional Council) that mainly consisted of former political exiles, dissident politicians and prominent local business leaders. They based themselves in the Tibesti hotel in central Benghazi. Gaddafi's well-armed and organised mechanised forces arrived in the east of the country with the aim of crushing the revolution before it spread across the country and the rebels began to lose ground.

Gaddafi's forces positioned themselves within a few kilometers of Benghazi's two entry points, the western and southern gates and began artillery shelling the city. Shortly afterwards, they simultaneously entered the city with their tanks. Rebel armoured units engaged the initial loyalist armoured column as twelve T72 tanks forged their way into the city, but by mid-morning, it seemed that Benghazi was in danger of falling to pro Gaddafi forces. The rebels commandeered an old, rusting tank and opened fire on the lead Gaddafi tank, damaging it and forcing its occupants to abandon the vehicle. The tanks behind the damaged lead vehicle began to withdraw from the area under rebel fire and retreated back to the city limits. The opposition fighters forced the first wave of loyalist forces out of the city, but Gaddafi's resources were much more powerful than the rebels' and it looked as though thousands would soon be slaughtered.

French fighter jets entered Libyan airspace and flew over Benghazi, conducting aerial reconnaissance missions and waiting for the green light from the United Nations and NATO to intervene. At the last minute, the UN sanctioned a non-resolution decision for Western allies to intervene. The permission came through just in time and coalition intervention began as a French fighter jet fired the first missiles and destroyed several loyalist armoured vehicles. Later, other French fighter jets destroyed at least a dozen other Gaddafi tanks. The international coalition stopped the regime's intended assault on Benghazi; undoubtedly saving many civilian lives in the process.

No matter how precarious the situation looked in the east of Libya, in the west the situation was worse. Gaddafi ordered his elite forces to move into the port city of Misrata, one hundred and forty kilometres from Tripoli. The forces moved in simultaneously from all three sides taking control of all the major intersections and moving snipers into as many high rise abandoned buildings as possible. At this particular time, Misrata was widely considered the most dangerous place on earth and in the midst of the most hard-fought battle of the war.

The Misratians are a proud people with a hard-earned reputation for their strength and entrepreneurism. The people were unhappy about the repression everyone suffered under the Gaddafi dictatorship and it was the home of many lawyers, accountants and successful businessmen. Together they organised and self-funded an uprising against the government forces in Misrata, joining those in the east of Libya in the country's struggle against Gaddafi.

The Battle of Misrata had huge strategic importance as it was Libya's largest major port and earned the reputation of being 'Libya's Stalingrad'. During the siege, the city saw very heavy fighting and came under daily assaults and shelling. The government forces took control of most of the city and port with bombardments that destroyed large sectors of the city and killed many civilians, but again with NATO involvement the revolutionaries drove back the loyalist troops. Rebel forces eventually regained control of the port and the city centre but were fighting the government forces on the three other sides of the city. As they retreated, Gaddafi's forces left the waters around the port heavily mined making it difficult for aid, food, medical supplies and reinforcements to come into the city and technically cutting the city off from the outside world. From the outskirts of Misrata, Gaddafi's troops were still bombarding the city with tanks, artillery, mortars and Grad multiple rocket launchers. As they moved back, they left booby traps and snipers in key positions that were killing men, women and children on a daily basis. Following NATO's initial military intervention in the Libyan civil war on the outskirts of Benghazi, they declared that breaking the encirclement of Misrata was now its top priority.

Over in the east of Libya a vast expanse of desert separated the two sides. The Benghazi rebels were now using technicals, which were modified pickup trucks mounted with anti-aircraft or heavy machine guns, running up and down the road mounting attacks against the Gaddafi troops. However, in Misrata the front line continually changed and was usually marked by the gap between a few houses or a road. This was urban warfare at its most fierce; often the rebels could actually hear the Gaddafi forces talking and smell what they were cooking. Constant brutal clashes were what would ultimately decide the outcome of this battle. It ranks as one of the longest and bloodiest battles of the entire civil war. This was the situation, when I first arrived in Misrata.

CHAPTER 15

BATTLE FOR MISRATA

Misrata was still in the midst of battle when I arrived from Malta by boat into the newly liberated port in late April 2011. I had been put onto an American businessman who I knew from the Iraq days who owned a small specialist international communications company. Gaddafi had closed the whole phone network down once the uprising started and the company had been contracted to work with the rebel forces to take control of the mobile phone network in Misrata so that the various groups could communicate with each other again. My job was to liaise with the rebel commanders on the ground in Misrata and to provide security advice as well as a layer of physical protection for the team of international engineers hired for the job.

These engineers were a mad bunch of 'misfit telecommunication mercenaries' from all over the world with great in-depth knowledge of communication systems. They were prepared to go into hot danger zones such as Libya for thousands of dollars a day to carry out such hazardous tasks as this. They were a unique bunch of individuals, a British guy who lived by choice in Freetown, Sierra Leone, a completely wild and nuts place at the best of times; a couple of old school South African Boers who thrived off the thought of war zones, and a British Muslim who was more wary than the rest put together, but clearly needed the cash. They were supported by a couple of Americans who were running the contract with specialised skill sets as well as the Libyan partner. They were brave, maybe a little foolhardy, but up for going into

Misrata in the midst of the battle to work on the communication network. I was just the nutter agreeing to go with them and provide the security support that could enable them to get the job done.

Some of our team, along with one other security advisor, had been down in Benghazi for the last month doing the same job there, so they understood what they were doing and had a taste of what to expect, even though Misrata was going to be a completely different challenge to Benghazi and far more dangerous. The plan was for me to bring the second half of the team with me by boat from Malta and to meet them in Misrata when they arrived from Benghazi. I made my way to Malta to meet up with the engineers and booked into a hotel before heading down to the port the next morning to confirm the details of the boat taking us to Misrata.

Three days later, it was finally confirmed that the boat had arrived in Malta and we would be able to depart for Libya sometime in the next forty-eight hours, once all the paperwork and arrangements had been confirmed. The boat was a one hundred-foot Italian fishing vessel, which had been rigged especially for this transit and I watched as they lowered an ambulance right onto the middle of the deck, which took up most of the room. Much needed food and medical supplies were then piled up around the ambulance and in almost every other available bit of space on the boat before we got an opportunity to load all our communications equipment into a spare corner that had been put aside for us and finally get on board ourselves.

At the port in Malta, there were dozens of Libyans from all over the world desperate to get to Libya to join the revolution. They were ordinary men in jeans and T-shirts, chain smoking cigarettes and just wanting to get over to Misrata to join their comrades in the fight against Gaddafi. The Captain told the crowd that he had limited space, and after the doctors and nurses were on board, he had capacity to take a just a few of them with us. The Libyans on the dock discussed, in what sounded to me like a typical heated Arabic argument, amongst themselves before deciding who would go and then six more climbed on board with their small bags. The boat was now fully laden; one more packet of fags and it was going to sink.

I gritted my teeth for the twenty-four-hour sea journey that followed, but luckily, the waters stayed smooth and calm. The atmosphere on the boat was incredible; the Libyan revolutionary volunteers were full of high spirits and were so excited about getting the opportunity to go over to fight with their fellow countrymen. They sang evocative Libyan songs all the way, mostly damming Gaddafi who they called 'Majoon', which meant mad in Libyan. It was an amazing feeling being with these guys and as an ex-soldier myself, I admired their bravery. Knowing very well that none of these young guys had any previous military training or experience or fully understood what they were letting themselves in for, I just hoped that they would all survive this adventure they were embarking on and live to tell the tale.

The following morning, Misrata port came into sight and the atmosphere of excitement turned into a nervous, quiet eeriness. We all knew that the waters around the port had been mined and even though the Captain had been informed that NATO dredge ships had now cleared the channel, it was still unnerving. As we drew closer to the port, the lack of people and activity around the dock struck me as strange. We expected at least a small welcoming committee of some sort but there was nobody there; all men of fighting age were of course up on the front lines fighting and supporting their comrades. The whole place was deserted. We slowly headed into dock and it was like entering a post-apocalyptic ghost town, there was not a soul to be seen. In the distance, we could see smoke rising above the city limits and hear the occasional explosion going off, but the port was completely abandoned. The mines in the water and on the land around the port prevented a lot of traffic from coming in, but NATO had done as much as they could to establish a small but safe route in to allow as much aid and as many fighters as possible to get there.

NATO now controlled the air above and around Misrata and government troops had been pushed out of the main city areas, but they still maintained the capability of battering the hell out of the place with rockets and artillery. They had Garratt multi-barrel missile launchers set up, which posed a constant threat and which NATO jets were attempting to locate and neutralize at every opportunity.

NATO were now in essence acting as the rebels' private air force, even though the UN resolution only really permitted them to protect Libya's civilian population from attacks by loyalist troops. However, the hard-pressed rebel leaders were still not happy and wanted more from them. There were many rumours doing the rounds at this time that the rebels were in direct touch with NATO who by now they had nicknamed the 'Storm Gods'. Apparently, a bunch of Libyan Air Force officers based in the Misrata air academy switched sides and quickly become the conduit between the rebel's command and NATO and helped to accurately identify Gaddafi loyalist targets for the NATO jets to attack and destroy. The greatest frustration to the rebels was the slow progress of NATO to identify and destroy the numerous Grad rocket launchers that were still battering the hell out of the city.

Using my satellite phone, I managed to get hold of our contact, one of the leaders of the rebel force, Yousef Ben Yousef, who later became the Mayor of Misrata and an influential figure in the rebuild of the city. For now, he was one of the key rebel leaders and he drove down to the port with a few of his guys to meet us. He took us to a place that used to be the old ministry of communications compound and showed us to our accommodation that turned out to be a decent and comfortable little villa. Over the next couple of days, we sat with him and worked out the plan of action. Yousef also drove us around the parts of the city that were classed as reasonably safe to get our bearings and a feel for what was going on. The streets were mostly deserted, but here and there, we saw women outside cleaning and tidying up. It was totally bizarre. There was destruction everywhere, buildings smashed to pieces, shells of former buildings and rubble everywhere, yet these women were sweeping the roads and painting the curbstones. The majority of the adult population was out on the front lines around the edges of the city, fighting Gaddafi forces, with everything they had. We came across a few supermarkets that were now amazingly back open and entering them felt like being on the set of an episode from *The Walking Dead*. Deserted of people, the shelves in the stores were near on empty apart from a few basics and, oddly enough, masses of tins of tuna. I liked tuna, which was very lucky for me as this was the main filling of every sandwich I ate over the next few weeks.

The revolutionary fighters were ordinary men and women, butchers, bakers, schoolteachers, accountants, lawyers and business owners with no real military training. I took my hat off to them and over the next few weeks I got to know some of them really well and went to the places from which they were operating. They might have been untrained rebels but, if nothing else, they were resourceful, determined and brave. When they captured the first Garratt missile launchers from Gaddafi troops, they had no idea how to operate the high technology pieces of equipment, but they soon worked out how to use them and managed to fire them back at their enemy with precision and skill.

Cal, who I was working with on this task in Misrata, and I, were invited down to the beach one morning by Yousef to see the rebels in action. He clearly wanted to show off their skills and at the same time get our advice on how they could improve. It had been the same with Yousef since we arrived, he was very proud of what the Misratian revolutionaries had achieved over the past couple of months, but still looked to us as former soldiers for acknowledgment of this and for advice, where it could be offered. Even though this was not what we were there to do, we always tried to offer support where we could. After all, these guys had our lives in their hands and we never knew if or when we may need to call on a favour if the momentum of the battle swung against them again and we found ourselves needing some protection or a quick way out of the city.

We arrived at the command post they had set up, strategically located a few hundred meters from the Garratt missile system itself, which was on the beach. It had been captured as the government forces had retreated in a hurry from the old front lines a few days previously. A few kilometers away on the new front line, the rebels had set up an observation post (OP) with eyes on a large warehouse that was being used by the enemy to store armour and ammunition. They worked out how to use the Garratt multi barrelled rocket launcher and using satellite phones they all remained in close contact with one another, pinpointed the target and clearly communicated the exact location of the target in latitude and longitude into the missile system computer. The order then came to fire and shortly after this an almighty burst of fire let loose from the Garratt as six missiles launched into the air and set off on route to their intended target nine kilometres away. I had never seen anything like it; it was an amazing sight. What seemed like an age passed by, then the news came back to them from the observation post that the missiles had not only found, but had also totally destroyed their target. The news was greeted by everyone with loud cheers and shouts of "Allahu Akbar" (God is great) and "Alhamdulillah" (Praise God). I was very impressed. As a trained military mortar man, I knew the difficulty of the set-up procedure and how complex it was to tie together all the required elements for success, the observation post, command team and missile system. To work as one perfectly oiled machine and hit the target with such accuracy was impressive to say the least. I felt great pride in my new friends, they were fighting for their lives and their families' freedom.

A few days later, we got the opportunity to visit the main road in the city called Tripoli Street. It was in the heart of Misrata and where most of the shopping and trading had previously taken place. It had now become the site of bitter street battles; it was the target of many incoming loyalist missiles and NATO airstrikes on Gaddafi tanks who had taken the area over and were hiding from detection under covered ways. The whole area had been devastated.

Buildings that had been there for years were now a mass of shattered ruins, many reduced to a pile of rubble. The once bustling commercial district was now filled with the twisted carcasses of Gaddafi's burned out T72 tanks with turrets blown completely from the main body and armoured personnel carriers ripped open like cans of sardines. The area was still receiving the odd missile fired by loyalist units who were in range and the number of Misratian casualties was very high. We ventured up onto the roofs of some of the remaining buildings with our heavily armed escort and could see milk crates still full of Molotov cocktails (petrol bombs) which the rebels had been throwing down on top of the Gaddafi tanks and infantry units when the battle for Tripoli street was at its most intense.

Gaddafi Snipers had caused havoc after they were sent in on 19th March, picking off civilians and rebels at will, and firing from the roofs of the buildings into civilian populated, rebel held areas. The Tameen office block, the city's tallest building, with a view right across Misrata, was captured after bombardment by rebel forces in late April, just as we arrived. Several loyalist snipers were either killed or captured during this rebel attack. Other buildings nearby were also cleared, leaving the rebels in control of the northern end of Tripoli Street.

Within the city, Gaddafi still had pockets of his elite troops so nobody knew whom they could trust or where they were totally safe and there were still snipers hiding in derelict buildings that the rebels had not cleared properly yet. Stories told that many of these snipers were women, mercenaries Gaddafi brought in from southern Africa and the Eastern Bloc. They were crack shots that hid in the bombed-out buildings trying to pick off key rebel leaders who were located in the area, but often killing innocent civilians. When these snipers were captured, they were killed, and I saw the body of one of them hanging from a lamppost in the street.

Everyone worked together; the sense of community was incredible. Nobody stole from any of the barely stocked supermarkets or from each other, despite the desperateness of the situation and the shortage of food and clean water. The older women cooked huge pots of stew and baked bread that was taken to feed the fighters on the front lines and every night an eighty year-old woman brought a pot of food and bread that she had made to our villa for our evening meal. The local take-away restaurants had all closed, but strangely enough later on a brave, young chef did his bit for the cause by setting up a kitchen, which was within missile range of the loyalist forces, and delivering hundreds of pizzas a day to the fighters on the front lines. It was a proper war effort mentality; a little like in WWII, I would imagine.

It was important for me to check out what medical resources were on hand just in case anything serious happened to my team or the engineers, which Cal or I could not deal with ourselves. We visited the rebels' main hospital, Al Hekma, which had been a private medical clinic before the war and had now become the world's busiest real-life A&E trauma centre. It was a horrendous sight. The whole place was full of injured people and many stricken fighters arrived on the back of pick-up trucks; the blood was running along the corridors, down the steps and into the street. Injured and dying were brought to the entrance of the hospital in ambulances and dropped off outside for the doctors to perform triage under a temporary tarpaulin tent which had been erected to act as the A&E area. Those that they could help were taken in for treatment or to perform surgery on, dependent on the severity of their injuries. I saw the body bags coming out of the back, piling up and waiting to be identified by their relatives before being taken off for burial. It was a surreal and traumatic feeling and really brought home the stark reality of war and the devastation it brings to the entire communities involved. I hoped that none of the guys I met on the ship during our voyage over ended up in this place. This was definitely not what they were expecting when they boarded the vessel in Malta with the dream of fighting alongside their brothers against the Gaddafi regime. However, I have to say that the hospital was extremely well run and the doctors and nurses, some from Italy, Malta and of course Libya, were totally inspirational and never flagged under the immense pressure. However, it was not somewhere I was going to go with any of my team members, unless the situation really got out of hand and no other option remained.

We were there to protect the engineering team and provide a workable environment for them to get their job done. We certainly were not there to soldier. Our responsibility was to ensure the engineers could get the phone system up and running, but the leader of the rebels asked us if we wanted to come out to the front line and see what was really happening. As a former soldier, it was impossible to turn his offer down. After a short and bumpy twenty-minute drive, we arrived at the holding area for the western front line. We were then carefully taken forward on foot to a group of trenches that acted for all intents and purposes as the forward position, with nothing between it and the Gaddafi troops apart from a rough expanse of barren waste ground. The sound of incoming rounds was heard on a couple of occasions as we made our way in and both Cal and I joined our Libyan guides in hitting the deck by the nearest bit of cover, hoping that the rounds didn't land on us. This was a proper front line, a flash back to the first and second world wars as I imagined them and a very small insight into what those fellows went through. We were now with all the fighters and could hear other incoming fire going over our heads towards the city as local women brought in cauldrons of stew for the rebels to eat. We were also hungry by this point and were invited to dig in and share some food; luckily, I had my racing spoon on me and didn't need to be asked twice.

There was no way I could get involved with the fighting, this was the Libyans' war, but while I was there, I came across a group of Libyan rebels who were trying to work out how to use an old French eighty-one millimetre mortar that they had set up. They had no clue how it worked, and I showed them as the battle raged around us. They did not understand how the baseplate needed to be bedded into the ground, so that it was held stable, so I showed them how to do this and how to guide the mortar rounds down the tube, rather than leaving them hanging in the top of the tube and causing misfires. All basic stuff to military mortar men, but these blokes were working on a kebab stand or in an IT shop a few weeks previously and did not possess the level of training or mentality that we had. Amazingly, the rebels were winning and gradually pushing the government troops further back. After lunch, I was invited into their forward OP. I crawled in slowly on my belly, keeping my head as low as I could in case enemy snipers had eyes on this position and I was handed a set of binoculars through which I could clearly see Gaddafi's soldiers, some of whom were only a few hundred metres away, running around like headless chickens in the distance. I could clearly see their faces and did think to myself what damage a section of Parachute Regiment soldiers could do to this lot, or even what I could do on my own with a decent weapon at my disposal like a GPMG and the means to use it.

The rebels appreciated our help, the fact that we were there with them on the front line at a time like this, and clearly loved to see us out there, mixing with them and joining in the banter. However, there was no way I wanted to be seen as a mercenary joining in the war. We were very conscious that there were many western media teams in and around the front line and the last thing we wanted was to get caught on camera and end up on the BBC or CNN looking like we were part of the rebel force, fighting on the front line as mercenaries, with our ugly faces plastered all over the UK papers the next morning.

A few weeks into the contract, the rebel leader moved us from the compound into a boutique hotel called Baraka, where he thought we would be more comfortable now that the city was considered a little safer and virtually clear of government troops. It was a strange experience; the hotel was very new looking without a single war scar on it from what I could see. The building itself had only limited running water and a few hours of electricity per day produced from its one generator, but it was very smart and modern. The furnishings were stylish and comfortable, and we were given an entire floor to ourselves with single occupancy rooms. We soon discovered that the other guests in the hotel were western journalists from networks such as the BBC and CNN with their own security advisors. Marie Colvin, a renowned journalist well known for her uncompromising attitude, eye patch and long blonde hair who was sadly killed in Syria in 2012, was there reporting for the Sunday Times.

Another journalist, Tim Hetherington and photographer Chris Hondros had sadly been killed in Misrata a few weeks prior to this and that had clearly focused the world's attention on the battle. The Misrata leadership was keen that the international journalists continued to report accurately to the world on what was really happening in Misrata and kept it in the news as a hot topic. They wanted them to show the success that the rebels were having against Gaddafi and the atrocities that his troops had carried out against the Misrata population.

During the day, the journalists were out and about with their local fixers reporting on events as they unfolded on the ground and in front-line locations and every evening they broadcast their live reports from the hotel roof with the local mosque or burning and smouldering buildings as the backdrop. I got to know them all well; every evening food was brought into the hotel for us and we all ate together. We stayed in the hotel for the rest of the time that I was there with the war raging in the distance. Every now and again, Gaddafi forces mounted counter attacks or managed to get their artillery or Grad missiles into range to fire a few rounds into the city, but luckily, our hotel was never hit. It was nerve-wracking stuff, but over time, these attacks began to fade away and became less frequent as the revolutionaries began to win the battle of Misrata.

One morning, our driver did not turn up and Yousef explained to us that his brother had been killed the night before on the front line during an incursion by Gaddafi forces. Our hearts dropped as the reality of war struck us again, the sadness of the situation and the fact that there was nothing we could do apart from carry on, get the job done and provide the people with the much needed phone network.

We were on a forty-five to sixty-day mission to support and protect the engineer team while they set up the mobile phone network and to do this, they needed to get to all the cell towers that covered the Misrata area. However, not all of them were located in rebel-controlled areas and were still in sight of and in range of Gaddafi forces, so the engineers climbed the towers at night when they had least chance of being seen. Up they went with minimal light to work on the electronics to connect the system and make whatever adjustments were necessary. These guys were brave and determined to get the job done, whatever it took. The idea was that when everything had been set up correctly, they just flipped a switch and a secure network would be operational and under Misrata revolutionary council control. There were a few issues and false starts, but eventually they were successful; the job was complete and the Misratians had their mobile phone network.

Once the contract was complete, I made my way back to Malta in a fishing trawler with a few of the engineers and we passed more boatloads of Libyans making their way over to Libya to join the fight against the rule of Gaddafi. This time, my journey took thirty-six hours in a much smaller boat and it was a hideous, rough crossing. I felt like I was on a constant fairground roller coaster and ate my pillow the whole way back, trying desperately to catch up on the sleep I had missed over the last few weeks.

On arrival in Malta, I was dropped off at a small jetty. As I had not been stamped out of Malta or into Libya in the beginning, I had no need to go through immigration or customs. It was a weird feeling and as I made my way up the beach, I felt like I was an illegal immigrant sneaking into the country. I was looking forward to getting home now and seeing Dawn. As I sat on the plane the next morning, my thoughts were still with the many new Libyan friends and comrades I had made over the last few weeks back in Misrata, still fighting for their freedom. I knew for sure at this point that I would return soon and going forward, I wanted one way or another to establish my new business properly in Libya.

CHAPTER 16

INTO TRIPOLI

After the contract finished in Misrata, I went home full of ideas about future business opportunities in Libya and how I could build the SNE Special Projects brand. The Misrata contract had come out of the blue, it had all happened so fast and had been so intense. I was so preoccupied with what I was doing in Misrata that I hadn't even had a chance to really think about how I could turn this opportunity into a proper business plan. Once I was back home, I had a real light bulb moment as I quickly realised from my experience of what had happened in Afghanistan and more so in Iraq that there was going to be a huge demand for security services once the revolution was over and I had a very real window of opportunity. Now was the time to get in there; the early bird catches the worm and all that. My plan was to really go for it, build something sustainable, and commit to a long-term business strategy in Libya.

In August 2011, despite vowing to fight on until victory or martyrdom and to purge the streets of the rebels he described as vermin, Gaddafi fled his Tripoli headquarters in the dark of night and effectively disappeared. The hunt for him began while some loyalist troops continued to attack the rebel forces in various parts of the country. The Rebels had momentum and with NATO air superiority on their side, they finally gained control of Tripoli and ransacked Gaddafi's palace, Bab-Al-Azizya, which was later flattened and turned into a marketplace. All over Tripoli, people defaced or destroyed symbols of the dictator who had been in power for over four decades. Tripoli turned very quickly, avoiding a full-on battle and the death and destruction that this would have brought upon its civilian population. Once the people knew Gaddafi had gone, the last of them openly turned against him and Tripoli was officially liberated with a big party in Green Square or Freedom Square, as it quickly became known. Free Libya was born.

Without any contracts lined up, I decided to fly back over to Libya and booked into the Radisson hotel in Tripoli where I knew a number of international businessmen and news teams were based and I picked up some adhoc work with one of the networks. They filmed from the roof of the hotel with a view of the scarred city and the constant sound of gunfire and artillery in the background.

Gaddafi had now been in hiding for nearly two months, but the fighting continued. Tripoli had become a total madhouse, with various armed militia groups all across the city quickly laying stake to as many former Gaddafi luxury villa compounds as they could and enjoying the spoils of war, as they saw it. It was like a scene from a dystopian movie; young, drunk, and often stoned out of their brains, the rebels were out of control, partying or sleeping in these former loyalist areas, all vying for power and money. The battle for control over Tripoli and Libya as a whole had moved into the next phase and Gaddafi had not even been found yet.

On 20th October 2011, I was up on the roof with a journalist when the news started coming in that Gaddafi had been captured and possibly killed. Since his disappearance, he had been constantly on the move with a convoy of hardcore loyalist supporters and the coalition had been desperately trying to track his whereabouts, getting closer and closer each day. They had spotted a large convoy travelling along the coastal road and NATO planes bombed the convoy. The net was closing in on Gaddafi. His vehicles split up, going in different directions but the planes succeeded in destroying a few more of them. Misratian rebels were in close pursuit and were chasing the convoy near the town of Sirte, considered Gaddafi's hometown, although he was in fact of nomadic birth. They knew that he must be nearby as they came across his destroyed vehicles and then began searching the immediate area. They finally discovered Gaddafi hiding in an underground culvert with a few of his loyal supporters. One by one they were dragged out pleading for their lives and subsequently killed. Gaddafi was pulled up last, paraded, filmed and beaten by the enraged gang of militia who had been fighting and tracking him for weeks. Finally, a young relatively unknown Misratian fighter called Ahmed

Muhammad al-Swayib shot Gaddafi in the head and killed him. The liberation of Libya was officially declared, but nobody realised then that the country was about to step into a new phase of mayhem with years of instability and civil war ahead of them. For me, that meant serious business opportunities.

I got to work on creating some marketing material and sent it off to various companies who I believed might have potential interests in Libya. One of those companies, an oil and gas firm got in touch and said that they were very interested in what I was offering. Once back in the UK, Dawn and I went up to London to meet one of the three Libyan brothers who owned the company. We arrived at the swanky address in central London where the driver was outside cleaning the Rolls Royce, and we were taken into a very impressive, oak clad, private office to meet Ahmed. The family was a well-known business family in Libya that had been involved with supporting the Western Mountain rebels during the revolution and was now keen to add a security arm to their business empire.

I instantly got on with Ahmed and I liked the way he talked and did business; we had chemistry and we discussed and agreed upon the foundations of our venture. He liked my ideas, wanted to be my partner and offered to support me in setting up in Tripoli with accommodation, office, vehicles, drivers and the support of their local Libyan network. In return for this, they expected me to use my contacts in the industry to win new international business and then deliver the security support to these potential clients across the country.

The next step was for me to meet Mustafa, another one of the brothers, in a London hotel. Ahmed explained the importance of Mustafa buying into this business plan and said that I had to sell the idea to him. We met with Mustafa a few days later at the Lanesborough hotel on Hyde Park Corner and he took us down to the meeting room where he said there would be a presentation. However, instead of asking me to present the plan, he gave me an overview of his company and what his vision for Libya was. It was abundantly clear that Mustafa had big political aspirations and wanted to be the next Prime Minister of Libya. After he finally finished, we got down to discussing the plan Ahmed and I had come up with and I laid out what we could do and the level of support and finance it would require to get it up and running.

Mustafa quickly lost interest and clearly did not want to invest any money whatsoever into the venture. He could not grasp what it would take to bring this plan to life. He clearly had a very short attention span and I knew that he was ready to walk away as he started to get up from the table. I knew this opportunity might not come again, so took control of the situation and told Mustafa to sit down and listen to what I had to say. I explained the experience I had in this field and how it had worked in Iraq and although a very different situation to Iraq, it could definitely work in Libya given the chance, the opportunity in front of us and with the correct level of backing. I emphasised that now was the time to commit and trust in each other to deliver. Through pure passion, force of personality and the will to not let this fail, I managed to persuade him to back the idea and he even ended up giving me the contract for his own personal security detail, which another outfit based out of London was running at the time. However, in our desperation to get this deal over the line, we did ignore some clear warning signals that the family business finances were not as solid as they made out and certainly did not live up to the image that the swanky house and fancy cars portrayed.

After a painful delay waiting to procure my new visa, off I went again all excited to set up our new business venture with the family in Libya. One of their people met me at the airport and took me to the villa that they had promised for our new base in Tripoli. This turned out to be an unfinished and sparsely furnished villa with a dodgy water and electricity supply based out on the airport road where the family was in the process, before the revolution, of building a new housing estate. Armed only with a weak plug-in Internet dongle for contact with the outside world, I did what I could in the first week to make the villa more habitable and fit for purpose, but it was hard going. Ahmed came down every few days to visit, but his priority was to channel any spare cash they had into getting the houses finished. They were far from being completed, and it was hard work getting any of their time, let alone support or much needed finance.

I told them that I needed a proper set up with resources and I presented them with a new simple to understand business plan, which I had designed to get us up and operational with the bare minimum amount of cash outlay, but they just did not seem to have the appetite or desire to pay for it whatsoever. They said I needed to get the business first, so we had a bit of a chicken and egg scenario going on. I spent a couple of months trying to get work, living off an unsustainable budget, with very little help from them. Although I did get some small jobs in and started to make some good contacts and headway in the relevant prospective client companies, not many were coming back into the country at this time. I returned home for a show down meeting with the brothers and tried to persuade them that I needed more support, but they were still not forthcoming.

From a personal perspective I got on very well with them all and had respect for their situation and more sympathy now that I had been on a couple of field trips with them deep into the southern desert to visit their old oil rig sites. When we arrived, I clearly saw how they had been destroyed during the revolution and looted of anything of any value. Ahmed was in tears at one of these sites and explained that the insurance companies were not going to pay out. The writing was on the wall and I could clearly see that this venture was never going to work. I finally decided to back off when I received a strange call from Mustafa late one night whilst he was in Dubai staying at the Burj Al Arab in his usual suite, courtesy of one of the Sheiks. He asked in a very roundabout way if I could possibly arrange for the capture or assassination of a high ranking relative of Gaddafi who was apparently hiding out in the Libyan desert. It was the most bizarre call I think I have ever received and maybe I heard him wrong. I can only assume he had drunk one glass too many of the expensive Glenfiddich single malt whiskey that he seemed to like and regularly got stuck into, but all the same, it worried me that Mustafa would even think that I would take on such a mission and stupidly say this over a phone line in Dubai. After all, I was a businessman and not a mercenary, let alone an assassin. It was never mentioned again. A few days later, I had a show down meeting with Ahmed to discuss how I was getting on and I stated that I was not happy and didn't think it was working. I thought it was best that we all went our own separate ways. Ahmed was very understanding, and we parted good friends. He said to stay in touch and let him know if I ever needed anything, which I very much appreciated.

While working with them, I met one of their local managers at the oil company and we spent some time talking about what could be done. We got on very well and once I had told the family that I would no longer be in partnership with them, I moved quickly to take AR on as my go to man and notional partner in Libya.

This time it was different and I decided to run things myself rather than have a contract in place with a local Libyan partner. I just worked with AR, paid him a monthly salary and owned, ran and financed the whole venture myself, taking no payments in country and only contracting with clients who paid us directly into our international bank account. It was a risk for sure, as there was now no short term support and I had to use every last penny I had to finance this move, but if it worked out, I would be in a much better position long term. We quickly got ourselves organised, updated the website and began to win a few pieces of work. Our first decent contract was with a British insurance company that needed to send in one of their loss adjustors to check out the damage that had been caused to four different oil refineries during the fighting across Libya.

Around the same time, Des, an old friend of mine from 1 Para and who had worked with me out in Iraq for a while, had arrived in Libya with his girlfriend, who was a journalist working for a non-government organisation (NGO). Des was a real free spirit, he had touched base with me a few weeks earlier and I had arranged a visa for him. He had now travelled into Libya on a whim, just wanting to see what it was like. It was great to have him in town. At the first opportunity, we ordered a crate of lager and a bottle of whisky, which my driver acquired from the Tripoli black market, and sat on the roof. We sat in the dark until we had drunk every drop of alcohol and smoked three or four packets of cheap Libyan cigarettes just reminiscing about the good old days and putting the world to rights. It was great to have my wingman in Libya with me.

I asked Des if he wanted to do the loss adjuster task with me. He did, and we consequently worked together in Libya for the next five years, until he very sadly died of a heart attack when in Bangkok on his time off in 2017. Des was an integral part of my team, always kept my morale up when things were looking grim and told me exactly how it was when I needed a wake-up call. He left behind his two daughters Kaitlin and Kenzie, and his son John. Des was one of the first friends I made when joining 1 Para, our friendship endured time and I still miss him to this day. Reading his eulogy at his funeral at the Garrison Church in Aldershot in front of over two hundred serving and former members of the Parachute Regiment and his family was one of the saddest and proudest moments of my life.

The loss adjuster task started from Benghazi and we drove from Tripoli to Benghazi in one day. It took fourteen hours and we really got a great feel for the dynamics and geography of the country. We were some of the first western security guys to go down there since Gaddafi's death and found it to be a very welcoming and friendly place. We picked the client up two days later on his arrival at Benina Airport and then set off on task with a two-vehicle team: AR, a driver from Tripoli, two guys from Benghazi, Des and myself. The job was great and took a couple of weeks as we drove right across the country and spent a few days at each refinery to allow the loss adjustor to inspect and write his preliminary reports.

We met lots of new, interesting people in the time we spent in the various areas. In Benghazi, I made many new contacts which would prove to be essential in the next phase of my plan, and in Misrata I consolidated relationships with people that I had met in my time there during the war, earlier in the year. We drove right across the country and back to Tripoli gaining some great knowledge of the lay of the land and, most importantly at that point, finally earning some money. Dawn and I were completely broke; we were only just surviving in Dubai, living in a friend's apartment and didn't even have a car. When that first invoice payment went in, Dawn went straight out and rented a car. It was a huge relief to finally have some money and to see my dream of having my own company starting to materialise.

CHAPTER 17

BENGHAZI

Back in Tripoli, I discovered that one of the large German international power generation companies was moving back into Libya. The security manager, who I had known for a long time and had worked with in Baghdad, was now in Tripoli heading up their regional security department based in Dubai. I got in touch with him to organize a meeting, but unfortunately for me, he had just taken out a new contract with a large Canadian owned security firm. They were working in Tripoli but had nothing set up in Benghazi at this time. I told him that I had just returned from Benghazi and had excellent connections in the east of Libya. I asked him to keep us in mind if they ever required any support in that region.

A week later, he called me to say that he had a team going to Benghazi to do a short survey on a power station. He told me that if I could prove that I could support his team with the required level of security and vehicle support, then he would give me the work.

We provided the level of satisfaction they needed, I got the job and we went down to Benghazi with the client team and stayed in a local hotel, which we recommended, and looked after them while they did their survey on Benghazi North Power Station. We received very positive feedback from the trip. The engineer team, mostly from Germany, was quite rightly sceptical about working so far east and in Benghazi, which was not really considered a safe and secure area yet. Des and I made sure that the engineers were well looked after, came away with a positive experience and most importantly, that they were happy to recommend that the longer maintenance contract on two of their turbines could take place. Soon afterwards, I was offered the contract protecting their main team working on the two-month contract and I was asked to supply a five-vehicle team consisting of a number of Libyans and two British Project Security Managers. These were, of course, Des and me. After that, the work just seemed to snowball. Initially, I borrowed some money from a friend to tide me over and bridge the gap between having the finance I required to support these contracts and the client paying us. We finally received the first big paycheck from the Germans and after paying back what I owed, we suddenly had money in the bank. Things were really starting to look good and our reputation was building.

We got a lot more work in Benghazi from other companies as well as the Germans, who by now had become our main and most important client in Libya, and we became known in the area as the Benghazi Kings. Clients started to come to us on recommendation and SNE Special Projects, which became known as just SNE, got some good traction as a reputable company that produced high quality results. At this point, it was all about the guys we used. We were small and could cherry pick the blokes we wanted to employ and pay them decent money. More importantly, I could oversee and run everything myself and make sure that the quality and personal touch was always there. Some of our larger more well-known competitors did not have this and were just run in country by employees who, with all the will in the world, would never put as much effort and passion into the business as a person like me who owned and ran their own company.

The country as a whole was still in total turmoil as different factions started to emerge with strong feelings about the power share of the country and who should have control in the new transitional government. Everywhere we went, there were rogue militias in villa compounds and former government buildings. There was a history of extreme Islamist and Al Qaeda influence in certain areas of Libya, mostly in the east, in and around the town of Derna and they posed a huge threat to Westerners along with a large number of rebels groups now with too much time on their hands and a lot of weaponry at their disposal. They sat around in compounds drinking heavily and shooting randomly in the air; regular skirmishes took place with other groups as the alcohol kicked in late each night. The country was out of control, in chaos; there were no reliable communication systems, no functional hospitals and moving around the place was difficult and dangerous.

With so much work in Benghazi, it was time to take the next step and set up a permanent office in the city to oversee and manage the running of all our contracts in the east of Libya. We found, rented and set up a good, discreet, three-bedroom, ground floor apartment in Benghazi with plenty of parking space. It had a few rooms that clients could rent from us and we hired a local Libyan manager, Nasser who ran it for us. Nasser had contacted me via LinkedIn at just the right time and proved to be an excellent addition to our team.

Back in Tripoli, we were also trying to win new contracts and compete with GW and CRG, so we rented a small apartment there as well and hired a couple of locals to work for us. The security manager for the client company had now moved back to his Dubai head office and had brought in a new British guy to run all the operations in Libya. He was quite a temperamental and strange character. One week he was happy with our competitor and gave them all his work, then they did something to upset him, and he called me to his office, openly ran the competitor down and then offered me all the work they had coming up over the next month or so. Then he swung back the other way without rhyme or reason. The funny thing was both the competitors and I usually got on okay, and we all laughed a little at how he and his new back to back did things, trying to play us off against each other, but we got used to their childish methods. At the end of the day, the Germans were tier one clients and had become key to our business within Libya. We were proud of our work and knew that we had always provided a great service and gone the extra mile for them, even if it wasn't recognised by those in the decision-making positions. I just had to suck up their churlishness and get on with delivering the best possible service we could, as and when we were in favour.

A friend in the UAE asked me to carry out a personal protection task for a former female American diplomat and prominent member of George Bush Jr.'s Whitehouse staff. In her new life, she now represented US businesses abroad and was travelling to Tripoli to meet with some prominent local businessmen, as well as Libyan government officials and the US Ambassador, J. Christopher Stevens. It was a very big deal for her to be going to Libya and so I was contracted to personally look after her during her visit. I met her at Tripoli International Airport and on the way to the hotel we were staying at during her trip, I gave her a quick briefing on the current security climate in Tripoli and Libya as a whole. I explained who I was and what she could expect from me during her stay. She spent a lot of time at the American embassy meeting with Ambassador Stevens and during this time, I had the opportunity to meet and spend some time with the Ambassador's personal security team.

One evening, she had an appointment to meet with the Libyan Intelligence Chief along with Ambassador Stevens for dinner. The Intelligence Chief had invited them to meet in a small, backstreet restaurant in Tripoli old town where he had arranged a private dinner for the three of them. We arrived just after the Ambassador's security team and I took her into the restaurant through a private side door and escorted her to the bottom of the stairs where I was stopped by one of the Intelligence Chief's bodyguards. They were having their private meeting upstairs over dinner and no one was allowed up there with them.

I sat down with the two US security guys at the bottom of the stairs and exchanged pleasantries. The Intelligence Chief had the nickname of Finger Cruncher, which I am reliably told was due to a technique he had used fairly regularly to obtain information from poor souls who happened to end up in front of him.

Finger Cruncher had four security guys downstairs with us; two more were upstairs, and a few more guys were outside in vehicles monitoring the local area. They were all older guys with stern, hard, unsmiling faces, unlike most Libyans I had met in the past, who were very friendly in general. They were all wearing long trench coats with huge bulges barely disguising the MP5Ks and pistols they were carrying underneath their coats. It was a weird, tense scenario and I felt as though I was in a scene from a Hollywood thriller movie.

The four-day trip went well and the lady seemed very happy on the way back to the airport the next afternoon. I escorted her through immigration and onto the plane and let her office know that it was wheels up on the plane and the Principal was on her way home.

I got on well with the US security guys, and we agreed to stay in touch. I thought that they could be very handy friends to have in this environment; you never know when you may need a favour from our US cousins. Just a couple of weeks after this job finished, I received a call out of the blue, in the early hours of the morning of 12th September 2012 from the Sky News' chief foreign correspondent who I had had dealings with in the past. He was calling to ask me what I knew about what had happened to Ambassador Stevens. He had heard that he'd been injured in an attack on the embassy in Benghazi. I was in Tripoli at the time and had no idea what he was talking about, as the news had not reached us yet. He was ringing me in the hope of more information and although I knew some of Ambassador Stevens' security team, I didn't feel as though it was right for me to call them. If something had actually happened, they would be busy dealing with it. I decided in the end to send a text message to one of the guys, just saying that we had some local guys in Benghazi and if they required any support to just let me know. I never heard back.

The correspondent called me back a little later to tell me that it was being reported that the ambassador had been killed, along with three of his security guys. It turned out that two of these guys were from the CIA Annex located nearby and had been killed in a separate attack. He asked me if I would be willing to let him interview me over Skype for a Sky News TV report. I knew it would probably be great publicity for my company, but at the same time, I didn't particularly want to become a high-profile personality on TV. I certainly did not want to be one of those people who appeared on TV from the country where something had happened, but not in the actual area they were talking about and ended up talking about conjecture and speculation, rather than fact. I was also worried that I would say the wrong thing, mess it up and make myself look an arse, which was always a possibility!

I discovered that the shocking and upsetting Benghazi attacks were said to be a coordinated attack by members of the Islamic militant group Ansar al-Sharia. They had attacked the American embassy in Benghazi and Ambassador Stevens became the first U.S. ambassador to be killed in the line of duty since 1979. U.S Foreign Service Information Management Officer, Sean Smith was also killed in the attack. In the early hours of the following morning, the group had launched another attack against a CIA annex about a mile away, killing Tyrone S. Woods and Glen Doherty, and wounding ten others.

At first, the CIA was under the impression that a protest had got out of hand leading to the embassy attack, but further investigations showed that the attack was planned, although rioters and looters may have joined in later. The U.S. filed criminal charges against several individuals alleged to have been involved in both the attacks, including Ahmed Abu Khattala, the Benghazi leader of Ansar al-Sharia. Later, in January 2014, the U.S. Department of State designated Ansar al-Sharia as a terrorist organization and U.S. Army Special Operations Forces eventually captured Khattala in Libya.

After that terrible event, things really changed; it left a rotten feeling in my stomach, a feeling of disgust, fright, and distrust. Overnight, diplomats left the country, international businesses thought twice about entering or investing in Libya and the Ansar al Sharia had clearly made their mark. From this moment on, business was even more difficult than before, but we had to be prepared for all the ups and downs that Libya presented to our fledgling company.

CHAPTER 18

LIBYA STRUGGLE CONTINUES

Following the model that we used in Iraq, I decided it was now time to set up a proper high-quality villa and operations centre in Tripoli, which would be SNE's flagship base in Libya. This time however, I did things a little differently. First, we had to find a suitable villa in a decent area with good access routes to the airports and the city centre. An old Misratian contact had a place that fitted the bill in the Hai Andalous district of Tripoli; it was discreet looking from the outside with plenty of space inside. With the current instability in all areas, hotels were not necessarily safe anymore and so I decided to rent out rooms in the villa for clients to live in and work from, for the short or long term. We kitted the bedrooms out with new fitted wardrobes, desks and comfy chairs and set up some offices. I brought in a Ugandan chef who cooked three high quality meals per day and a cleaner who provided a daily laundry and ironing service. They were both introduced and recommended to us by the local church Pastor and his wife Veronica. We then went about setting up the villa like a small high-end boutique hotel, whilst the security team lived down in the basement or in the roof top room. This way we could provide a safe and comfortable environment for our clients in the main living area. The villa soon started to fill up, so we converted part of the basement into a new large operations centre and meeting room to free up more space upstairs for client offices.

Dawn flew over from Dubai for her first and only trip into Libya just after I secured the villa and things in Tripoli were fairly stable. Dawn was pretty robust and had a real eye for detail. She spent three weeks with me, and we were able to send her out with one of our local drivers around town to buy soft furnishings and other items she required for the villa. Dawn managed to transform the villa into a modern, attractive and inviting place to stay for our international clients.

Together, Dawn and I got the chance to visit a few of the local sites. One of these was the famous and spectacular ancient city of Sabratha. It was a lovely day and we walked around the incredible Roman Amphitheatre and through the remains of the ancient settlement that led down to the stunning coastline. In such peaceful and picturesque surroundings, it was hard to imagine the hostilities that were raging across the country but as a stark reminder of the dangers of where we were, just a few weeks later, two expats were found murdered on the beach, right next to where we had been.

Dawn met AR's wife and his mother at his home and I was also planning to take her with me to Benghazi to meet Nasser and his family, but trouble broke out in the east and the airport in Benghazi was looking like it may close. Des took Dawn back to Tripoli airport whilst I was out on a task in Misrata and she headed back home to Dubai to run our office there. It had been a great experience for Dawn and I had loved having her there with me. It also provided her with an invaluable feeling of what it was like to live and work in Libya and gave her a distinct advantage and level of respect when talking to our clients about life in Libya.

Even though the number of international companies now heading back into Libya was a lot less than we had anticipated or hoped for by this point in the plan, SNE as a company was doing really well and we had established a good loyal client base who were keeping us busy and profitable. I had gone on a business development trip to Washington DC a few months earlier and had picked up work from a few American NGOs whilst there. They were proving to be great clients; guys and girls who we all really enjoyed working with and who were now providing us with lots of repeat business and long-term contracted work.

In early 2014, I made one of my regular trips down to Benghazi to see Nasser and this time we also visited one of our power station projects an hour and a half away to the west of Benghazi, just outside a town called Ajdabiya. We needed to leave the city via the Western Gate checkpoint in order to get to the power station to catch up with my project manager and have a chat with the client representatives; it was just the usual face time which kept them happy and showed that I cared about them. All went well and after three hours at the site we headed back to Benghazi, making sure we left enough time to arrive back before last light. Like anywhere in the world, once the sun goes down, the bad guys tend to come out to play. As we neared the Western Gate checkpoint, we could see that something was going on and the traffic was a lot heavier and moving slower than normal, far slower than when we passed through it a few hours earlier on the way out. We couldn't work out what was happening and we were now stuck in a queue of slow moving, heavy traffic. We gradually moved forward to where the checkpoint area began and suddenly realised that the black flag of Al Qaeda was now flying on the main building and on the heavily armed technicals now parked around the checkpoint and to our flanks. The black standards with the white shahada written on them fluttered in the breeze and my heart rate moved up a few notches as I looked at Nasser and realised there was no way of turning around, we were boxed in and we were committed to going through the checkpoint.

While we were out of the city, Ansar al Sharia, an off shoot of Al Qaeda in Libya and those responsible for the murder of US Ambassador Stevens in 2012 had moved in and taken the checkpoint over from the Libyan National Army (LNA). There had been very little resistance as this aggressive and ballsy move took everyone totally by surprise.

We edged closer to the gate and as we drove forward, a scary looking guy, armed with an AK47 and wearing a long Islamic beard synonymous with Al Qaeda put his hand up to stop us. He gestured for us to slow down and as we stopped next to him, he was momentarily distracted by one of his comrades, so he did not fully look into our vehicle, at us. Nasser was of course a Libyan guy, born and bred in Benghazi, but he was a liberal and was clean-shaven. I was sitting next to him in the passenger seat with a short beard, a shemagh around my neck, and sunglasses on, desperately trying to look as inconspicuous as possible. Luckily for me, I've always had a Mediterranean look and blended in reasonably well in these types of environments. As our bearded Al Qaeda friend glanced away to find out what his mate had said, Nasser stepped gently on the gas and started to move past him. I saw the guy quickly glance back at us and do a double take, as he looked straight at me. Either he was not sure if he could believe what he had seen, or he just did not want to look like an idiot having let a western expat through his check area, but either way, we got past. Nasser kept our vehicle moving, there was no way we were sitting still long enough for them to realise that it was a westerner sitting in the passenger seat. He put his foot down and accelerated through the checkpoint and drove quickly away and into the city. I breathed a huge sigh of relief. For sure, if they had realised straight away that I was British and subsequently that I was a former soldier, they would have taken me, and this story may well have had a different ending. It was another close shave for me, and not the sort of position I ever liked to find myself in; I had very little control over what was going on and I was just hoping for the best.

This was the start of another battle to get rid of Ansar al Sharia from Benghazi. We got back into the city centre and broke the news to our teams and clients in the east and west of Libya. A new battle for Benghazi had begun, and I was to witness the destruction and desolation of large parts of this ancient city as the different factions fought it out over the next few months and years.

The power struggle for Tripoli had been gradually building and bubbling away under the surface for a few months. July 2014 saw Misrata make their long-anticipated move to seize power from Zintan and gain control of the country's capital. Hundreds of families were forced to flee neighborhoods around Tripoli international airport as the fighting intensified in the fiercest battle since the 2011 revolution.

From our roof in our Hai Andalous villa, we witnessed the tank shells, rockets and artillery raining down on the airport and surrounding districts as the Misratians fought the Zintanis, who had been in control of the airport since the revolution.

Many of the commercial airline planes, which had been stranded on the runway and near the terminal building, were left damaged or on fire, and some missiles had even hit the apartment blocks in nearby areas. Clouds of smoke rose from the airport as the battle spread into the western districts and, across the city, the noise of artillery and ground-to-ground Grad rockets could be heard.

The two warring militias were two of the most powerful groups in the country that had toppled Muammar Gaddafi in the 2011 revolution. Zintan is ninety miles southwest of the capital, and the people were known as the Hill Billies of Libya. Misrata, one hundred and forty miles east of Tripoli, had accused Zintan of holding the airport illegally and had aspired to control it themselves since the start of the conflict. I, of course, knew the Misratians well and had a deep affiliation and great respect for them. In my opinion, they were a far better option for bringing some much-needed stability to the capital than the Zintanis, who only seemed interested in partying or getting what they could from the situation by hook or by crook.

A week or so into this fight the casualty rate was rising and much of the airport was now in ruins, with at least thirteen planes destroyed or damaged and all flights into Libya now suspended. The fighting was part of a wider struggle between a loose coalition of Islamist-led militias and an equally loose coalition of nationalists. Both sides were also battling in Benghazi, the eastern capital. In-fighting between nationalists from General Khalifa Haftar's Libyan National Army (LNA) and the Islamist Al Qaeda orientated brigades left more than two hundred dead.

Misrata had overwhelming power in the end and pushed Zintan out of the airport and Tripoli as a whole and back to their homeland up in the western mountains. The reign of Misrata had started and was to go on well past my time in Libya.

Once this battle was over and Misrata had taken control of Tripoli International Airport (TIA), I was lucky enough to have the opportunity to be one of the first expats to get into TIA to support a British loss adjuster who had to carry out a survey on some of the damaged planes and helicopters. I was excited to see what the actual extent of the damage was, as rumours had been flying around for a while about how severe it had been. One of the local reps from Libyan Insurance took us in and showed us around. He did talk about the possibility of getting into a few of the planes to see the extent of the damage, but I warned him that I had chatted with some of the UK Special Forces guys based in the area. They had told me that Zintan had booby-trapped a few of the planes and some of the entrances to key airport buildings before they vacated the airport. They said it would be wise to stay well away from these areas for now and also to be very careful about unexploded ordnance (UXO) such as rocket and mortar rounds which had landed and not exploded and if tampered with, could go off at any time. We saw a huge amount of UXO all over the place, mortar rounds sticking out of the soft ground in and around the runway and nearly all the planes had some sort of damage, shrapnel holes in the fuselage or entire tails missing. Sadly, all the helicopters apart from one had been totally burned out and even the surviving chopper had damage to its rotor blades.

On our direct advice during the lead up to this battle, which many had been predicting for some time, many of our clients had taken what flights they could out of Libya. However, once the fighting started, several of them who had not departed yet found themselves unable to get out and needed to be locked down with us at our villa. We collected and congregated those requiring support and held them with us until we knew it was safe to travel by vehicle convoy to the border crossing point into Tunisia at Ras Jdair. We crossed with them and took them to safety in Djerba or the capital, Tunis.

We carried out several of these land evacuations over the next few years. The international airport never opened again. Every time General Haftar made threats and moves towards Tripoli, the international companies would quite rightly get jittery and look to pull their staff out of the country. If the temporary Mitiga airport closed, which happened on several occasions due to bombs landing in and around the perimeter, then land moves became the last option.

After one bombing raid on Mitiga airport, they tried to blame the Egyptians who they said were in league with General Haftar and to prove this claim they produced an Identification card (ID) of one of the Egyptian pilots who they said had dropped it as he flew over the airport and had been found on the runway. Whether the Egyptian air force was involved or not, I could not say for sure, what I am pretty sure about is that they don't have open cockpits anymore and certainly would not drop their ID cards as they flew over. This summed up the Libyan mentality for me and the tit for tat conflict in which they were involved.

In January 2015, Islamist terrorist groups such as Islamic State (IS) began to really make their presence known in Libya and they were becoming a real threat as they spread across from Iraq and Syria. One of the clients that SNE was supporting at the time was a large American NGO. We provided them with a security manager called Richie who was living in the NGO villa that was just down the road from our place.

There were two major hotels in Tripoli at the time that were geared up for hosting conferences, the Radisson and the Corinthia, where most foreign officials and government workers tended to stay when in Tripoli. The Corinthia Hotel was holding an exhibition and early on the morning of 27 January, Richie was making his way to the hotel with some of the NGO clients. He was running late because one of the clients had been delayed and they left twenty minutes or so later than scheduled. On route, he received a call telling him that shots had been fired at the hotel. He pulled the vehicle over in a safe area and began making enquiries.

Members of the Islamic State (IS) detonated an IED in the car park of the hotel and then in the chaos, five terrorist gunmen killed the hotel security guards and ran inside the hotel shooting at random and killing innocent guests.

Security forces secured the outside of the building leading to a drawn-out hostage situation. Richie took a call from one of the NGO's local Libyan employees who was actually in the hotel whilst the incident was ongoing. He was speaking to Richie from a hiding position under the stairs as the gunmen ran amok shooting at anybody and everybody in the building. Richie passed this information onto us in the SNE Tripoli operations centre and we then disseminated it to all the other security companies and client organisations we knew, telling them what was happening and warning them to stay away from the hotel.

Sadly, five expats died in the attack, one American, one Frenchman, and three Tajiks. The American, David Berry, was working as a contractor for an American security firm. Five Libyan security personnel were also reported to have died in the attack. If Richie had not been delayed, he and his clients would have been in the hotel when the attack took place. This is an example of the fine margins we dealt with on a day to day basis in Libya at this time.

Members of the Islamic State "Tripoli Province", who are believed to have been natives of Libya, took responsibility for the attack. They stated their objective was revenge for the death of Abu Anas al Libi, a Libyan Al-Qaeda operative who was involved in the bombing of two American embassies in 1998. He was captured by American Special Forces inside Libya in 2013 and had died in an American hospital a few weeks earlier.

Every incident that occurred in Libya, especially in Tripoli, had a knock-on effect on the local economy and international business in the country. After the Corinthia hotel attack, business slowed down again, many companies pulled their international staff out or stopped new ones from coming in. It seemed every time we built up any momentum, something would happen to derail it. These were the risks of operating in turbulent countries such as Libya.

A few months later, while taking a few days off in Cyprus with Dawn, I received a call from one of my trusted guys in Tripoli telling me that he thought my Libyan partner AR was up to no good. He told me that he thought he was in cahoots with Ben, an English guy who had worked for me for some time; I totally trusted both of them. I did a bit of digging around and spoke to a few people I knew and found out that both of them had been seen having a meeting with a client representative of mine and we suspected that they were trying to form a breakaway business and steal this contract as their method of startup. Unfortunately, it was an all too common story in this industry of jealousy and blind ambition getting the better of professionalism, integrity and loyalty.

I jumped on a plane and flew straight over to Tripoli to sort it out. Ben had gone home on leave, so sacking him was a no brainer and no loss at all, even though I would rather have done it face to face. However, AR was another story altogether. It was a real shame and a huge blow as he had been with me from the very start. I considered him a good friend and both our families were very close. He was also a key element to my operations in Libya and my link to the local staff. AR did not know I was coming over and his face was a real picture of guilt when he walked into the meeting room to see me standing there. I sat him down, told him that I knew what he had been up to with Ben, and asked him to explain himself. AR was such a nice guy and he was so embarrassed and apologetic. Very typical Libyan behaviour. However, the trust was gone, and you can't get it back, so we agreed a deal to go our separate ways and that was the end of that.

I quickly moved to promote Nasser, who was my Eastern Libya manager, to be my Libyan partner. I had always liked and respected Nasser and knew how intelligent he was, actually far more switched on than AR and his English was much better, so all in all it turned out well. Nasser proved to be a great business partner and stayed with me until the end. AR went his own way, he attempted to set something up and running with another group of international guys, but it never got off the ground due to the turbulence in the country at the time. I kept hold of the client they attempted to steal and my original idea of controlling my destiny and holding all the cards rather than share in the traditional way with a Libyan partner proved to be the best move I ever made. Splitting with AR was much easier than it would have been otherwise.

Libya remained extremely volatile and we were involved in several client evacuations during our time operating in the country. Tripoli seemed to be under the never-ending shadow of General Haftar's threats to seize power from the east, and this had a negative effect on big, international business coming back into the country. However, throughout this period, we somehow managed to forge great relationships with several key clients and were successful in winning more than our fair share of any new business coming into Libya. We were proving to be a real success, built from nothing and against all the odds. It was something I was very proud of indeed.

IS were starting to grow in power in the east of Libya and there was a lot of talk about them attempting to gain a foothold in the Sirte area to form a caliphate. The international community and good Libyan people were certainly not going to sit back and allow this to happen. After forty-two years of Gaddafi tyranny, they didn't want to just swap it for a so-called Islamic State of brainwashing and manipulation. A ground offensive mainly led by the Misratian revolutionary groups was underway, backed by western air assaults. The troubles were far from over for the people of Libya.

CHAPTER 19

END OF THE ROAD

In 2014, word got around that I was open to selling my business and I got a call from Dale, the owner of another security company based in Iraq. I first met Dale in Iraq in 2003 and he had supported our team when we came under attack in Baghdad. We got on well and had a similar way of looking at things. I knew what he was like and how he operated and I was excited to hear what he had to say. Dale had recently sold the majority of his own company to a group of American investors based in Texas, who now wanted to build their operational capacity. Buying SNE was a way of getting into the Libyan market. We agreed to meet in Dubai to chat over the possible opportunity.

In the past, I had been approached indirectly by one of my larger competitors to find out if I was interested in selling. I saw it as a compliment when someone looked at my company in this way, however, that deal never got off the ground as they were looking to buy SNE predominately to remove us as a competitor in Libya. If I was ever to sell, I wanted to stay on as part of a close-knit team taking the project forward.

Dale and I met in the Marina Mall in Dubai and he explained what he had done with the Texan investors, what sort of guys they were, and that his plan now was to expand across the region. I laid out what sort of deal I would be looking for, if I were to sell, and left it with Dale to broker the subject at his next board meeting and see where it went.

His next meeting with the Texans was a few weeks later, and apparently, some of them were on side with the concept of the acquisition of SNE but one or two were more sceptical and required further information and persuasion. I armed Dale with some figures and a future forecast before he flew over to meet them. During this meeting when the Libya conversation was raised, one of the Texans read off his Blackberry that Tripoli Mitiga airport had been bombed the day before by General Haftar's Libyan National Army forces and that Tripoli was in lockdown again. This sent a wave of uncertainty through the room and it was eventually decided not to pursue the potential acquisition at that time and to revisit it at a future date once things in Libya had stabilised.

The deal was now off the table. This was disappointing news and Dale assured me that we would stay in touch and speak again when the time was right. I quickly got back to business and put it out of my mind. We had a great little company that was making good money with excellent profit margins and a loyal, growing client base. I knew very well that the bombing of Mitiga airport and the constant flare-ups between the various power groups was just part of life in Libya. Any potential buyer would have to understand this and be willing to accept the risks that came with operating in a country such as Libya along with all the great business potential that came with it.

A year later, Dale got in touch again and explained that his situation had changed and that he had now been bought out again by a larger already established American Security and Demining Company called Stirling. The Texans had sold all their shares and made a tidy profit. Dale had moved over as part of the deal and he was now their new Vice President of Commercial Business. He also had the ability and support behind him to push his original plan forward to buy SNE and amalgamate us into the new company setup. The plan was to build a large, powerful company with the capability of operating in all the various sectors of the security market and mutually support each other in this aim. It was an exciting idea, and if run properly with the correct people involved steering the ship, it would place us at the top end of the security market sector and enable us to compete with the big players in the industry at that time like GW, CRG, Constellis and G4S. It was something with which I was keen to be involved and wanted to hear more.

We set up a meeting with some of Dale's guys in Dubai to get the initial paperwork moving and then made arrangements for me to fly over to the US to give a presentation to the Stirling Senior Leadership Team (SLT).

I flew the fourteen hours from Dubai to Washington DC, and then caught an internal flight down into Knoxville in deepest Tennessee, followed by an hour taxi ride to a small motel in Lenoir City. This was close to where Stirling had their home office and more importantly it was where all their senior leadership team lived. It was an idyllic little place to live, very green with some beautiful lakes. I could instantly see why they liked living and working from there. They did have a corporate office in Washington DC for business purposes, but this was where the real decisions were made.

The plan was that I would meet them at their office the next morning at nine and give them a presentation on SNE. I had spent the last week preparing an in-depth, informative and, hopefully, interesting power point presentation. Dale had forewarned me about a guy who had presented to them a few months before who had bored the pants off them. I wanted to hit the right notes and get the relevant info over to them in the two hours I had allotted to me. Figures were, of course, the key to selling a business, and we genuinely had excellent figures for the past few years, which showed year on year continuous growth, and our forecast for 2016 was encouraging. I had to make sure that I covered all this at the end of the presentation and left them with an upbeat and positive feeling in their minds.

I got up early the next morning, ironed my shirt and put on my smartest suit to make a good first impression. I was too nervous and excited to even eat breakfast. I knew this would be a big day for my business and I had already invested a lot of time and money in getting over there and preparing for this meeting. I ordered a cab and set off for Stirling's office.

Twenty minutes later, I arrived at the huge, log cabin style structure surrounded by forest in the back of beyond. It was surreal. Tammy, who was their executive PA, had just arrived to open the executive building and she took me into the meeting room and helped me to set up. Whilst I was setting up and having a coffee, a guy dressed very casually in jeans and a Polo t-shirt came in and asked me how I was getting on. I assumed that he was the IT guy and talked about making sure that there were no hitches with the projector and Powerpoint presentation. He then introduced himself as Alan, the Stirling COO, and that broke the ice!

They clearly dressed very informally in the office and all of a sudden I felt very self-conscious in my smart suit as if I was a salesman. I guess I was on that day! However, Alan was a great guy, very welcoming and he soon made me feel at ease. He was very laid back, but he also had an intense desire to make the company as successful as he could and had a clear plan of how to achieve this aim. Part of this plan was to identify and acquire small businesses with lots of potential growth as well as key personnel in strategic locations to build the new company capability and global coverage. I got on very well with Alan from the moment we met, and I had a huge amount of respect for him and the way he did business.

I gave the presentation to Alan, Matt, who was the CEO, the CFO, their corporate lawyer, and their senior strategic advisor, a former ambassador, who was listening in and asking questions from Washington DC via a video link. It went very well. At the end, there were around two hours of Q&A and I was pleased because they were not ripping apart what I had told them about Libya, which was a good sign, but even more so because they were drilling into the figures and future forecast with a genuine interest.

Once we had all finished, Alan offered to give me a lift back to the airport in his truck. A truck, which incidentally had more weaponry and firepower in it than we had in our security vehicle teams in Libya or even Iraq. The Americans love their weapons and, in Tennessee, it was absolutely normal to have a handgun with you at all times, another sort of automatic weapon in the truck and a full armoury at home, just in case of Armageddon. Alan invited me to the range next time I was in town to test my marksmanship skills, I thought this might be an interesting challenge; I had always been a good shot. But what if I lost to him? How embarrassing would that be? During the drive back, he talked a lot about where he saw SNE, as well as me personally, fitting into the company structure and the long-term vision, which left me with a very positive feeling of how things had gone.

When I arrived back in Dubai a day later, I took a call from Dale who said that he had chatted with Alan after he dropped me off at the airport. Alan had said that he liked me and thought my presentation was one of the best he had seen. He wanted the deal to be done as quickly as possible to get me on board and amalgamate SNE into the new company brand, which was to be called Janus Global Operations (JGO). This was great news, the price I had asked for had been agreed in principle and now the lawyers from Stirling would carry out their due diligence. If all went well with this phase of the negotiations and my lawyer could get all the terms and conditions agreed upon in time, then the plan was that I would officially become part of the new JGO company team on the 1st January 2016, and have my sale money safely in the bank.

I then flew off to Cyprus where Dawn and I were due to be married on the 31st October 2015, Halloween. Dawn was already there, finishing off the final preparations. The news of the probable company sale was perfect timing, it provided us both with a great boost and was the perfect wedding present. We had a great ten days in Cyprus with all our close friends who flew over for the Stag and Hen nights as well as the wedding. Luckily, the Stag night was forty-eight hours before the wedding day itself as there were some heavy heads the day after, not least my own. For my Stag, a dozen of us had hit Paphos town in world dictator fancy dress outfits, we had Hitler, Saddam Hussein, Genghis Khan, Pol Pot, the Ayatollah and me as Colonel Gaddafi of course, amongst others. I drank the world's quota of whisky and other spirits, which don't sit well with me at the best of times. Carl, aka Genghis Khan, managed to snort the entire bar's supply of helium and the party was in full swing. God knows how I got back to the wedding venue where I was staying that night. It was a great few days and a perfect wedding. Dawn and I then flew off for our honeymoon.

The Stirling lawyers were dragging their heels a bit and a few days before the end of the year, the deal was still not complete. The agreement we had in place to finalise the contract, expired at midnight on New Year's Eve and in an attempt to add some spark into the proceedings, I made it clear that they needed to get their arse in gear and get it done or else I might feel differently in the new year. Then, like all deals such as this, things suddenly moved very fast and sure enough on New Year's Eve, three hours short of the midnight deadline, I received a call from Alan in Lenoir City stating that everything had been finalised, the contract had been signed and payment had been wired to my account. We raised a beer to each other via Skype, both wished each other a very happy new year and said that we were looking forward to working with each other next year. I was with Dawn and both my parents in their flat in Bournemouth. We popped open the champagne and raised our glasses to a job well done and a very happy 2016.

Once the New Year celebration hangovers had cleared, I got to work and installed two guys as my new country management team in Tripoli. Paul and Richie were both excellent, but very different blokes who I felt understood how to run my business and had the capability to take us to the next level and reach our financial targets. I had now been set clear turnover and, more importantly, profit targets by JGO, which I would have to meet in each of the next two years to receive the second and third parts of my buyout payment in full. To achieve this, I needed them to work closely with me to keep our outgoings under control and maximize our profitability. I sat them both down in Tripoli and clearly explained the targets for the next two years and inserted a clause in their personal service agreements so that they would also receive bonuses from me if we met all our targets. This way, all three of us were working as a close-knit team towards the same goal and we were all professionally and financially incentivised to achieve it.

One of the hardest decisions I had to make was to remove my existing Libya operations manager. Pete was a lovely guy, he had been with me for a few years, had hung in there holding the fort in Libya under some very testing and dangerous conditions and never let me down. The clients really liked Pete, he was loyal and hardworking. Unfortunately, I needed a different breed of manager at this time, someone who really understood the business and financial side of life, and who could handle the heavy paperwork load and reporting timelines which were about to begin with JGO. I headed up to where he lived to give him the news in person. Pete took it very well, acted professionally and continued to work with us as our senior project manager on some other key projects. In the years that followed, Pete set up his own business in Libya and went on to achieve great success in his own right, which I was very pleased to see happen, and we are still good friends today.

I was now spending more time in Dubai with my new colleagues from JGO. They had moved into our office and were starting to try to impose their methods and ideas upon Dawn and me. Considering that I had owned my own business for the last six years, had not had to answer to anyone and definitely had never wanted to work for anyone else ever again, I was actually really enjoying working for Dale and Alan, for whom I had huge respect. I knew what they were trying to achieve and I had totally bought into the long-term vision. However, the same could not be said for some of the other guys who I now had to work with in the Dubai office, and they were starting to test my patience. I worried deep down inside that things would never work with people like that involved in JGO.

Back over in Tripoli, I shielded my team the best I could. All was going well and the team was relatively unaffected by the new JGO ownership and we were pretty well left alone at an operational level to continue doing what had to be done. There were a lot more procedures and reports, but Richie and Paul were taking care of them and sending them direct to the US. The most important part of the business was the client relationships that I mostly dealt with and controlled myself. The Libyan part of the business was doing better than ever, and our monthly, quarterly, and then first yearly figures bore this out.

At the start of 2017, the yearly start up meeting was held in a Dubai hotel. All the so-called country managers and key figures in the JGO commercial set up were invited and given a forty-five-minute slot to present how their individual business sectors were doing, explain the future forecasts for the next twelve months, and most importantly, provide a breakdown of their respective year-end financial figures.

Alan came over from the US for this two day get together to see how we were all doing and have a bit of social time in the evenings with us all, which he always seemed to enjoy, maybe a bit too much. Our commercial business development manager, who in my view did not have the personal qualities or contacts in the industry to fulfill such an important role, was in charge of setting up and running the two-day meeting.

The event went smoothly enough, but it clearly highlighted the weaknesses in the commercial side of the company and where it needed strengthening, which was normal practice and the aim of gatherings such as this. The only problem was that even though it was continually identified that we really needed support on the business development side, it never came. This was disappointing because it was one of the main reasons, I chose to sell to JGO. I had hoped that they could add that extra level of support to our business and enable us to grow and compete against our larger competitors on an equal sized playing field rather than having to punch above my weight as I had been all the way through with SNE.

One morning in early 2017 whilst I was in Tripoli, I received a sad and distressing message from Dale saying that Alan had been sacked and was no longer part of JGO. For me, this had come out of nowhere and it was a real shock. Alan had a long-term vision for winning some of the large government contracts, and to aid in those wins he had invested carefully in acquiring and building certain strategic country-oriented businesses like SNE in Libya. However, the powers that be in JGO were becoming restless with this approach and were, for whatever reason, not willing to give it the required time to come to fruition and had brought the guillotine down on him. As soon as I heard this news, I knew that this would be the start of the end for me in JGO. Alan was a key part of what I had signed up to and without his personality, energy, drive and support, I could not see the business achieving what it had set out to do. On top of that, I genuinely liked working with him and had a personal bond with Alan due to his part in the acquisition of SNE.

Alan was firstly replaced by an interim COO. The reason for this was lost on me, as the company required stability with long term planning and leadership. Six months later a new permanent COO came on board, who I never met. I had no personal relationship or bond with the new man and I was not inspired in any way whatsoever to go that extra mile. I was now starting to feel excluded and on the periphery of the company and could not see where this was going or how it may end up; the JGO I had bought into was starting to change and disintegrate.

We had a large demining project running in Misrata, which was brought to the table by the old Stirling team in the US and set up and enabled using my contacts and knowledge in Libya. Contracts like this were the whole reason Alan had purchased SNE in the beginning and I was excited by the opportunity for all parts of the JGO business to finally work together and compete at the big boys' top table. My side of the business was tasked to plan and run the project and provide the expat security, medics, local manpower and armoured vehicles to support the contract. A huge amount of work went into this and, thanks to my Misratian partner, we managed to locate and acquire a great compound in the west of the city which was formerly a holiday park for rich Libyan families. We took on some discreet local Misratian security guys and then employed some expat paramedics and security team leaders. I was keen to keep the bar high, and as our budget was healthier than other similar tasks in country, we took on some of the guys who were already working in Libya for other security companies who had up to date experience of the situation and knowledge of the ground. We devised a security plan and put it in place using all of our experience and local contacts in Misrata and Tripoli; something that we were very proud of and which would have been virtually impossible to pull off without us.

However, when the demining experts arrived in Libya, an internal struggle for power quickly started. My team and I found ourselves spending more and more time dealing with their petty personal gripes and continuous moaning about their living conditions or standard of food; the coffee machine was too complicated to work, there was not enough variety of cereal, no ice cream or diet coke. It just went on, with no understanding of where they actually were. Their living conditions were far better than anyone else had in the company. They spent too much time complaining rather than actually focusing on the job they were really there to do. The new project manager seemed to think that he had total power to dictate what we should be doing, and I had to then waste a lot of my precious time sorting him out rather than getting on with my job and the things that really mattered. Fortunately, from an operational perspective, the project was going well. JGO was training a group of Libyans in demining techniques with an aim to then deploying them down to Sirte. Once the city had been finally freed from the grip and tyranny of the IS fighters, they could start to clear the huge amounts of UXO and booby traps that had been left behind and allow the civilian population to get back into their homes and on with their normal lives again.

Dale's time at JGO was coming to an end and he was looking at moving to a more relaxed advisory role within the company. I was told that I was in the running, along with two or three others, to become the new VP of Commercial Operations. It was a position that interested me as I saw it as a huge challenge to take the helm after Dale and keep the company's commercial arm on the upward curve that he had had us on for the last few years.

For one reason or another, the current JGO Business Development Manager somehow ended up getting the job. To be honest I was not that surprised and had already pretty well made my mind up to leave the company when my buy out period was up in March 2018.

Nearing the end of the year, I was offered a few roles within the company to keep me involved. On the list of positions I was offered and told I could choose from was the Business Development Manager position as well as Head of Special Projects, which would be a new position created for me, if I took it on. This would include the responsibility of getting JGO into Syria and building the business there.

If I'm honest, I was slightly tempted to take on the business development manager role, if only to make the point and show them how it should be done and actually go out there and win some new business for the company. The special projects' role was genuinely interesting and under normal circumstances, and if Dale and Alan were still involved in the business, then maybe that would have been something that I would have taken on once my contract in Libya had come to a successful end. However, at the end of the day, I decided that there was no way I could work with the new management team. It was time for me to clarify my position, put in place plans to move on, get out whilst the going was good, and start my new life with Dawn in Cyprus.

My contract was up on 31st March 2018 and it was agreed that after the festive and New Year holidays, I would start a gradual hand over to the person we all agreed would take over from me in Libya. I went to the 2018 yearly start up meeting that was run by the new commercial VP. The CEO had come over and had a chat with me one evening over a beer. He said that he could not imagine me sitting on the beach in Cyprus doing nothing. He said that he would like me to stay on and reiterated that if I wanted to, I could choose from whatever positions were available if it meant I stayed with JGO in some capacity. I thanked him and said that I would think about it, but I had pretty well made up my mind. It was time to move on and start the next chapter of my life.

It was confirmed that Paul was going to be promoted from Libya Operations Manager to Country Manager and that I would start a gradual handover to him from mid-January up to when I left at the end of March. This required trips to Egypt and Tunisia to meet with the local partners, a range of client meetings in Dubai and London, and then a substantial amount of time in Libya handing over all my responsibilities to Paul. I had made a deal with a new Libyan landlord at the end of 2017 for a fantastic new compound in Tripoli, which had three villas, a swimming pool and a large gym area at a great fixed price for the next three years. This would enable JGO to continue the growth path that I had started all those years ago with an established top-notch villa and operations compound in Tripoli. I wanted to leave Paul in as strong a position as possible and also to make sure that all my staff both local and expats who had worked so hard and loyally for me over the past few years in Libya were okay and kept their jobs secure.

Paul and I got on very well and shared the same military sense of humour. One day when I was in London and Paul was in Tripoli, I arranged a conference call with him and a potential client from a female NGO. The chat was going very well and I explained how we could provide support in the area she required. She then asked if we had any female operators and, trying to be funny, I replied that I would get Paul to put a dress on. I immediately imagined Paul, a six foot, six inch monster of a man, in a little, tight dress. Paul and I chuckled away on the call until we realised that she was not joining in and finding it as funny as we were. Needless to say, we never heard from her again, but it has given us many a laugh since.

As part of the final handover, Paul and I went down to Benghazi and spent some time with Nasser. I was keen that Paul and Nasser bonded properly and built the same level of trust between them as had always existed between Nasser and I. This was key to the success of the company in the east of Libya.

Nasser took us around the areas of Benghazi that had been the epicentre of the fighting between the LNA and Ansar al Sharia. I knew about the destruction from seeing the daily reports, but this was the first time I had the opportunity to actually go down and see it with my own eyes. It was unbelievable and heartbreaking to see. Large areas of housing had been destroyed; only dusty, crumbling rubble and blackened ruins remained. It was like walking through a ghost town that had been abandoned centuries before, every window had been blown out, roofs collapsed down onto exposed interior floors and any remaining outer walls were riddled with holes from bullets and shells. Twisted rebar stuck out from shattered concrete, rubble, burned-out cars and tanks blocked the streets. I was deeply saddened; it really brought home the scale and ferocity of the fighting that had taken place in Benghazi. I had not been able to get down over the last year or so due to the instability in the area and the beautiful Benghazi I remembered so fondly from when I first went down there in 2011, and had fallen in love with during those early years, had been changed forever.

On 1st April 2018, my time with JGO was finally over and I was back in Cyprus, with Dawn. I woke up in our villa, walked out onto the veranda and sat with the sun shining down from above, a cup of coffee in one hand and a cigarette in the other, looking out over my pool and taking in the views across the valley and down to the sea. I felt a huge sense of relief. All the pressure and heavy burden I had been carrying on my shoulders for the last eight years of running SNE, and the stress of making the difficult decision to leave the Paras twenty years ago nearly to the day was lifted. Joining the security circuit had proven to be the correct move and now I didn't have to check my emails to see what drama or problem had to be dealt with today, or really worry about anything too much apart from what to have for breakfast.

However, at the same time, I felt a great loss and a huge hole in my life. The reality hit home that my business, which I gave birth to all those years ago and was the baby that I had nurtured, fought for and developed into what it was today, had finally gone. I actually had nothing to do with it anymore, and never would again.

I now had to find something to fill this huge gap in my life. I had thrived on adrenalin every day for so many years and now I had nothing to replace it. I knew I needed to quickly learn how to embrace the new way of living that I had worked so hard to acquire and which I had dreamt about for so long. I now needed to appreciate the fruits of my labour. It was time to relax, kick back and enjoy life with Dawn, to eat, drink, and work on my golf handicap. The next phase of my life had well and truly started.

The Long Road to Libya proved to be just that, a real mixture of Danger, Excitement, Tenacity, Resilience, Opportunity and Success. In hindsight, we would all change some decisions we have made, and I, of course, regret hurting anyone along the way. But this was my journey and I was proud of what I had achieved. All that was left now was to one day put it into a book.

AFTERWORD

Writing this book was a long road in itself and far more difficult than I anticipated. However, it gave me the opportunity to look back, reminisce, and carefully consider my journey to this point in my life. I really enjoyed the process and I learned a lot about myself as I went along. Things that I didn't maybe see at the time, due to being caught up in the moment of the sometimes chaotic and crazy life I lived, became much clearer.

My journey has been a fantastic experience. I was lucky enough to work in many places around the world and I always made a point of trying to be one of the first into countries opening up after conflict. I quite honestly did my best work when these countries were entering the post-conflict stage, and I really enjoyed being there at such a dynamic point in their history. I had to think outside the box in order to survive and be successful and this is something that I have always found to be a thrilling and rewarding process.

In all of the many diverse and challenging environments that I worked, I always relied heavily upon the guys I operated with and the excellent local staff we employed, who all had my back. I was honoured to operate alongside some of the best that the British Armed Forces have to offer, and the security circuit could provide. I worked with and met so many interesting and unbelievable people along the way and saw so many things that changed my view on society and humanity. I hope that in the troubled areas that I worked, I helped those around me to get through the experiences we endured, was able to leave behind some semblance of good, and, in some small way, improved the lives of the local people we left behind.

It seems to have been a similar story everywhere I went. A war or short conflict to remove a dictatorship or rogue government was followed by a lull when international reconstruction and private businesses moved into the country. A resurgence in violence then ensued as Islamic terrorism grew, or local militia groups fought over the spoils of war and argued amongst each other about the future governance. The only losers in this process seem to be the innocent local people trying to go about their daily business, living hand to mouth as they attempt to survive and protect their families. Do we leave dictators in place to continue to repress and murder their people, or do we remove them, only for them to be replaced by something that seems in many cases to be far more chaotic and worse? I wish I knew the answer. Only time will tell who was right and who was wrong, but I am a firm believer in doing something rather than nothing, and bullies at any level must be dealt with one way or another.

What I do know is that we are very lucky in the UK and other similar run democratic countries. Those who moan, gripe, and continuously look to undermine our governments and our way of life have no idea what it's like in the majority of the world to live and survive on a daily basis with no political rights, freedom of speech, medical care or a social welfare system. We need to be stricter, if anything, to maintain our way of life at all costs, and honour the veterans who have fought and helped to protect the freedoms that we all enjoy today.

My time on the security circuit was about protecting the clients whose safety was entrusted to us. What really mattered was making sure that those people, who were just in the country to do a job, went safely back home to their families at the end of their contracts. We were not trigger-happy madmen. The weapons we carried were only there to use in desperate situations, as a last resort, and usually meant that all the other systems and procedures we had put in place had already failed. I am proud that no one was ever lost on my watch, but I pay homage to those who did pay the ultimate price in the line of their duty: they will never be forgotten.

As I've stated in this book, I was lucky and dodged death or serious injury by very thin margins, on more than one occasion. Others were not so lucky, and I have to say that there are outcomes that no amount of skill or experience can avert. Even with the best laid plans in the world and the most highly trained and well-funded security teams that money can buy, if you are in the wrong place at the wrong time, then that is that. This is the life of a private security contractor on the circuit.

ACKNOWLEDGEMENTS

There are so many to thank and acknowledge that I apologise in advance if I miss anyone out. Every bit of support and encouragement that I have ever received along my life journey has been very much appreciated – thank you all.

Firstly, this book would never have actually happened if it were not for Sian M. Williams bringing the idea to life. I would like to thank her for her help and guidance in developing the manuscript and for bringing out the reluctant writer in me. Damien Lewis for taking the time to read my manuscript, give good sound advice and then endorsing the book. Phil Campion for writing an excellent Foreword, Ollie Ollerton for his support and endorsing my story. The team at Matador Books for turning my Manuscript into a real book and Billy Allinson for designing an awesome book cover.

Mum & Dad, thank you both for bringing me up to know right from wrong and for your gentle, constant guidance and support, even when I was being pig headed.

My daughter Chelsea, I am hugely proud of the woman I see you growing into today. It is my greatest honor in life, to be your father.

My wife Dawn, without whose unwavering support, multi-faceted skill set, hard work, firm hand, and love, the business and I would never have flourished as we both did and for this, I am forever grateful. Caroline & Jo for all you have done for me.

Stu & Des for thirty years of friendship and stepping up to the plate, when others would not. Andy for giving me the opportunities and for being a great loyal friend. Carl and Paul for coming on the journey with me and all the laughs along the way. PB for providing a young man just out of the army with an opportunity. Francis for your guidance and mentorship. Phil, Chris & Jack for the crazy times in Afghan. Ollie, Marcus and TC for having my back through some mad years in Iraq. Lee H, for his friendship in those early days when we first became civvies, Mark R for the use of his sofa and long friendship, Tony R & Tom, for their great company at Wormsley and Trev R for the many exciting times we spent together.

My team and all who worked for SNE Special Projects for their hard work and loyalty, especially Paul, Richie, Pete, Tucker, Ems, Matt, Tony H, Esther, George and all my excellent Libyan staff. My business partners in Libya, Abdul & Nasser as well as my partners in Egypt and Tunisia.

Dale and Alan for making the sale happen and for the good times since.

The numerous members of the Private Security Industry, who I have worked with and alongside on The Circuit and who carry out such an important and unseen role in the security and prosperity of our way of life.

My Airborne brothers from the Parachute Regiment, far too many to mention. Every Man An Emperor, 'Utrinque Paratus'. I am proud to have been a small part of this regiment's illustrious history.

All members of the British Armed Forces serving across the world, who fight the good fight, risk their lives on a daily basis and sometimes pay the ultimate sacrifice to keep us all safe in our beds at night, and who never seem to receive the recognition or after-support they so much deserve.